THE
NORDIC SOUND

Explorations
into the Music of
Denmark, Norway, Sweden

by

JOHN H. YOELL

Foreword by Antal Dorati

CRESCENDO PUBLISHING CO.

BOSTON

The North is most assuredy entitled
to a language of its own.

— ROBERT SCHUMANN

ACKNOWLEDGMENTS

Numerous individuals contributed advice, information and encouragement toward completion of *The Nordic Sound*. Without the year in, year out support from Mr. Per Olof Lundahl of the Swedish Music Information Center and Miss Bodil Russ of the Norwegian Composers Society, this project would have been impossible. Valuable assistance also came from Prof. Dag Schjelderup-Ebbe, Mr. Dan Fog, Mr. Sven Wilson, Dr. Herbert Rosenberg, Mr. Jon Embretsen, Miss Hanne Wilhelm-Hansen, Klaus Egge, Finn Mortensen and Knut Nystedt. Visits to Scandinavia became more memorable because of the warm hospitality offered by Mr. and Mrs. Harald Saeverud, Mr. and Mrs. Vagn Holmboe, Mr. and Mrs. Jan Carlstedt, Mr. and Mrs. Bent Lorentzen. Mrs. Louise Hart gave expert help in manuscript preparation, and Miss Jane Browne brought this book to the attention of the publishers. To these as well as many others — librarians, composers, secretaries, antiquarians and friends — the author expresses his most heartfelt gratitude.

FOREWORD

The influence of environment upon all facets of life is well recognized and exhaustively studied. The one somewhat neglected sphere of that study would be perhaps the relationship of the arts to their physical local climate.

John H. Yoell's book *The Nordic Sound,* besides being a valuable collection and exposition of data, provides — at least to this reader — a welcome "launching site" for further thoughts on that subject.

It is from personal experience that I — born in a moderate climate but a southerner by temperament — know the very real and very special musical sound of the North. A very important span of my life was dedicated to the task of recognizing that sound and learning how to make it blossom forth.

In order to make the reader of this book aware of the emotional forces behind its narrative, I would like to describe for him here the Nordic Sound. But words, as always when it comes to the essence of music, prove to be scarce and inadequate. One has to turn to nature and its infinite resources — both to experience and depict — for help.

Nature's great, perhaps greatest, exciting phenomenon in the North are the shining nights. I am not referring to the short yearly wonder, the sensation of the midnight sun, — but to the summer nights in general, — to the feverish alertness of these "ever-awake" times, where night and day mix — one is tempted to say: copulate — in a pan-erotic elimination of borders — to that overpowering beat of a gigantic pulse of those almost-alike days and nights, which store up the strength, the juices of survival, as it were, during the oncoming long dark winter months.

It is that light, that white fever of these summertimes which shines in the best music of the north.

The material that Dr. Yoell's book offers should kindle the desire to transcend "knowledge," transform it to experience — in other words, to hear the Nordic Sound and to find the quality and that enchantment that lies within.

Stockholm   ANTAL DORATI

iii

PREFACE

The Nordic Sound aims to supply handy information about Scandinavian music. The book is for the general listener and record collector, not the professional musician or musicologist. Since so much music from the North lies outside the so-called standard repertoire, the author's primary intent is to supply an introduction for the inquisitive listener, a map leading him to the vast resources available for reproduction on the modern home sound system.

Historically, music from Denmark, Norway and Sweden has shown an erratic pattern in concert halls and public favor. But the long-playing record, tape and high-fidelity reproducing equipment have turned the music world right around. Concerts no longer count as the principal means for musical communication; discs and tape have become the new arbiters of musical taste. Within one generation, the dazzled music lover has been granted access to mankind's total musics, a technological fact with far-reaching implications. Whole styles and periods formerly the private preserve of connoisseurs and musicologists — the baroque era, for instance — have been resurrected, recorded and popularized. Bach and Vivaldi have joined the stream of mass consumerism. Works from all nations seldom sounded in public may now be enjoyed by any music lover to his heart's content. As a result, the serious listener soon realizes that the many byways of music can prove just as fascinating and meaningful as the heritage from the "great masters." *The Nordic Sound* is offered in this spirit.

Scandinavian music covers a broad field. Selectivity rapidly became necessary in the preparation of the present survey. Being phonograph-based, *The Nordic Sound* devotes most attention to composers backed up by a reasonable number of works in available recorded form. Regrettable omissions of some composers occur in order to keep a balance between the broad panorama of Scandinavian music and detailed information about specific compositions which the author feels important for a first grasp of the subject. The opinions of others, however, have been taken with a grain of salt; with few exceptions, every composition evaluated is on the basis of firsthand listening.

The Nordic Sound makes no pretense at encyclopedic coverage. For this reason, biographical data has been pared to essentials. Tedious recitals about a given composer's qualifications to compose will not be found here. Instead, emphasis falls on what general listeners and high-fidelity enthusiasts really care to know: something about the artistic position of Scandinavia's composers, their relationship to Western music as illustrated by a listener-to-listener evaluation of specific works in non-technical language.

Violent issue might be taken with any book about Scandinavian music failing to range beyond the products of Danish, Norwegian and Swedish composers. Where is Sibelius? What about Finland? Iceland?

Apologies may be in order, but the author made an early decision to limit the ground covered to music from the three heartland kingdoms — an arbitrary approach in no way intended to undermine the substantial contributions from Finland or the proud and active musical life of the Icelandic people.

Does a term like "Nordic sound" have any real meaning?

Thanks to mass media, the world's stock image of Scandinavia is of a sub-Arctic socialist utopia populated by luscious blondes and pornographers, where sex, sauna and suicide reign supreme in that order. The very idea that the northland enjoys a lively creative and performing musical tradition of its own strikes too many people as esoterica of peripheral importance.

In the past, the Scandinavian peoples contributed at least a few composers whose music met widespread appreciation; since the mid-1950s, the dawn of "the new music," the collective strength and international recognition of northern composers have grown. Beyond that, Scandinavian music can show traits as specific as anything from Russia or Spain. Edvard Grieg was correct when he emphasized that his music was "Norwegian," not "Nordic." Like others, he recognized national variants within a broader regional culture; the "Nordic sound" rises above national boundaries and runs far deeper than local color. It has even been exported, repackaged and shipped back — Lalo, Delius, Stravinsky and even Smetana are among the more prominent foreigners tempted to dabble in sounds from the North.

This listener's concept of the "Nordic sound" was deepened by field trips to Scandinavia, including Dr. Burney-like visits to the homes and workshops of most of the leading composers. When asked the direct question, these men generally agreed that such a thing as a "Nordic tone" existed in music, if hard to define. Some of these composers talked freely of their work; others spoke of many things apart from music. But in all instances these informal, cordial encounters gave this listener insights impossible to obtain by other means.

This book argues no armchair musicological proposition. It does not advance the brief that every scrap of music out of Scandinavia amounts to a neglected masterpiece. But should the educated listener become more aware of music in the North? Has this area contributed any worthwhile symphonies, operas or chamber music, anything beyond a few established classics from Grieg or Sibelius? No pat answer is given, but these pages can lead the inquisitive listener straight to the music. There is where the answer lies.

JOHN H. YOELL

Los Angeles, California
November, 1973

CONTENTS

PART I: HISTORICAL PERSPECTIVES

PART II: COMPOSERS GALLERY

PART III:
SELECTIVE INTERNATIONAL DISCOGRAPHY

Illustrations follow p. 138

PART I

HISTORICAL PERSPECTIVES

ANCIENT WELLSPRINGS

Music, along with the visual arts, is basic to human society in all parts of the world from the dawn of history to the present. In many cultures the beginnings of music are assigned to some act of the gods, often with explicitness. But even the mythological origins for the Nordic sound lie veiled behind a misty past. Finnish legend boasts a prominent Orpheus-like figure in Väinämöinen, but the otherwise detailed, intricate labyrinth of Norse mythology becomes blurred at this point. Almighty Odin fathered poetry and was held to be a marvelous musician whose songs caused the very rocks to expand. But Odin wore many hats, with music among the lesser ones.

Nordic music at the morning of time also received a contribution from Heimdal, the great White God sometimes considered a son of Odin. Heimdal's job was to watch over Asgard, home of the gods; should danger threaten he would lift his gigantic *Gjallarhorn* ("echoing horn") to his lips to send forth resonant blasts of warning throughout all the worlds. If nothing else, the Nordic sound seems to have been born with lusty vigor.

The facts of cultural growth in the far north of Europe have emerged slowly, piecemeal and with much mystery. Traces of migratory hunters flitting across northern Norway as early as 10,000 B.C. have been identified, but more substantial settlement belongs to the Late Stone Age (3000–1500 B.C.) when comparatively advanced farming people trickled in, apparently out of Central Europe.

During this long settlement period musical practices are largely conjectural, but it seems reasonable to assume that untold generations of hunters, fishermen, farmers, traders, artisans, shipbuilders, warriors and priests — the whole human panorama filling the ten thousand years of Scandinavian pre-history — were, like people everywhere, fully susceptible to the charms and magical powers of music.

Music of the Reindeer People

The mysterious Lapps may or may not be direct descendents of the aboriginal population of Scandinavia, but one thing is certain: they have been moving back and forth along the rim of Europe's Arctic waters for a long, long time. Their surviving folklore, the subject of intensive research in modern times, may furnish at least a few tantalizing clues about the nature of ancient Nordic music. A few experts have even proposed the controversial view that Lapp music shows links to cultural elements of Stone Age hunters. Others see traditions absorbed from earlier sub-Arctic peoples. But whatever occurred to mould the music of the Lapps, the peculiar type of vocalization it represents shares certain musical characteristics with other ethnic groups, notably the Eskimos and even certain tribes among the North American Indians.

Central to Lapp music is a type of song known as the yoik (or *joik*). The sole Lappish instrument is the drum, usually the property of the shaman, artfully inscribed with symbols relating to the magic-oriented substructure of Lapp religion. Although part of a semi-nomadic tribal and family community, the Lapp is basically a loner, at least when it comes to his music which he feels belongs out-of-doors, outside his tent or dwelling in nature. Here, when he feels like it, the Lapp yoiks alone.

To modern listeners, even those with tolerance for raw, primitive folk music, yoiks sound particularly crude and charmless. These outdoor solo songs with intervals monotonously chanted in a faltering voice usually accompany words about some particular place, animal or person. Often the Lapp regards his yoik as personal property. Confined to a narrow tonal range, the yoik commonly rises in pitch as the singer drones on with peculiar ornamentation thrown in unexpectedly to make the contours of Lapp melodies difficult for the average European-trained ear to grasp.

The yoik, as known today from field research, cannot be put forward as "pure" ancient music. Too many years of interaction between the reindeer-herding Lapps and their culturally different Scandinavian neighbors have had an effect. Swedish, Norwegian and even Danish folk and popular songs have diluted the yoik; today, with radio and television available to most Lapps, the end of the yoik itself is almost certainly at hand.

But the seemingly flat and unemotional nature of the yoik tells the listener something very deep and primordial. Although sounding to strangers like so much hoarsely rasped Chinese singsong, the yoik can convey an eerie sense of timelessness. These are touching songs of loneliness, childlike in their simplicity, sung by men and women whose eyes traditionally scan endless, white horizons. Imperfect as it is, the yoik forms the closest living link to what we may presume to have been the actual sound of prototypal Nordic music. Beyond the yoik, speculation becomes lost in primeval silence.

Instrumental Artifacts

Incredibly, many listeners (not excluding some misguided music critics) have succumbed to the myth that until the advent of Grieg and Sibelius the Scandinavian countries were a musical blank — a notion off-target by several thousand years. A case can be made that at various points in history the northland has suffered from varying degrees of musical backwardness, but man and his music have existed side by side in Scandinavia as intimately as anywhere else. Countless instrumental artifacts such as bone flutes, "trumpets" made from animal horns, and rattles of various types have been dug from the Scandinavian past. Although not a true musical

4

instrument, strictly speaking, ancient man's "bull roarer" — a bit of stone, flint or wood whirled overhead on the end of a string — has been found in northland soil. The whirring or buzzing sound was presumably intended to invoke the gods. One example, found in Denmark, is believed to date back some eight thousand years to the depths of the Stone Age.

During the Nordic Bronze Age (1500–500 B.C.), the Scandinavians experienced a series of forward cultural leaps. Most of the fascinating rock pictures strewn about the northern landscape date from this brisk period. Nordic lithic art pays great attention to religious symbols, notably the sun, along with weapons, tools and ships. But rock carvings also furnish hints of musical activity, such as representations of humans in dance postures, apparent depictions of events connected with the hunt, fertility rites and other forms of cultic worship. However, the clouds surrounding northern prehistoric music part for a brief but glorious moment upon mention of the *lur*.

The *lurs* of Scandinavia are among the most important discoveries in musical archeology. Nothing certain can be said about the antecedents of these graceful bronze horns first pulled from Jutland's peat bogs some two hundred years ago. At first they were thought to be old viking instruments, but as further specimens came to light in Norway, Sweden and a few spots around the general Baltic area, their true antiquity was established. The bulk of the recovered *lurs* (several dozen in various states of preservation) lay in Danish soil, giving Bronze Age Denmark credit for being headquarters for *lur* manufacture and use.

The frequent recovery of *lurs* in pairs, at times with asymmetric tubing, correlates with rock pictures showing horn players in groups of two or more. Can this mean ancient northerners practiced unison sonority or even part harmony? The question remains unanswered. Another speculation suggests that *lurs* with common pitch might have transmitted and received long-distance coded signals — a sort of Bronze Age telegraph system. Intriguing speculations aside, the main use for *lurs* seems to have been in religious rites, and perhaps they were even carried into battle.

When the *lur* is held in playing position, the contorted "S" shape resembles a cobra ready to strike. The instrument itself consists of five to eight feet of carefully fitted cast bronze; the mouthpiece, amazingly modern in design, testifies to a remarkable degree of metallurgic skill among the ancient Danes. Chains and pendant plates equip some *lurs,* adding a shrill tinkle to their harsh, trombone-like timbre.

No evidence exists to indicate that Bronze Age players could produce more than natural tones from their *lurs* (like the modern bugle), but restoration of several horns to playable condition has tempted present-day brassmen to coax a full range of notes from them. Of course, actual knowledge of what Bronze Age men played on their instruments is nil, but the visitor to Copenhagen's National Museum can stand before the crowded *lur* showcase, press a button and just about be blown off his foot by the massed power of three thousand-year-old Nordic sound.

5

Saga Days

The fabled vikings were not a race apart, but merely those northerners who for some reason got the collective itch to leave hearth and home for long periods outside Scandinavia. The Viking Era (700–1000 A.D.) brought rapid expansion of the Nordic world which at its peak stretched as a network of trade routes from the Caspian Sea to the shores of North America. Pillage and plunder cannot be denied, but it is sometimes forgotten that the vikings were as adept at barter, exploration and colonization as they were at warfare and piracy. Reliable information about viking musical life is fragmentary; much of it depends on inferences from the sagas which were written centuries after the events they describe. As with much of Europe in the Dark Age, the people of viking lands recognized no sharp distinction between music and poetic storytelling.

During the lengthy gloom of winter, when their sleek ships lay idle, the Norsemen seem to have devoted themselves to two principal pastimes: mead drinking and poetic entertainment. They would gather in the great hall of their *jarl*, or chieftain, to feast and then indulge in the art of the *skalds*. The Old Norse passion for poetry encouraged the development of a school of bards called *skalds*. Most of them were Icelanders and, induced by cold cash, they would call regularly at the courts of kings and *jarls* (often little more than glorified farmsteads) throughout the North. They presented two main types of songs: the *drapa*, a song of heroic praise, and the *flokk*, a short poem in simpler, lighter style. When the bard performed, the raised voices of all assembled often formed an enthusiastic chorus. Instrumental accompaniments were also customarily provided, most commonly from the harp or lyre, but ancient fiddles of the *rebec* type were in regular use after the eighth century.

On a grimmer note, the twelfth-century Danish chronicler Saxo Grammaticus tells of blood-reeking religious rites at the large pagan temples close to modern Uppsala where some form of elaborate priestly incantation and the "unmanly clatter of bells" accompanied human sacrifices to the fertility god Freyer.

The only known firsthand account of early Scandinavian music in action, the childhood of the Nordic sound, comes down from Al-Tartushi, a Moor on a business trip to Denmark about the year 950. He reported: "I have never heard such horrible singing as that of the Slesvigers — it is like a growl coming from their throats, like the barking of dogs only still more brutish." Since the people of viking times left no written music behind or commentaries of their own on this subject, the impressions of a traveling salesman must be taken at face value. On the other hand, perhaps Al-Tartushi merely took in a poor performance.

The Middle Ages

For all their remarkable attainments, the Scandinavians of the Viking Era belonged to a barbaric culture: humanism — the hallmark of true civilization — lay just beyond them. But starting about the year 1000, events moved swiftly to change this situation. Conversion of the northern peoples to Christianity meant no victory of an alien civilization; instead the North merged with Western Christendom when vitality and creative energy had reached a peak.

With the adoption of Christianity, hastened by native leaders like St. Canute in Denmark and St. Olav in Norway, musical resources in the North became enormously expanded. Soon after the introduction of plainsong into Scandinavia, the new faithful could be found worshiping in the Roman style in their own cathedrals as far north as Nidaros (now called Trondheim) in Norway. During the Middle Ages music literally traveled with the Church; no surprise, then, to learn of well-schooled choirs singing God's praises throughout Sweden, Norway and Denmark. Monks and clerics were dispatched to study liturgical music in such centers as Paris, Cambrai and Prague; many returned to practice their acquired skills on home soil.

Communion between Rome and her northern faithful lasted over five hundred years, too long a time to assume that the music heard at Mass would stay entirely within church or monastery walls. Diffusion of elements from Gregorian chant through all strata of medieval society was inevitable. In more remote regions of Norway, Sweden and even Denmark, the practice of religious folk melodies improvised by the congregation sprang up, a tradition which endured for centuries. Besides fertilizing the rootstocks of Nordic folk song, Gregorian chant and Roman hymnody in turn absorbed some features of the skaldic style. The extent to which this interaction influenced later Nordic art music remains highly controversial, but the music of the Roman Church was not the least of the streams joining to form the Nordic sound.

To claim the existence of a true "Nordic school" during the Middle Ages is an exaggeration, yet the few surviving musical documents from this era give reason to believe that the northerners not only learned much from their southern colleagues, but at times demonstrated considerable boldness of their own. Much quibbling has taken place over the suggestion that part harmony originated in the North which for cultural purposes then included a good portion of the British Isles. For example, the virile two-part, euphonic hymn to St. Magnus (*Nobilis humilis*), discovered in the library at Uppsala some years ago, apparently represents the work of a Norwegian monk passing through the Orkney Islands during the thirteenth century. More than a musicological curiosity, this splendid "Magnus Hymn" is probably the earliest piece of authentic Scandinavian music enjoyable by listeners today, a sort of Nordic counterpart to Britain's *Sumer is icumen in.*

Polyphonic music finds mention in Uppsala choir statutes dating from 1298, while organs entered regular use in Swedish churches as early as the fourteenth century. Sweden's St. Birgitta (St. Bridget) inspired many liturgical sequences, hymns and rhymed offices, although most of these melodies are derivative. Denmark's oldest musical documents — Latin

7

hymns and sequences for the Office of St. Canute (Knut Lavard) — go back to the twelfth-century days of Absalon, Bishop of Lund and founder of the city of Copenhagen. The earliest known notation of a secular song in Scandinavia occurs in a late thirteenth-century collection of Scanian laws (Scania: a province in southern Sweden); the words are written in runic characters, the melody in medieval square notes. Other scraps of evidence might be cited, but this is enough to convey the point that Scandinavia's alleged isolation must be taken with a grain of salt. By the Middle Ages, the North enjoyed a good supply of highly competent musicians in firm contact with the European mainstream.

The richest type of secular music to appear in Scandinavia during medieval times took the form of the ballad, with Denmark as the flowering garden. Patient research and a certain amount of reconstruction enable the interested modern listener to enjoy old Nordic balladry, but not usually as a recreation of the original experience. The very word "ballad" stems from the Italian *ballare* (to dance), stressing the crucial truth that popular ballads of medieval times comprised more than song; they drew song, poetry and dancing invariably together. About the only living link to medieval ballad practice in the North appears in the hours' long, chanted dance marathons of the Faeroese Islanders, descendents of the old Norsemen, who inhabit a windy sheep run halfway between Iceland and Denmark.

A clear idea of the importance of balladry to subsequent Scandinavian music presents difficulties because the interests of literary people, not musicians, dominate most of the available information. We simply do not know the name of a single ballad author or what his tunes originally sounded like. The chivalric ballad, or its prototype, apparently spread north from France in the form of courtly entertainment. But eventually ballads caught the fancy of the common people and merged with grass-roots folklore. This meant transmission from generation to generation within the oral tradition with uncertain effect upon the original material. By a curious turn of fashion, however, collecting ballad poetry became a hobby with many high-born Danish ladies during the Renaissance. Thanks to this fluke much Danish balladic material escaped the commercial corruption of later years when printing presses and street corner hawkers distributed tons of so-called ballads in the form of single sheets or broadsides.

In general two types of Scandinavian ballads may be distinguished: the chivalric ballad with roots in the old French "carole," and the heroic songs or *Kjempeviser* which were most enthusiastically cultivated in Norway. Some of them, notably the venerable Norwegian *Draumkvede* (Vision of Heaven and Hell), seem to have originated as far back as the fourteenth century. Various subtypes of the chivalric ballads have been defined, such as the historical ballad so popular in Denmark, the mystical ballad dealing with witchcraft and fey happenings, and the religious or moral ballad.

Thanks to modern research, good representations of Scandinavian ballads are now available on phonograph records in renditions as authentic as possible. These enable the listener to round out his composite view of the main rootstocks for the Nordic sound. Apart from the Icelandic sagas, only the ballads mirror the secular music and poetry of the Scandinavian Middle Ages although "through a glass darkly."

The decline of the Middle Ages found Nordic music robust and spread through all levels of society. Besides enjoying full participation in the rich heritage of the Church, traditions of secular song became well founded through the popular appeal of the ballads. These answered the need for narrative entertainment so dear to the northern peoples while providing a good excuse for dancing despite strong disapproval from churchmen. Instruments became liberated from mere song accompaniment. The *Ynglinga Saga,* for instance, mentions that King Hugleik of Sweden had all manner of musicians at his court playing on harps, viols and assorted fiddles. Although pictures of medieval musical life in Scandinavia as presented in the pages of the sagas probably lean toward excessive idealism, there seems little doubt that these centuries saw the foundations for the Nordic sound well laid.

Disaster in the form of bubonic plague struck fourteenth-century Scandinavia with unusual severity, the heaviest blow falling on Norway. Over half that country's population died; noble families were all but extinguished; the line of royal kings was broken. Almost completely sapped of her former strength, Norway fell weakly into the arms of Denmark and merchants of the monopolistic Hanseatic League. For slightly more than a century (1397–1523) the North's three crowns joined for the only time as one political entity, the so-called Union of Kalmar. But this uneasy relationship eventually split apart to usher in an almost interminable series of bitter wars between Denmark-Norway and Sweden.

Basic change also accompanied the Reformation. Catholic power in the North terminated. The Church's once-impressive musical establishment fell apart, although some Gregorian influence lingered a while in Sweden, where the Jesuits made a strong bid to recoup Catholic fortunes. But after considerable strife the royal houses of Scandinavia firmly supported the precepts of Martin Luther. The Reformation not only meant a new view of Christian worship and the type of music the congregation experienced at services, but Lutheran emphasis on congregational singing greatly stimulated musical expression among the common people. Then, too, political reorientation led to sharper national definition; royal power became increasingly centralized as the Danish and Swedish nobles were brought to heel. These events also meant centralization of all culture. As a result, the royal courts at Copenhagen and Stockholm became almost the sole havens for art music in the North for some 250 years.

COURTLY PATRONAGE

Seventeenth-century Denmark

Colorful Christian IV, still Denmark's favorite king, missed few of life's pleasures, coarse or refined. During his long reign (1588–1648) music held a leading position at his court, for among innumerable other projects Christian expanded his orchestra and staff of dancers until the Danish musical establishment came to rival the splendor of any in Europe. Royal largesse also attracted several distinguished foreign musicians to the court for prolonged visits, among them such masters as John Dowland and Heinrich Schütz.

Native talent also received Christian's blessing. Promising young Danes were sent to Gabrielli at Venice to master the new monodic (single-voiced) style at the fountainhead; this eventually replaced Netherlandish polyphony in the music for the Royal Chapel. Among Gabrielli's Danish pupils *Mogens Pedersøn* (c. 1580–1623) ranks today as the most important and the first individual Danish composer worthy of note; Pedersøn's major work, a collection of Masses, hymns and motets called *Pratum spirituale,* left the press in 1620.

A particularly fine memento of Denmark's sumptuous court musical life under Christian IV remains for all to see in the chapel at Frederiksborg Castle, an hour's ride north of the capital. Here sits a beautifully cased organ built about 1610 by Erasmus Compenius for the princes of Braunschweig and presented a few years later to the music-loving monarch by his sister. Unlike many organs built by master craftsmen of the baroque era, the instrument now at Frederiksborg escaped "improvement" by later generations and kept its original equal temperament tuning. The chapel has therefore become a mecca for anyone appreciating the reedy tone quality of a genuine pre-Bach instrument. Recordings cut at Frederiksborg hold a special interest for music-lovers who fancy true baroque organ sound.

The actual birthplace of the great organist and composer *Dietrich Buxtehude* (1637–1707) cannot be specified with absolute certainty, but all major possibilities were towns then under the Danish flag. Most probably Buxtehude was born in Helsingborg (now in Sweden), then moved across the narrow Sound to Helsingør (Elsinore) where he grew up. During his youth Buxtehude served as an active church musician in both places, but no organ compositions from his own hand at this time have

10

been discovered. At least one gem by Buxtehude belonging to the composer's early Danish years has come to light, however: the delightful little church cantata *Aperite mihi portas justitiae* (Open the Gates of Justice to Me) for three voices, two violins and basso continuo. At twenty-one, Buxtehude crossed the frontier to settle permanently in Lübeck; from this point on he properly belongs to German musical history.

Seventeenth-century Sweden

On June 24, 1523, Gustav Vasa led his victorious army into Stockholm, marking the birth of the modern Swedish state. Interestingly, all the early Vasa kings displayed various degrees of musical ability. Gustav Vasa was a passable lute player while his ill-fated son Erik XIV tried his hand at polyphonic composition. Services in the royal chapel were elaborate, with works from Continental masters of the period such as Lassus, Hassler, Isaac and Senfl familiar to the choir. But other excellent choir schools also existed in the Swedish realm, the most notable located at Åbo (Turku) in Finland. Here the student Didrik Peter of Nyland compiled a book of over fifty secular and religious songs published in 1582 as *Piae Cantiones,* many of which survived as Latin school songs well into the nineteenth century and still enjoy favor with Finnish choral societies. While the Italians sang innumerable madrigals, Swedes and Finns enjoyed their own less sophisticated *Piae Cantiones* which even today sound fresh and utterly delightful. This famous collection, incidentally, furnished the tune for the Victorian Christmas carol "Good King Wenceslas."

The new unity of Swedish nationhood stirred royal ambition during the seventeenth century when the country's warrior-kings broke from the periphery of European politics into the very center as they forged a Baltic empire and made deep stabs into Russia and Poland. Gustav Adolph, initiator of Sweden's "Great Power" period, also made pioneer efforts to encourage native composers and strengthen the musical resources of his court, a wise precaution since appropriate ceremonial apparatus lay at hand when his bullet-riddled body came back from the Thirty Years' War.

Gustav Adolph finally found permanent rest among the gloomy tombs of Ridderholm Church while a double choir intoned his funeral ode *Pugna Triumphalis,* composed for the occasion by *Anders Düben* (1590–1662), a former pupil of Sweelinck and organist at Stockholm's German Church. His son *Gustav Düben* (1624–1690) may be considered the first consequential Swedish-born composer, member of a dynasty active in local musical affairs for many generations.

The enigmatic Christina, daughter of Gustav Adolph, ascended the throne in 1644 at eighteen. With typical thoroughness this brilliant scholar-queen brought her forceful personality to bear on what her courtiers saw and heard in the way of entertainment. Queen Christina's whole approach to music seems to have been more cerebral than passionate; she made an excellent impressario. Personally, Christina preferred intimate chamber ensembles and private theater parties to the pomp of state occasions, but she exhibited a high level of taste and imported excellent talent. Least of her interest went toward church music, although *Vincenzo Albrici* (1631–1696), a visiting opera producer, composed a mellifluous *Fader Vår* (Our Father) for Christina which has come down to us as the oldest preserved major composition with Swedish words.

In 1654 Christina caused a sensation by converting to Roman Catholicism, abdicating her throne and moving to Rome to continue her patronage of the arts under the southern sun. Upon her departure Swedish musical life became less colorful; however Gustav Düben and German colleagues maintained high standards. Further variety came from visiting French troupers bringing in "Lulliste" opera.

Recent years have seen some of Gustav Düben's music released from archival slumber to confirm his historical reputation. Besides sets of stately court dances and a very fine choral piece, *Veni Sancte Spiritus* (1651), listeners might also find his *Odae Sveticae* (1674) of interest as compelling examples of seventeenth-century song writing. These latter take their texts from the venerable Swedish poet Samuel Columbus.

The arts, however, found little favor from the last of the warrior-kings, Charles XII. Early in life he declared that the only music he wanted to hear would come from whizzing musket balls, a wish the gods readily granted, although when idling in Turkey he attended an occasional concert. But when a bullet finished Charles in a Norwegian trench, Sweden's overextended imperial ambitions also came to an end. With the burden of almost continual warfare lifted off their shoulders, the Swedish people turned toward more careful cultivation of their own garden.

In music the most significant change during Sweden's new "Age of Freedom" was an opening of doors. The well-traveled Handelian epigone *Johan Helmich Roman* (q.v.) stepped to the forefront of Stockholm's musical life through the initiation of public concerts that did much to abolish the stuffiness and royal exclusivity of Swedish music up to this point. Roman also conclusively demonstrated the value of the Swedish language in vocal music. For these and other reasons the worthy Roman became dubbed "the father of Swedish music," an honor fully deserved.

Somnolent Norway
From the fifteenth through eighteenth centuries a creditable, if not crushingly original, musical tradition grew up alongside the royal courts in Copenhagen and Stockholm. What was going on in Norway during these years? "Not much" makes a fair reply. Norwegians are by no means devoid of creative genius, but political and economic reverses conspired to punch a hole in their country's history. During the baroque and classical eras the cultivation of music depended on a leisured aristocracy; but no Esterházys lived in Norway.

Only after the grip of the Hanseatic League had been broken and the Norwegians were allowed to develop their own resources and mercantile system could artistic currents flow easily to Norwegian shores. With the revival of trade in the eighteenth century, the west coast port of Bergen began to stir more vigorously in cultural matters. In 1765 a group of public-spirited Bergensers founded an orchestral society, the *Harmonien* — still in existence as one of the world's oldest symphony orchestras. The society's records, going back as far as 1792, indicate a library containing a surprising number of Haydn scores as well as good representation of Mozart.

Further north, at Trondheim, the local church organist wrote orchestral and chamber music in the *galant* manner, but *Johan Heinrich Berlin* (1741–1808) was a rare bird; in those days Norway could support few professional musicians and these worked in widely scattered posts. The governing upper crust of Dano-Norwegians naturally looked to Copenhagen for musical stimulation, leaving Norway's "national voice" slumbering in the ignored world of folk music.

The Rise of Danish Music

Until the eighteenth century art music in Scandinavia showed no appreciable differences from what was current in the rest of Europe, but gradually changes began to appear, very slight at first, like tendrils sprouting from a parent tree. As with their languages, the three Nordic kingdoms own a common musical background with growth leading to three distinct but closely intertwined traditions. The Nordic sound is regional, but it has three main variants. Danish music was the first to establish its identity.

During the early and middle decades of the eighteenth century, the nobility and well-to-do of Copenhagen shared Europe's passion for opera. At first the ubiquitous Italian type predominated, but later the city's musicians brought forth worthy comic and dramatic examples of their own. The capital's musical ferment owed much to numerous resident foreigners, mostly Germans and Italians but with a good sprinkling of Frenchmen and others. The most potent cultural figure in town, however, originally hailed from Norway — the incisive dramatist Ludvig Holberg, sometimes called the "Molière of the North." A competent musician himself, Holberg encouraged the presentation of public concerts sponsored by the newly affluent merchant class and he made ample room in his popular plays for songs, dances, interludes and other musical numbers. Holberg was also largely responsible for the restoration of Danish as the official language of the court and army where German had long held sway. In a real way, Holberg sparked a new birth of Danish national consciousness.

The two kingpins of Italian opera in Copenhagen were *Paolo Scalabrini* (1713–1802) and his formidable rival *Giuseppe Sarti* (1729-1802), perhaps best known to musical history as the teacher of Cherubini. For a while these two carried on a lively "war of the theaters," but the exceptionally gifted Sarti washed himself out of the country by foolish dabbling in court intrigue. Not long after, Italian opera fever subsided, with its replacement as theatrical entertainment coming in the form of a new type of comic opera more adapted to northern tastes.

13

Singspiel, a German word meaning "song play," can claim several sources for origin, but full growth of this type of popular music drama came about mainly in Germany in the hands of composers like Johann Hiller. The chief innovation rendered by singspiel was the appearance in the theater of folk-like songs coupled with familiar plots using colloquial dialogue, homespun informality giving the public relief from the increasingly sterile mannerisms of Italian *opera buffa*. Singspiel took deep root in Scandinavia; in fact, the North became its final refuge.

Some of the early Danish singspiels dwelt on national subjects, a considerable novelty at the time. *Johan Ernst Hartmann* (1726–1793), a German immigrant and patriarch of Danish music, is remembered as the first composer to bring a clear-cut "Nordic note" into music, notably in his two most celebrated singspiels, *Balders Død* (The Death of Balder) and *Fiskerne* (The Fishermen), on stage around the time of the American Revolution. Hartmann founded a distinguished musical dynasty in his adopted country, with its influence felt to the present day.

Edouard Du Puy (1773–1822), born in Switzerland, displayed many talents both in music and among the ladies. Copenhagen knew him in several guises: violinist, conductor, composer and tenor. In 1806 Du Puy gave his public the ballad opera *Ungdom og Galskab* (Youth and Folly), one of the most durable of all Danish singspiels. Du Puy greatly admired Mozart (he sang the North's first Don Giovanni) and his merry overture for *Youth and Folly* shows it.

What can be accepted as the true groundwork for a distinctive Danish variant of the Nordic sound, however, followed from the example of *Johan Abraham Peter Schulz* (1747–1800), a baker's son from the little town of Lüneberg in Germany. Schulz spent only eight years in Denmark, but these were crammed with activity. Upon accepting the post of court conductor, Schulz came straight to Copenhagen from Berlin where he had been at the center of a circle of poets and musicians fostering the idea that the song style of the common people held artistic merit. This group of preromantics demonstrated less interest in folk-song collecting than in producing their own popular songs in folk-song manner adapted to current native verse. Simplicity and naturalness were their aim; they desired songs of a "quasi-familiar" nature as Schulz himself described them. Just before his move to Denmark, Schulz published his collection *Lieder im Volkston* (Songs in Folk Style, 1790), a seminal work in the German lieder tradition.

Once engaged in his new duties, Schulz promptly saw that Danish folklore offered intriguing musical possibilities. While he produced no Danish songs comparable to what he had published in Germany, he brought local folk tone (or folk "mood") into singspiels such as *Høstgildet* (Harvest Festival) and *Peters Bryllup* (Peter's Wedding); both encountered great success. In Schulz' theater music, native audiences discovered something delightfully fresh, yet at the same time entirely familiar, coming at them across the footlights. In effect, Schulz had found the secret key to

Danish musical sentiments: simplicity, the breath of old ballads, homespun charm and the lilt of folk song. Schulz blended these to form the substrate of Danish song, and song forms the germinating core of Danish music.

The Gustavian Flowering

Stockholm, toward the close of the eighteenth century, demonstrated all the dismal features of an overcrowded provincial seaport and capital of an impoverished nation. Debauchery, drunkenness and human wretchedness lay at every hand. Yet, under royal leadership, this same city supported a remarkable feast of the arts. King Gustav III, the prime mover, saw himself as Sweden's cultural Messiah and went about his role with uncommon zeal. What funds he could lay his hands on went for lavish court entertainments. Gustav imported scores of musicians and theater people and to insure the quality of his offerings founded the Academy of Music in 1771 and the Royal Opera two years later.

Opera was Gustav's overriding passion; he adored Glück. For the all-important post of opera director, the king summoned *Francesco Uttini* (1723–1795), long resident in Sweden and a skilled composer with lively command of the court theater style. But Uttini's administrative abilities seem to have been inferior to his musical qualifications, leading to his dismissal and the arrival of his successor *Johann Gottlieb Naumann* (1741–1801). Sweden was but a sidelight in Naumann's brilliant career. He was among the most celebrated musicians of his day, one of the few German classical masters to win fame with serious opera in Italy. Naumann's two visits to Gustav's court were brief but highly significant. Aside from providing Italian-style opera (some using Swedish librettos), Naumann wrote the music for the historical epic *Gustav Vasa* (1786) with libretto by Johan Kellgren, apparently from a draft prepared by Gustav III himself. Both musically and dramatically this pioneer Scandinavian national opera has shown sufficient strength to survive its era.

But opera and drama did not entirely dominate the Gustavian flowering. Of the able musicians at court, both *Joseph Martin Kraus* (1756–1792) and the itinerant *Georg Joseph Vogler* (1749–1814) contributed their share of instrumental pieces. Today's listener is likely to find Kraus' music of more than passing interest, particularly his outgoing string quartets and the bold, high-strung Symphony in C minor (1783) with its affinity for the *Strum und Drang* of Haydn's middle period. Even more impressive is Kraus' last work, the heartfelt *Funeral Cantata for Gustav III* (1792), a tribute by the composer to his assassinated patron, but, as fate decided, his own requiem as well.

The friends and disciples of Kraus and Vogler included *Johan Wikmanson* (1753–1800), organist, longtime lottery clerk and perhaps the most informed native-born composer in Stockholm since the days of Roman. Wikmanson's well honed music deserves rescue from the history books. Of his small number of works, some sonatas and other keyboard pieces exhibit imagination along with rococo charm, but Wikmanson's three smoothly reasoned string quartets remembering Haydn are on a considerably higher level.

Competent and enjoyable as their music may be, composers like Kraus and Wikmanson count as minor figures working in the farther reaches of eighteenth-century *Empfindsamkeit* ("marked by feeling"). The true genius of Gustavian art — *Carl Michael Bellman* (q.v.) — took a much different path. The subtle blend of humor and irony in his songs more surely captures the flavor of Gustavian Sweden than all the king's operas strung end on end.

Pure chance has preserved an important focus for much Swedish theatrical and musical activity of the eighteenth-century. From downtown Stockholm the Drottningholm Court Theater is a short boat ride which turns the clock back to plant the visitor in the world of Kraus and Bellman. The theater, a small outbuilding off to the side from the main palace, seems plain enough, but the romance awaits inside; an intact rococo theater complete in every detail, with original sets, costumes and stage machinery. Restored to operation in 1922, the Drottningholm Theater carries on like a ghost from the past presenting a regular season of operas by Pergolesi, Glück, Handel and their contemporaries in an authentic milieu. The Gustavians have long since vanished, but their little theater at Drottningholm remains behind, the living memento of a resplendent artistic era.

ROMANTICISM AND NATIONAL ASSERTION

The abused term "romanticism" has been applied so widely as to include almost any piece with clearcut melody and emotional feeling. "Romantic" more literally refers to a particular historical movement from the first half of the nineteenth century when a revolutionary spirit swept through the arts, especially north of the Alps. Robert Schumann, one of the first to fully grasp this new cultural phenomenon as it affected music, personally disliked the term "romantic," but he indicated that his view of musical romanticism should include originality, fantasy and a touch of the poetic.

Almost every aspect of German romantic music ramified in Scandinavia with proliferation of such typical forms as the "character" piano piece, the art song and to lesser degree the tone poem. In many ways the new wave meant liberation of native ideas and national consciousnss in the North rather than slavish devotion to the German ideal. Although partly derivative, Scandinavian romanticism developed a distinctive flavor drawn from deep roots of its own. For almost five hundred years the Nordic peoples had received a steady flow of foreign ideas. They showed some flashes of response in science and literature, but musically they had largely remained a colony. But by glorifying the ancient past, romanticism caused the resurrection of the entire panorama of the old Nordic world. Read again after centuries of neglect, the sagas and eddas gave the modern Scandinavians a badly needed link with the past to bolster their cultural confidence. An extreme view, but one based on more than fantasy, showed the Scandinavians as the direct heirs and rightful guardians of the whole Germanic tradition.

Folklore, the "living" past and presumed key to ethnic identity, broke like a dam to release a flood of previously disregarded songs, dances and tales to enrich both music and literature. The twin rivers of romanticism and nationalism began flowing together. In the North, this manifestation proceeded most strongly in "underdog" Norway and may be compared with similar developments then arising among the Poles, Czechs and Russians. Less intensely, Sweden and Denmark also showed vigorous stirrings of renewed national pride. By no means does all worthwhile Scandinavian music fall within the romantic era, but this was a time when northern composers began to put their best foot forward; for the first time, a few of them even managed to draw the attention of the entire world.

Romanticism in Denmark

The opening shot of Scandinavian romanticism boomed in 1802 when Adam Oehlenschläger wrote his celebrated poem *Guldhornene* (The Golden Horns). A "Golden Age" of Danish letters swiftly followed, filling Copenhagen's streets with a host of literary aspirants whose reams of verse and stacks of plays cried out for musical alliance. Christian Winther, B. S. Ingmann, N. F. S. Grundtvig and Hans Christian Andersen, to name but a few of the more prominent authors of the day, all contributed to the substance of Danish romantic music. *Christoph Weyse* (q.v.) stands as the most important composer in forging the critical link between Danish romantic poetry and music. By refining the folk tone idiom of his teacher and mentor J.A.P. Schulz, Weyse gave the Danish song, or *romanse,* its classic profile. Strong collateral support also came from the style of French operatic plays of the day which were introduced and imitated in Denmark.

Scandinavian art songs are often referred to as lieder, but in general the German *lied* and Nordic *romanse* are not synonymous. True lieder lost all innocence after Schubert; by the time of Hugo Wolf, German song showed attributes of miniature music drama. Piano accompaniments developed into full partnership with the vocal part, both of them probing the depths of poetic meaning. Scandinavian romantic song rarely achieved such intensity; exceptions occur, but Nordic song tended to remain far simpler, almost pre-Schubertian. Danish songs particularly seemed content to breathe softly and rock on billowy rhythms not too far removed from the noble strains of balladic ancestors. Romantic song in the North developed along channels of its own, not as mere spillover from the German watershed. By and large the aim of the *romanse* is the evocation of poetic mood; true lieder covers a broader emotional range and comes to grips with poetic meaning.

As another point of difference, the Scandinavian *romanse* kept close ties with the theater through singspiel. In this area Weyse encountered competition from *Friedrich Daniel Kuhlau* (1786–1832), a one-eyed fugitive from Napoleon's recruiting sergeants, who fled to Denmark from his native Germany in 1810. Kuhlau brought the idiom of Beethoven and Weber with him, well-exemplified by his sturdy C major Piano Concerto. His fleet-fingered sonatinas for piano and copious opus numbers for flute have retained a fair degree of international currency, but in Denmark Kuhlau's fame rests on *Elverhøj* (Elf Hill, 1828), a well-fabricated singspiel which popularized the air *King Christian Stood Before the Mast,* later taken up as the Danish National Anthem. If the Danes can be said to own a true "national opera," *Elverhøj* most closely fills the bill.

New heights in Danish romantic song appeared with *Peter Heise* (1830–1879). Like so many of Scandinavia's nineteenth-century composers, Heise trained at the Leipzig Conservatory, but his best songs lie well within his native tradition, particularly when he set the poems of Christian Winther. His late cycle *Songs of Dyveke* with text from Holger Drachmann has been considered an outstanding example of Danish musical romanticism. The spirit of medieval balladry, with perhaps more than a touch of Wagnerianism, runs through *Drot og Marsk* (King and Constable, 1878), Heise's best-known opera.

Outside Scandinavia, most music lovers would doubtless point to *Edvard Grieg* (q.v.) as the high priest of Nordic romanticism, but that position more properly belongs to his considerably older colleague *Johan Peter Emelius Hartmann* (1805–1900), whose life covered virtually the entire period. Grieg worked from a narrower Norwegian base. Hartmann crossed national boundaries to follow the broader currents of pan-Scandinavianism which held great interest for cultural leaders in the North until Bismark's army crushed abandoned Denmark in 1864 to reveal the whole idea as a dream. Hartmann composed in all forms, but this illustrious scion of Denmark's foremost musical family most firmly established his name as a composer through songs and works for the stage. As time goes on, Hartmann's most ambitious efforts have largely receded into silence (concert overtures, ballets, dramatic pieces), but Hartmann, above all composers, was first to earnestly and consciously cultivate the Nordic sound. A beautiful example occurs in the opening measures of his melodrama *Guldhornene* (1832) where Oehlenschläger's rolling lines are cloaked in rich yet gloomy sonority. Hartmann's vivid, theatrical style has been likened to the clash of viking shields and the heroic meter of the ancient sagas. In fact, Hartmann mined Old Norse literature on several occasions, culminating in his cantata for male voices *Vøluens Spådom* (Sayings of the Prophetess, 1872) based on the opening section of the *Poetic Edda*.

On the other hand, Hartmann could turn on pure Danish charm when the occasion demanded as in the repeatedly performed opera *Liden Kirsten* (Little Kirsten) with libretto from H.C. Andersen. In songs like *Flyv, Fugl, Flyv* (Fly, Bird, Fly) and *Du, som har sorg i sinde* (You, with Sorrow in Your Heart) he moved right to the heart of Danish romantic poetry.

The lack of attention paid to J.P.E. Hartmann's music outside Denmark contrasts with the situation of his son-in-law *Niels W. Gade* (q.v.), who quickly gained and held an international reputation. Early in life Gade came under the wing of Felix Mendelssohn, who warmly welcomed him to the Leipzig inner circle. Here Gade proved an able lieutenant; he conducted the Gewandhaus orchestra, befriended the Schumanns, heard his works praised by Europe's musical elite and when the sorrowful hour arrived he helped carry Mendelssohn's casket to a premature grave.

Political friction between Denmark and Prussia, however, terminated Gade's Leipzig idyll and prompted his return to Copenhagen. Once back home, he pursued lifetime careers as organist, conductor, teacher and composer. In 1852 he married Sophie, daughter of J.P.E. Hartmann, cementing his relationship with the kingdom's leading musical family, and although his young wife died within a few years, Gade reigned on as the lion of Scandinavian music.

Two generations of Nordic composers passed directly or indirectly within range of Gade's critical glance. When they were no more than promising youngsters both Grieg and the Funen peasant boy *Carl Nielsen* (q.v.) encountered his sometimes gruff but helpful paternalism.

One junior composer, however, found Gade anathema. This was Grieg's Danish classmate at the Leipzig Conservatory, *Christian Frederik Emil Horneman* (1840–1906). Horneman's almost pathological antagonism toward the mighty Gade undoubtedly damaged his own career and possibly prevented his creative potential from being fully exercised. But a fair idea of his abilities may be gleaned from his masterful, incisive *Aladdin Overture* (1864), one of the high points of nineteenth-century Danish orchestral composition. Twenty years later he completed his grand opera *Aladdin*. The vigorous orchestral technique displayed in *Aladdin* pointed directly toward Carl Nielsen, who once referred to Horneman as "The flame, the separating fire in Danish music."

Tivoli, Copenhagen's downtown park filled in summertime with floral, gastronomic, theatrical and musical delights, came into existence during the reign of Christian VIII, Denmark's last absolute monarch. An entrepreneur persuaded His Majesty that citizens offered a chance to amuse themselves at public expense might prove disinclined to ponder politics — bread and circuses with a Danish twist. Some outmoded fortifications in the center of the growing capital came down for Tivoli, opened officially for public pleasure in August 1843. Well over a century later these gardens have become hallowed with musical memories for Danes and legions of visitors alike.

Music was meant to be an integral part of the fun at Tivoli from the very beginning. The choice of *Hans Christian Lumbye* (1810–1874) as Tivoli's first musical director paid fast dividends. As a young army bandsman, Lumbye lent a thoughtful ear to the new ballroom dances brought to Copenhagen by a visiting Austrian orchestra. Soon he had formed a group of his own to exploit the style perfected by Vienna's Lanner and the Strauss family, as well as by Musard in Paris. By no means a mere imitator, Lumbye added a few tricks of his own to the presentation of dance and novelty numbers, proving to his Danish audiences that native confectionary could taste as delectable as imported musical bonbons. Other members of the Lumbye family carried on, building a reputation for Tivoli in the field of light music recognized throughout the world.

Lumbye has been dubbed the "Johann Strauss of the North," but in all fairness his inspiration rarely soared to such heights as the immortal *Blue Danube*. Much of the fresh bloom once on his music has wilted with time. In recent years the Danish younger generation has grown frankly bored with it; reared in the world-wide mass culture, Danish youth goes to Tivoli to hear rock music, not Lumbye. Like much else from a bygone era, the old Tivoli spirit which is inseparable from Lumbye's music may be on the way out. But if decidedly "square," the music of Hans Christian Lumbye liltingly paints an authentic picture of nineteenth-century Danish sentiment. Lumbye was capable as a waltz composer, but his real forte was the galop. The valiant swing of his best marches is also memorable. For listeners who may be unfamiliar with Lumbye's often delightful music, a few starting points are suggested: *Christian IX Honor March, Amelia Waltz* and the irrepressible *Champagne Galop.*

Mid-nineteenth-century Denmark witnessed the flowering of another famed national institution. The Royal Danish Ballet can trace origins back to Christian IV or even earlier, but the greatest organizing genius in its long history was undoubtedly August Bournonville (1805–1879), the son of a French dancing master but born in Denmark. Enormously energetic, Bournonville devoted his entire life to the Royal Ballet and left a lasting imprint on nearly all its productions. Only in later years has the company been able to pull beyond Bournonville's magnetic influence. During his long tenure, Bournonville assumed full responsibility for almost 150 productions. Of these some dozen remain active in the repertoire, with *La Sylphide* and *Napoli* heading the list. When Bournonville reigned supreme, Copenhagen's composers fluttered about him as moths around a flame.

Norwegian Resurgence

The bursting patriotism readily apparent to visitors in Norway stems from an age-old struggle against nature, the memory of a heroic past, and a specific set of political circumstances. Modern Norway followed in the wake of Napoleon's exit from history, a time of territorial reshuffling all over Europe. The victorious powers punished the Danish losers and rewarded their Swedish allies with Norway as the pawn. The upshot for the Norwegian people meant quasi-independence, a compromise that allowed them to keep their liberal Constitution of 1814 along with a parliament (*Storting*), but ultimately the reins were pulled from Stockholm. Culturally speaking, however, the uneasy century of Swedo-Norwegian union saw the Norwegian half surge ahead toward ethnic reaffirmation under the banner of national romanticism.

The main thrust of the Norwegian revival came from literature with Henrik Wergeland and then Bjørnsterne Bjørnson in the vanguard, but music grew increasingly important in the national romantic movement. A modest start began with *Waldemar Thrane* (1790–1828), first of several Norwegian composers to spring from the conservative drawing rooms of the merchant class. Thrane's compositions are of slight importance with the exception of *Fjeldeventyret* (Tales of the Mountains, 1824), a singspiel about vacationing university students and their rustic girlfriends. Here, in one number called "Aagot's Song," a clear-cut Norwegian melody surfaces for the first time in Norwegian art music.* Rearranged in Swedish as *Fjällvisan* (Mountain Song), Thrane's little slice of local color became a staple number in the repertoire of Jenny Lind.

Norwegian national romanticism received an enormous boost from the fabulous *Ole Bull* (1810–1880). Of his many roles, his proudest was "That Norwegian Norseman from Norway." Before Ole Bull could read or

---

*Kuhlau's piano variations on "God Dag, Rasmus Jansen," Op. 15 (1817) is another example of pioneering with Norwegian folk song.

write he had steeped himself in the tales and tunes of rural Norway. Later in life, as a celebrated violinist of the Paganini breed, he brought some of this music (or at least his version of it) to the concert stages of three continents at a time when the existence of a country called Norway was barely recognized. His countrymen, slowly feeling their way toward independence and national consciousness, could not have been better represented than by this unofficial, vociferous ambassador. His flamboyance and exploits gave birth to countless legends; when Ole Bull stepped up to draw his bow, men were known to weep and their ladies to swoon.

Less can be said of Ole Bull the composer. Only a tiny fraction of his compositions has survived; the bulk of them consisted of flashy potpourris or arrangements of popular airs bent to the service of his pyrotechnical manner of playing. Shrewd critics like Eduard Hanslick saw through Bull's razzle-dazzle to pronounce him "The immature product of a fantasy in hopeless ferment." Yet in a few pieces such as the wistful *Saeterjentens søndag* (Seter Girl's Sunday), Ole Bull clearly demonstrated his genuine affinity for Norwegian folk tone. All in all, this impulsive genius rendered great service to Norway's music even if he sometimes presented it tinged with the smell of the circus.

Among the first to follow the path pointed out by Ole Bull and take a close look at Norwegian folk music, *Halfdan Kjerulf* (q.v.) carved a niche for himself in the musical reawakening of Norway which is sometimes undervalued. Kjerulf restricted himself to small forms, but some of his songs rank with the finest music from the North. A more systematic approach to folk music was undertaken by *Ludvig Mathias Lindeman* (1812–1887), son of an organist and scion of a family long at the heart of Norwegian musical affairs. Lindeman's search for authentic folk music led him to some of the remotest parts of Norway and the accumulation of a monumental store of native songs and dances. Lindeman's published folk-song collections played a seminal role in the distinctive romanticism of Kjerulf, Grieg and others.

Credit for Norway's initial romantic symphony belongs to the almost totally forgotten *Otto Winter-Hjelm* (1837–1921), but orchestral music in nineteenth-century Norway really got its start with *Johan Svendsen* (q.v.), whose best pieces with their careful blend of national color and cosmopolitanism have held up remarkably well. The arch-romantic flamboyance of Liszt and Berlioz found a Norwegian echo in *Johan Peter Selmer* (1844–1910), but his vivid imagination an as orchestrator failed to sustain his tone poems alongside the national romantic school. Mention should also be made of *Johannes Haarklou* (1847–1925), the composer of four romantic symphonies and five operas.

The generally dismal story of opera in Norway brings up *Martin Udbye* (1820–1889), whose struggles to get his efforts mounted on the stage ended in nothing but heartbreaking futility. Grieg and Bjørnson's bid for a "national opera" (*Olav Trygvason*) was similarly abortive. The climate was favorable, but Norway produced no Smetana or Mussorgsky.

According to most reference sources, *Rikard Nordraak* (1842–1866) played a crucial role in the development of Norwegian national-romantic music by supposedly pointing young Edvard Grieg in the right direction. But when the facts are examined objectively, this "Song of Norway" relationship contains a generous amalgam of myth and distortion for which Grieg himself must share some blame.

At best, Nordraak appears as a dilettante with promising musical talent, at worst a flash-in-the-pan feeding off the endless fantasies of Ole Bull. His few completed works (songs, piano morceaux and some theater music) show an ultra-simplistic melodic idiom in which naive handling of cadences and timid employment of harmonic coloration merely skim the surface of folk music. There has been much written about the alleged importance of Nordraak, but attempts actually to hear any of his music or obtain scores can prove frustrating. Only a tiny fraction of his music has been commercially recorded to date. The sole exception, of course, is *Yes, We Love This Land,* Norway's National Anthem, where Nordraak's hymnal tune sets words by his cousin Bjørnstjerne Bjørnson.

Although Nordraak and Grieg became fast friends during the course of a fruitful interlude in Copenhagen, comparison of the two young composers puts Nordraak at decided disadvantage. When death snatched him at the age of twenty-four, the differences between his dreams and the actual attainments of Grieg were already painfully apparent.

As for Edvard Grieg, a modern biography critically examining his accomplishment and free of national bias is badly needed.* Grieg's undeniable position as a link between romanticism and the impressionistic origins of modern music deserve to be more widely appreciated.

All his life Grieg experimented with harmonic coloration, pushing the frontiers of tonality forward in his constant employment of complex chords, unusual dissonances, bitonal and bimodal passages, sudden shifts from key to key, and waverings between major and minor. These features, as much as short-breathed phrases, alluring melody and virile rhythms, lie at the root of Grieg's inimitable style.

Grieg's involvement with Norwegian folk music happily remained free of pseudo-philosophizing or pedantry; in fact, he returned to native soil more than he mined from it. A legitimate question has followed: Did Grieg's music become increasingly Norwegian, or did Norwegian music become more "Griegian"? No matter what the reply, Grieg's wonderful music should be taken for what it is, not as others wish or imagine it to be. His art demands no hero worship. The ardent nationalist might feel disappointment that his country's greatest composer left behind no monumental symphonies or operas for the greater glory of Norway; in truth, the dreams and visions of Ole Bull and Rikard Nordraak remain unfulfilled. Instead, Grieg showed the mettle of a great artist by remaining true to him-

*For a scholarly investigation of Grieg's early career, however, see Dag Schjelderup-Ebbe, *Edvard Grieg: 1858-1867* (London: Allen & Unwin, 1964).

23

self. He had limitations, and swallowed them hard, but from his inner struggles a purer voice emerged, one decidedly Norwegian yet at the same time rising far above parochial confines.

The national school consolidating around Grieg was badly weakened by the departure of Svendsen for Copenhagen, leaving only comparatively minor figures working alongside The Master, yet an occasional song or short instrumental piece sometimes brings one or another of these satellite composers to mind. Despite Grieg's great prestige, romantic music in Norway was by no means his monopoly. Orbiting about him were *Ole Olsen* (1850–1927), still remembered for his *Solefaldssang* (Sunset Song); the conductor and choral composer *Ivar Holter* (1850–1941); and *Per Winge* (1858–1935), whose songs helped carry on the Kjerulf tradition. A true Norwegian flame brightens the modest but charming songs and chamber music of *Sigurd Lie* (1871–1904) and the Oslo organist *Eyvind Alnaes* (1872–1932), whose many fine songs carry fertile melodic inspiration.

Norway is the only Scandinavian country showing prominent women composers starting with *Agathe Backer-Grøndahl* (1847–1907), almost an exact contemporary of Grieg. Solidly trained in Germany (including a spell with Liszt at Weimar), Backer-Grøndahl became a concert pianist of international renown. Her reserved creative sensitivity may be readily appreciated from songs like the celebrated *Mot Kveld* (Towards Evening), but her unjustly neglected "concert études" and other works for pianoforte sometimes show remarkable poetic insight and resourcefulness. Although less a beguiling melodist than Grieg, her subtle use of folk tone coloration and harmonic boldness rival his while the sheer elegance of her technique may actually dig deeper.

Little is heard any longer from *Catharinus Elling* (1858–1948) or *Gerhard Schjelderup* (1859–1933), but both held leading positions in late-romantic Norwegian music. Elling was an erudite folk-song collector as well as symphonist; Schjelderup fell in love with the ideals of Richard Wagner. He fought valiantly in Germany, but his music dramas failed to gain more than a toehold on the stage.

Other minor composers might be added, but these are enough to indicate that during the nineteenth century, under the sway of romanticism and nationalist fervor, the Norwegians more than took up the slack in music; one might say they did it with vengeance. Today, few will claim that all this music merits instant revival, but the sheer industry of Grieg's numerous Norwegian contemporaries and immediate followers not only commands respect, but whets the appetite for deeper exploration.

Romanticism in Sweden
Compared to her Nordic neighbors, Swedish romantic music got off to a sluggish start. A firm literary basis lighting the way toward romantic ideals was held back by partisan squabbling, while the dynastic shift to the House of Bernadotte diverted attention from music. Even the Royal Opera lay dark for a few years. At the Academy of Music a condition resembling

rigor mortis had begun to set in until Crown Prince Carl Johan took an active interest, but not until the middle of the century were his intentions of a well-equipped conservatory along French lines fully realized. Laws limiting theatrical performances and musical publication also exerted a contrary influence on the spread of new ideas. Although Swedish music lay in the doldrums in the early decades of the nineteenth century, the assumption should not be made that musical culture failed to advance at all. The emergence of internationally-renowned performing artists like Jenny Lind and Christina Nilsson (both born before 1850) indicates that the Swedes had not run out of talent.

The university town of Uppsala became the germinal center of Sweden's romantic movement largely due to the presence of *Erik Gustav Geijer* (1783–1847), a many-sided savant whose considerable talents also included folk-song gathering and musical composition. Geijer's songs, chamber music and piano pieces speak with romantic restraint, at times recalling Mendelssohn. Other composers more or less affiliated with Geijer's circle include *Otto Lindblad* (1809–1864), *Jacob Axel Josephson* (1818–1880) and the clarinet virtuoso *Bernhard Crusell* (1775–1838). A few of their works, chiefly songs and choral pieces, retain minor positions in the present Swedish repertoire.

Early romanticism's brightest flame, however, worked apart from the Uppsala atmosphere. *Carl Jonas Love Almqvist* (1793–1866) was primarily a writer, one of the most original and erratic literary geniuses ever produced in the North. He was somewhat like Wagner in that his jostling stream of thoughts demanded musical as well as literary outlets, so he also became adept at composition. While Almquist failed to master sufficient technical equipment to qualify as a professional, he cannot be dismissed as a stumbling amateur. In austere, unaccompanied songs which he collectively called *Songes* (Dreams) and free fantasias for piano, Almquist presented a remarkable attempt to fuse musical and poetic ideas. Almquist's own life could have come from one of his fantastic novels and included an episode when he fled to America under a charge of murder.

A more consistent level of inspiration came from *Adolf Fredrik Lindblad* (1801–1878), who read the signals of Robert Schumann more clearly than most composers in the North. Lindblad's Symphony in C (1831) earned much admiration while his opera *Frondörerna* (The Critics) gained an historical niche as the vehicle for Jenny Lind's stage debut. But the best of Lindblad may be found among his estimated two hundred songs and warm, intimate choral works such as the cycle *Drömmarne* (The Dreams). As a songwriter, Lindblad committed few sins of taste or workmanship, although some issue might be taken with texts often drawn from his own inferior poetry. On the credit side, Lindblad proved himself the first professional Swedish composer fully attuned to the romantic movement and with fastidious craftsmanship to match. Sure feeling for telling lyricism and breadth of melody were his strong points. His song *En sommardag* (A Summer's Day), for example, has been cited for having one of the loveliest melodies in all Swedish music.

Until well into the nineteenth century much of Sweden's musical life was borne on the shoulders of amateurs and dilettantes, a large group of unschooled townsmen with tastes running to parlor songs and male quartets. Too often music was cultivated by their ladies to ward off boredom or used to accompany a reception in the home. Sometimes music was relegated to a mere interlude between acts of a play; some hapless pianist would play to a distracted audience or even a movement from a Beethoven symphony would be given, mainly to drown backstage noise during scene changes.

Yet many encouraging signs appeared as well. The Royal Opera continued to function while concert societies and chamber music groups showed signs of revival. Best of all, the cultivation of music in cities other than Stockholm had begun to bear fruit and provided some balance against overcentralization. This was particularly noticeable in Göteborg (Gothenburg), Sweden's thriving west coast port sometimes called "Little London" because many residents claim British descent, but a large population of Dutch, Germans and Jews also called this city home. With affluence came the desire for the amenities. When Bedřich Smetana, then a comparatively little-known musician, arrived at Gothenberg in 1856, he found a community eager to support his efforts as a pianist, teacher and organizer of concerts. Smetana remained five years in Sweden, mostly in Gothenberg but with concert tours ranging as far as Stockholm. His relationships with native composers seem to have been cordial, if not particularly close, but his influence on elevating performance standards set a new mark in what, at that time, was a provincial community with limited cultural horizons.

Choral singing gradually became established tradition at Uppsala and the other university town of Lund, in southern Sweden. Names looming large in this connection include *Johann Haeffner* (1759–1833) followed by *Gunnar Wennerberg* (1817–1901). The mid-century brightening of Swedish musical skies also owes much to renewed interest in music on the part of the royal family, not only from the monarchs Oscar I and Oscar II, but particularly the short-lived *Prince Gustav* (1827–1852), a talented composer in his own right, whose student songs live on.

Against this background of provincialism and spotty musical activity, Sweden suddenly produced a composer of true genius: *Franz Berwald* (q. v.) The Berwald clan originally hailed from the region around Königsberg in East Prussia, a generally hard-bitten breed boasting a family tree dripping with able professional musicians. By the end of the eighteenth century a Swedish branch of the family was flourishing with several members in the court orchestra. In keeping with family custom, Franz Berwald's musical education began early, at the tender age of five; he made his debut as a violinist at nine followed by a public concert in Stockholm the following year.

As a composer, however, Franz Berwald soared far above his family's honest kapellmeister heritage. Yet for years on end his native Sweden returned him nothing but rejection and discouragement, forcing him to support his wife and children through a variety of nonmusical business enterprises where, like Ives and Palestrina, he revealed a certain shrewdness in commerce.

Franz Berwald was never drawn into the romantic vortex; his music diverged from current styles of the period. Some critics found it old-fashioned, others commented sourly on its modernity. The chief features of his idiom seem born out of Beethoven and pre-romantic French opera with eyes fixed on a revitalized classic ideal. Paradoxically, the dramatic element in Berwald's creative makeup served well for his tightly-knit symphonies, but bogged down when he wrote for the stage. The successful opera which might have put Berwald over the top during his lifetime failed to materialize. Instead, like Berlioz, he suffered gross audience misunderstanding. Passages in Berwald's symphonies (notably his slow movements) embody a "pure" form of the Nordic sound, that is, a characteristic tonal atmosphere without obvious folk-song coloration. Berwald composed in all forms but was at his peak with the orchestra and string quartet. Posterity has safely judged Franz Berwald as Sweden's greatest composer of the nineteenth century.

Sweden paid a high price for spurning the genius of Berwald; the climate necessary to generate large-scale symphonic music was delayed for years. A few of Berwald's admirers made some effort in this direction but neither *Albert Rubenson* (1826–1901) nor *Ludwig Norman* (1831–1885) packed the punch needed to develop Swedish symphonism. The estimable Norman, however, may be likened to Denmark's Niels Gade in some respects. He proved a dedicated conductor whose activities did much to bring Swedish concert life out of the stagnation of dilettantism and provincialism. His own compositions, polished reflections from the Leipzig Conservatory, nevertheless show considerable strength, particularly in his string quartets. The operatic front found *Ivar Hallström* (1826–1901) and then *Andreas Hallén* (1846–1925) rising to local fame in the period after Berwald, but Hallström's charm and Hallén's worship of Wagner have failed to sustain their memories apart from the chronicles of Swedish music.

Compared to Norway, developments in Swedish national romantic music seem tepid and unspectacular until taking the measure of *August Söderman* (1832–1876), who roughly compares with Norway's Kjerulf. Both composers trained at Leipzig and outwardly led quiet lives; both appreciated folk song but avoided bellicose nationalism at all costs. Söderman, however, produced a great deal of theater music, notably for *Peer Gynt* (written before Grieg's) and his spirited overture for Schiller's *Jungfru von Orleans* (The Maid of Orleans). His piano pieces, some of which paraphrase Almquist's fantasias, show rare wit. But the most vital aspect of Söderman's work appears in his works for chorus, particularly the invigorating, infectious cycle for male voices, *Ett bondbröllop* (A Country Wedding, 1868), which recalls the composer's close tion with choral singing at Uppsala. This piece has been described as the most Swedish of all

27

Swedish music. On the other hand, Söderman's true masterpiece may be his rarely-heard *Catholic Mass* (1875).

If Grieg had a Swedish counterpart during the days of the Swedo-Norwegian Union, that composer might well be *Emil Sjögren* (1853–1918). Like Grieg, he too enjoyed pulling chords apart to seek fresh coloristic effects and contrasts. Many of his songs (often using non-Swedish texts) are close to German lieder. Perhaps Sjögren's most lasting work, however, may be found in his three violin/piano sonatas; these glow with the warm emotion and poetic expansiveness of a true romantic soul.

FOLK TRAILS

The population matrix of Scandinavia has remained comparatively stable for almost two thousand years. Major shifts have been largely limited to outflow — southward tribal wanderings as the Roman Empire declined, overseas colonization by vikings, and the heavy nineteenth-century exodus to America. Yet within Scandinavia, ethnic profiles have tended to remain sharply drawn. Industrialization has exerted a profound effect in moving people from farm to city, but a large number of families have stayed put. Some inhabitants of Jutland, for instance, bear a striking resemblance to the fantastically preserved bog man ("Tollund Man") on display in the little museum at Silkeborg, a gruesome memento from the Iron Age two thousand years ago. Population fixation as much as geographical remoteness, therefore, gave the Scandinavians an ideal crucible for the evolution of folklore.

Most Scandinavian folklore found today came into being after the Middle Ages but before the 1850s. Since then modern technology, by putting an end to village isolation, has checked the flow. Old ways have largely succumbed to railroads, telegraph and telephone; radio, motion pictures and, finally, television have delivered the coup de grâce. Fortunately, interest in peasant culture formed a major tenet in nineteenth-century Scandinavian romanticism which led to efforts at preservation and collection just at the time when serious threats to extinction began to appear. Men rode saddleback through the fields and mountains of Norway and Sweden, visiting isolated hamlets and farms to get songs and tales straight from native lips. Danish folklorists coupled patience with a sense of urgency as they sought out diminishing numbers of rural elders who could still recall the old songs and stories. The Danes were, in fact, among the first to bring phonograph recordings to their aid before many folk traditions had flickered out altogether.

Originally, thirst for folk-song collecting served chauvinistic interests searching for national identity. But as time passed and collections grew, musicological problems appeared to further seize the attention of scholars. The scientific study of folk music (ethnomusicology) has become well-developed in the Scandinavian countries, particularly in Norway. The wealth of material brought to the libraries, museums and universities in the North could enthrall the interested student for a lifetime, not to mention

29

opportunities for field work both in Scandinavia and its population extensions overseas.

Free use of native songs and dance music in serious composition has been going on for well over a century in Scandinavia, obviously an important contribution to the Nordic sound. Certain precautions, however, must be taken before referring to a given piece of art music as "typically Danish" or "strongly Norwegian." Such references may bear no relationship to specific folkloric content. Scientific evidence has accumulated to dilute the romantic era view that folk music necessarily reflects the unique "soul" of a people. Melodic lines, natural scales and metrical rhythms may show striking similarities in rural cultures hundreds of miles apart; the diversity of European folk song may be more apparent than real. Even an alert music-lover might easily confuse a piece by Grieg for one by Bartók or vice versa. While Scandinavian folk music has remained "pure" in some respects, it must be seen as part of a general European cultural complex. Only gradually, over slow centuries, did more specific national traits emerge.

Apart from ballads and hymns from the Middle Ages, the oldest types of Scandinavian folk songs arose from utilitarian functions: lullabies, work songs and herd girls' calls. The latter category possesses more than glancing interest, especially those calls from Norway and Sweden related to the age-old practice of sending girls and cattle to upland pastures (called *seter* farms in Norway) during the summer months. Seter farms have been the focus of much indigenous folklore celebrated in literature, painting and music. The seter girl could draw upon a large number of calls and signals to summon her animals, ward off wolves and trolls, and communicate with the parent farm in the valley below. She might take up a long wooden horn wrapped in birchbark, called a *lur* (no relation to the Bronze Age instrument) for these purposes or execute the Scandinavian variant of yodeling by sending out her calls in a high falsetto voice with vocal cords drawn tight. Although seemingly crude and primitive, Scandinavian cattle calls often reveal elegant melodic garnishment which some consider a remnant of the Gregorian alleluia.

Scandinavia's traditional dances and instruments form an inseparable combination which has deeply impressed composers because of rhythmic drive and color. The term *slått* refers to the classic peasant dances from Norway, separating them from nineteenth-century accordian-based interlopers like the polka, waltz, Shottisch and Rheinlander. *Slåtter* largely replaced the leader-chorus pattern of the ancient dance-ballads by the seventeenth century, and some of them give evidence of derivation from continental court dance prototypes. The principle *slåtter* are: the *Halling* (an acrobatic men's solo in even time), the *Springar* or *Springdans* (for two partners in 3/4 time) and the more stately *Gangar* (for paired couples in 6/8 time).

Slåtter accompaniments customarily are borne by the *hardingfele* (Hardanger fiddle), especially in West Norway. More than just an instrument, the Hardanger fiddle approaches a national symbol, like the bagpipes of the Highlanders. A northern cousin of the venerable *viola d'amore,* the Hardanger fiddle attained its present form in Norway about 1600. The instrument's unmistakable skirling, "screechy" timbre depends on a set of four or five underlying steel strings acting as sympathetic vibrators; a flatter bridge than found on the standard violin facilitates polyphonic effects and the production of sharp dissonance by double or triple stopping so typical of *slåtter* tunes. Tuning of the Hardanger fiddle is said to correspond to that of ancient harps mentioned in the sagas.

In Sweden, the folk fiddler generally plays the standard violin. In days gone by he occupied a central position in many old peasant customs. Besides playing for dances and weddings, itinerant fiddlers were commonly summoned to march the local militia off to drill, enhance seasonal festivities, help lighten manual labor and generally be present for all events in the village calendar. An important feature common to all Scandinavian folk fiddling is the individual player's imaginative use of syncopations, ornaments and embellishments. In many instances this "dialect" or "personal signature" readily identifies a given fiddler's home district.

The *hambo,* a Swedish dance of the polka type, displays some native characteristics, but the country's hard-core traditional folk dance remains the *polska.* The Swedes know the polka too, but their *polska* consists of an entirely different dance in 3/4 time somewhat like the Scottish reel. Origins, however, for both dances may have been Poland which might account for the similar names. *Polska* meter, either in eighth- or sixteenth-note phrases, dominates a large portion of all Swedish folk music.

Folk fiddling continues to flourish in places like Telemark in Norway and Dalecarlia in Sweden as part of continuing or revived interest in old country ways, but use of other homespun instruments has largely died out. Some playing of the *langeleik* (long-harp) reputedly lingers in Valdres (a district in East Norway); tuned strings set in motion by means of a plectrum produce the *langeleik's* droning sound. A similar instrument, the *nyckelharpa* (key-fiddle), holds an honorable place in Swedish folklore although its sound is produced with a bow. Both these instruments chiefly found use as accompaniments for singing. Other types of harps and fiddles, along with willow flutes, animal horns, Jew's harp and bagpipes, go far back in the musical history of Scandinavia's country people.

The small kingdom of Denmark may lack the vast scenic heartland of its Nordic neighbors, but in the realm of folklore the country is a powerhouse. The Danes have never been outstripped in their zeal to gather and evaluate native traditions. The main brace of Danish folk song has been the medieval ballad. When studied afresh in the nineteenth century these old songs of courtly origin had acquired rough-hewn contour but the frequently grim and bloody texts generally hung on. More recent types of Danish folk songs tend to be cheerful or salted with sarcastic humor, although many exceptions may be found, as in the tender Zealand air *Det var en lørdag aften* (It Was a Saturday Evening).

The ancient balladic chain-dance has long faded from Denmark, although some remnants in the form of a "Beggar Dance" and "Bear Dance" were reported in use late in the nineteenth century. The majority of really old Danish dances gave way after 1800 under the wave of popular music entering the country from abroad, so what passes for Danish folk dance today often discloses waltz tempo or a suspicious "Oom-pah-pah." Local fiddlers, however, have woven fanciful accompaniments around these newer tunes, and dancers have worked in many steps of their own, so a distinctive native flavor may still be said to exist. The only purely regional dance left in rural Denmark seems to be the *Sønderhoning* from West Jutland, for the great majority of Danish peasant dances are known all over the country. Some one thousand of them have been documented, while the Danish folk fiddler can draw upon a repository of as many as ten thousand tunes for accompaniments.

Folk chorales form one of the richest sources for the Nordic sound. Hymn books, first from Luther's' Germany, then from native presses, spread to almost every Scandinavian community as part of the Reformation. Yet traces of Roman plainsong did not entirely fade from memory or completely disappear from the new order of church services. By the seventeenth and eighteenth centuries many Protestant hymns and chorales had entered the folk music hopper to become radically altered. In many instances original cadence and meter were adorned with flowing melisma and modal phrases, especially in poorer parishes lacking organs. Numerous examples of the folk chorale have come to light in Denmark and Norway, but some of the choicest specimens developed in Dalecarlia where the tradition of improvising on a hymn tune has run exceptionally strong.

Scandinavian music "in the raw" makes interesting, if variable listening. As mass media overwhelm the North, what folk music remains owes its existence to scholars and artificial respiration at the hands of folk revivalists. As a rule of thumb, the folk music of the different Nordic nations can be expressed by means of a simple diagram, as was drawn by the indefatigable Danish folklorist Andreas Bergreen in the nineteenth century. He showed Norwegian tunes as a jagged line representing agitation; the Swedish song curve came out as an undulating line; the softer, more idyllic nature of Danish song formed a straight line.

As for "national traits" in Scandinavian folk songs, the listener should beware of quicksands. Yet if Danish tunes often sound "sweet and innocent," those from Norway "quaint" or "hearty," and Swedish examples "melancholic," there are vague but valid reasons why. A good starting point for the exploration of Nordic folk song is *Ack, Värmeland du sköna* (Oh, Beautiful Värmland), a Swedish air sometimes cited as the finest folk song in the world. Although it is not absolutely essential, the general listener with some folk music background can more deeply appreciate the full flavor of the Nordic sound.

LATE ROMANTICISM AND
PROTRACTED CONSERVATISM

The romantic movement ended or dimmed out at various times and in various ways. In Scandinavia, literature heralded the shift in cultural direction. Perhaps most significant was the change toward social realism and phychological insight projected with world-shaking consequences by the problem plays of Ibsen, seconded by the dynamic, radical teachings of Georg Brandes and the brilliant experimentation of August Strindberg. Comparable responses, however, came very slowly from Scandinavian music. For a long while few composers ventured beyond middle period Wagner, and although Grieg represented an immediate forerunner, the significance of Debussy largely escaped them. Some composers reworked the vein of national romanticism while others fell under the sway of the neo-romantic reaction which characterized much Nordic culture during the 1890s. Yet the so-called post-romantic era saw great activity and fertility in the North; a few composers of international caliber emerged to mark Scandinavia's musical coming of age.

Denmark and the Nielsen Generation

Late-romantic opera and instrumental music, as cultivated in Central Europe, failed to establish a bridgehead in Denmark despite some impact on Norway and Sweden. Mahler, Richard Strauss, Reger and other contemporaries received scant attention. Instead, the Danes wrapped themselves up in their own cozy blanket comforted by such lovable teddy bears as *Peter Lange-Müller* (q.v.) and *Fini Henriques* (1867–1940). The fantasy and nostalgia of both composers appealed immediately to the Danish public. Henriques, a native son despite his name, became a widely acclaimed concert violinist and the person'fication of Danish geniality. His smiling score for the H.C. Andersen ballet *Den lille Havfrue* (The Little Mermaid, 1909) remains, not surprisingly, his most beloved work.

For a short while European ears turned to Danish opera thanks to the almost forgotten *August Enna* (1859–1939) whose personal struggle against bitter poverty added a knowing note when he wrote his masterpiece, *The Little Match Girl* (1897) based on Andersen's poignant story. Today, even the Danes might consider Enna hopelessly sentimental, yet at his best he packed the punch of a seasoned music-dramatist and master orchestrator. Although less widely appreciated, *Haakon Børresen* (1876–1954) enlivened Danish contributions to opera with *Den Kongelige Gaest*

(The Royal Guest, 1919) and his imaginative, full-scale epic of the Greenland Eskimos, *Kaddara* (1921).

Recent years have seen Danish conductors paying closer attention to *Rued Langgaard* (1893–1952). Chronologically, Langgaard should be considered a "modern" composer, but his idiom belongs to an earlier era, although in a singular way. This eccentric organist at Ribe gained a reputation as a crank. A crotchety personality all but isolated Langgaard from the musical world which seemed all right with him. He turned out sixteen symphonies and numerous other large works like the elaborate tone poem for voices and orchestra *Music of the Spheres* (1918). Hearing this music might remind listeners of Debussy or Holst. While still very much a special case, Rued Langgaard may yet emerge as another important discovery in Nordic music.

The unquestioned giant of Danish music during the opening years of the twentieth century — or at any other time, for that matter — was Carl Nielsen, a country lad from the plains of Funen. This rugged individualist bridged the romantic and more modern eras by means of an assertive, athletic style in instrumental composition with roots in diatonic harmony but with a bold, far-ranging sense of key relationships. His was an unshakable belief in the fundamental guts of music: interval and rhythm. For Carl Nielsen, music meant nothing less than the life force. The energizing power and elemental resilience found in Carl Nielsen's six symphonies and other works are hard to resist. He has less in common with late-romantic German opulence than with the independent outlook of such contemporaries of his as Leoš Janáček and Albert Roussel.

In the formation of his style Nielsen took something from the northern school, notably Svendsen, and some clues from Brahms, but comparing him to Jean Sibelius (born the same year) serves no particular purpose in furthering better understanding of either master's achievement. Two entirely different personalities, each in his own way, brought fresh blood to the post-romantic symphony as they raised the northern contribution to new and imposing heights.

Norway after Grieg

The zestful national spirit propelling Norway's astonishing resurgence began to wane with the arrival of full independence in 1905. Bjørnson, Ibsen, Grieg: a potent triumvirate which led the sons and daughters of the new Norway to the attainment of the impossible, proving to the world at large that "underdog" Norway owned a viable culture which really mattered. This meant, in effect, an intoxicating realization of Peer Gynt dreams. But forward momentum slackened considerably. A few authors (Knut Hamsun, Sigrid Undset) drew well-deserved foreign admiration, but on the whole cultural affairs in Norway showed signs of slipping back into parochialism.

When Grieg died, a Norwegian national romantic school stood where next to nothing existed before. Several inheritors were available, but only one of them had what might be considered the necessary commanding personality; the mantle of leadership therefore settled onto the shoulders of *Christian Sinding* (q.v.). But Sinding's outlook and background had deeper roots in German rather than native traditions. Norway's national romantic cause was pushed forward by other hands.

Besides Sinding, the best-known name in early twentieth-century Norwegian music belonged to *Johan Halvorsen* (1864–1935), the portly longtime director of music at Oslo's National Theater. Almost every listener, at one time or another, has been exposed to Halvorsen's *The Entrance March of the Boyars,* a bumptious but effective theatrical tidbit dating from the composer's earlier years in Bergen. String players may know his baroque revampings, notably a Handelian *Passacaglia.* Otherwise, Halvorsen's music has largely stayed at home. A fast-working theater composer, Halvorsen churned out much easy-to-take music often heavy with exoticism. As for local color, he "out-Grieged" Grieg in *Fossegrimen* (The Old Man of the Waterfalls), one of his most enchanting works usually heard as a suite in which the Hardanger fiddle makes its debut as an instrument in the modern symphony orchestra. Essentially a lyric romanticist, a true disciple of Grieg and Svendsen, Halvorsen also kept the faith in three highly enjoyable Norwegian Rhapsodies.

The sunset glow of national romanticism further reflected from another of Grieg's spiritual children, *Arne Eggen* (1881–1955). While not a particularly productive composer, Eggen's music is of thoroughbred Norwegian character. He also stood guard over native musical tradition through his organizational activities. Eggen's affinity for folk tone found complete realization in his delightful dances for the Hulda Garborg play *Liti Kjersti* (*Little Kirsten,* 1924). In *Olav Liljekrans* (1940), an operatic recasting of an early Ibsen costume drama, Eggen entered a strong contender for what several critics have judged Norway's greatest work for the lyric stage. What small fragments this listener has heard so far from the opera suggest a Norse Puccini.

A special place in Norwegian music must go to *David Monrad Johansen* (q.v.). More than a mere follower of Grieg, this unpredictable and complex figure has renewed himself on more than one occasion in his restless search for stylistic synthesis. Johansen epitomized the best in Norwegian music between the two World Wars, but he has more than held his own in the radically different postwar climate.

Although David Monrad Johansen's contemporary colleague *Ludvig Irgens Jensen* (1894–1969) carried a high reputation in Norway, too much from him seems preoccupied with the past, heavily serious neo-Gothic works holding common ground with the Max Reger and Hans Pfitzner school of baroque worship. Jensen's involved note-spinning can become tedious, not to demean some splendid pages in his better orchestral pieces (Symphony in D minor, *Partita Sinfonica, Theme with Variations*).

Social Ferment

Industrialization irrevocably altered the pattern of Scandinavian life by the time of World War I. Social pressures caused by famines or sagging business cycles could no longer be relieved by the safety valve of emigration to America. As Sweden gained industrial strength and Denmark revolutionized the farming business, parallel social reforms were demanded by the electorate. Precarious neutrality was maintained through the 1914–1918 upheaval, but the three Nordic kingdoms shared postwar economic repercussions with the rest of Europe. Strikes became severe, particularly in Norway, where the real threat of Communism shook the politicians of the 1920s. Farmer-labor coalitions formed to usher in the socialistic welfare state. But as the industrious Scandinavians went about the formation of their proletarian democracies, new danger loomed close by when Adolph Hitler took control of a snarling Germany. The worried Swedes chose rearmament as their guarantee of neutrality, but the defenseless Danes could only rely on treaties with the Third Reich. In Norway partisan squabbling delayed appropriate military preparedness until the nation was set on a collision course.

Against this background of social ferment and nervous affirmations of neutrality, the music of the North entered a period of protracted conservatism. Rapid changes evident elsewhere in Europe pointing to the imminent break-up of tonality made only scant impression in the Scandinavian musical establishment. The record shows brief visits to the Nordic capitals by Schoenberg, Stravinsky and Bartók, but more than token interest in these leaders of modern music only became generally apparent after 1945.

Denmark after Nielsen

Following the impact of Carl Nielsen, Denmark lay musically groggy; audiences felt they had received ample "modernism" for a while and they needed time to digest Nielsen's difficult mature idiom. Very few pupils passed directly under Carl Nielsen's instruction, and the vistas opened up by his final works attracted few disciples. While *Jørgen Bentzon* (q.v.) did extend Nielsen's ideas about the individual character of instruments and became one of the first composers in Scandinavia to deviate from the major/minor tonal system, the dominant factor in Danish music from the 1920s through 1940s turned out to be neo-classiciam.

The impudent clowning of "Les Six" in Paris found response in Denmark's post-Nielsen generation. Messages from Paris traveled to Copenhagen in the person of *Knudaage Riisager* (q.v.) who beautifully adapted neo-classical precepts to the Danish temperament. Fashionable modernism also attracted *Flemming Weis* (b. 1898) whose work increasingly took on studied objectivity, frequently coupled with humorous touches. The Nielsen pupil *Poul Schierbeck* (1888–1949) devoted much time to vocal music; he may be sampled at his best in the vivacious opera *Fête Galante* (1931).

These composers, along with others of the post-Nielsen generation, all produced some extremely attractive and often witty music, but their youthful outlook and cosmopolitan interests which might have sired a viable Danish avant-garde in the 1920s and 1930s sputtered out. All of them drifted into conservatism, even *Finn Høffding* (q.v.) who displayed some early radical tendencies. By pulling in their horns, they emerged jolly Danes after all. This situation, in retrospect, was not totally unexpected; the Danish mentality frowns on extremism in any form.

Events in Norway

By contrast, music in Norway during the interwar years showed flashes of a more pioneering spirit. In 1939 a shy, scholarly archivist retired from his librarian's post in the music department at Oslo University, presumably to spend his last years quietly growing roses on the family farm in the western part of the country. Actually, retirement for *Fartein Valen* (q.v.) meant the freedom and seclusion he craved for his final push as a composer. For many years Valen had been vainly trying to obtain recognition for his personally developed atonal idiom, music years ahead of anything in the North. His reward was usually hostility by the press and expressions of almost brutal public indignation. Despite vast erudition and unshakable artistic convictions, Valen proved neither a fighter nor a leader. His influence on the Nordic sound while he lived was approximately zero.

But Valen did not stand entirely alone in seeking musical materials beyond fjord and folk song. New directions in European music as a whole became a personal crusade for *Pauline Hall* (1890–1969), who carried out her missionary work for modern music in Norway primarily as an outspoken newspaperwoman in revolt against the reactionary nationalism she found in Norwegian music between the World Wars. In 1938 Pauline Hall was largely instrumental in setting up the Norwegian chapter of the International Society for Contemporary Music (ISCM) and served long as president under her motto "Look to Europe!" Curiously, her own musical style is more pleasant than pugnacious; her numerous theater scores, chamber works and lightweight orchestral sketches such as the engaging *Circus Pictures* (1933) skirt atonality and take their cue from French models. Had Pauline Hall and Fartein Valen been one person, however, the course of modern music in Scandinavia might have proven considerably different.

Simultaneously, a completely reverse philosophy appeared in Norway — fanatic ultranationalism personified by *Eivind Groven* (q.v.) whose "back to the soil" movement has never swerved from his unshakable belief that Norwegian art music must rest on Norwegian folk roots. Any other position, for Groven, amounts to heresy. Disciples sharing this limited view include the prolific *Geirr Tveitt* (b.1908) mainly known for his *Hundred Folk Tunes from Hardanger* (1954) and *Olav Kielland* (b.1901) who must take responsibility for a maddeningly ethnic *Concerto Grosso Norvegese* (1952).

Sweden's Musical Rebirth

Like England, Sweden bears a fallacious reputation as a land without music. Comments have also been made that Swedish humanism shows up best in visual rather than literary or musical form. No doubt such debatable views partly derive from Sweden's lack of a "big name" nineteenth-century composer. This is an historical fact, one the Swedes themselves are first to acknowledge and regret — no single figure comparable to Grieg, Nielsen or Sibelius. They further realize and accept the plain truth that native efforts proved too feeble to win widespread attention against the gush of competitive national music which poured from Russia, Bohemia, Hungary and — bitter pill — their own co-kingdom Norway. By the time Swedish composers had sifted through their folk traditions to catch the melodic inflections, rhythmic patterns, color and cadences for operatic and symphonic purposes, the whole issue of national romanticism had begun to grow stale. Foreign audiences, satisfied that Grieg and then Sibelius amply stated the case for the North, turned their ears elsewhere, leaving Sweden's position on the national romantic bandwagon one of too little too late.

While not a particularly powerful force in world music, Swedish national romanticism nevertheless leads the interested listener down an attractive byway. *Hugo Alfvén* (q.v.) and *Kurt Atterberg* (q.v.) were chief exponents of this school. Both tackled the larger forms with courage and more than competence even to the point of arousing a measure of international acclaim. The general indifference shown toward these two Swedish composers since the 1940s, however, may be understandable but remains deplorable.

A neo-romantic literary revival, the so-called 1890s movement, provided the stimulating atmosphere for a somewhat differently oriented group of national romantics on Swedish soil. This wave saw the dynamic *Wilhelm Peterson-Berger* (q.v.) and the dream-filled *Ture Rangström* (q.v.) riding the crest. Appropriately, both possessed highly developed literary tastes along with exceptional melodic gifts.

Romantic trends in Swedish music continue up to the present day, but among the host of lesser figures drawn to folklore, especially the preserved treasures of the province of Dalarna (Dalecarlia), few are more typical or appealing than *Oskar Lindberg* (1887–1955).

While not a national romantic composer in the generally accepted sense, a snapshot of the Alfvén generation lacks completeness without *Otto Olsson* (1879–1964), a Reger-like organist preeminent in the field of sacred music. His potent Organ Sonata in E, Six Latin Motets for mixed choir and *Te Deum* for full forces cause revision of any narrow view of Swedish musical capabilities.

In retrospect, the full flowering of Swedish music did not lie with her late-blooming national romantics like Alfvén or Atterberg. First inklings of modernism stem instead from the personality and work of *Wilhelm Stenhammar* (q.v.), friend of both Nielsen and Sibelius. Stenhammar's own, often distinguished compositions stand at the fringes of the great Austro-German tradition, but their Nordic cast is unmistakable. He largely avoided folkloric coloration, for Stenhammar squarely faced the enormously changed social, political and cultural conditions in Sweden at the end of the

38

nineteenth century. He lived when his country felt the overwhelming impact of industrialization and, like many others, watched sadly as the curtain came down on an age-old agrarian way of life. To mix folk song with serious music under such conditions might only represent a futile attempt to turn back the clock. (Of course his contemporary Vaughan Williams and others like Béla Bartók and Carlos Chavez showed how ethnic material could fertilize a modern compositional style, yet Stenhammar's distrust of revived folklore in an urban, technologically oriented society represents an equally valid viewpoint.)

Personal contact with Stenhammar largely determined the course for *Hilding Rosenberg* (q.v.), the unquestioned father figure behind the growth of modern music in Sweden. Rosenberg formed the nucleus for a small phalanx of young composers banding together as the "1920s group." Acting together, they forced open doors toward progress and defied the entrenched conservatism guarding Swedish concert halls. Although quite familiar with Schoenberg's activities, Rosenberg kept his linear-polyphonic idiom within a tonal system, but this did not spare him scalding criticism from press and public. His fight to bring Swedish music abreast of the times was long and difficult. To win, he was forced to set an invincible example both as teacher and as composer. He piled skill upon technique until he attained encyclopedic mastery of his craft to the point of being possibly the most erudite composer ever produced in Scandinavia.

Rosenberg counted two steadfast allies within the "1920s group," but neither *Gösta Nystroem* (q.v.) nor *Moses Pergament* (b. 1893) had the creative stature of their leader. Nystroem, long resident in Paris, brought the cachet of French elegance to much of his work; he developed a type of Nordic impressionism that drew its chief strength from endless visions of the sea. Pergament, by no means the only Jew to make a name for himself in Nordic music, escapes ready classification beyond "general modernist." While he may not display a sharp stylistic image, Pergament served the "1920s group" as an able mouthpiece both at home and abroad.

Forward momentum became evident in Swedish music after World War I, not only due to the radical agitation of the Rosenberg circle, but also because a counterforce appeared which more or less held to middle ground. This second cluster of composers demonstrated willingness to move with the times, but not at the expense of alienating the public. The enormously popular *Lars-Erik Larsson* (q.v.) lies at the center of this loosely organized group as does *Dag Wirén* (q.v.). Larsson's most characteristic music combines flawless Nordic lyricism with neo-classic transparency. Wirén's carefully manicured scores indicate a style in which cool melodicism gains from the salt of wry humor. Both turned to sterner stuff, however, as they entered the 1950s.

Erland von Koch (b. 1910) also attracted a strong local following. In contrast to others of his generation, Koch did a complete about face — a neo-classicist reverting to mellow romanticism. Folk songs from Dalecarlia and sea breezes off the archipelago constitute Koch's prime inspiration.

Of his many works, including much for motion pictures, the *Oxberg Variations* for orchestra and a fluent Saxophone Concerto may be cited as better examples. Another romantic soul, *Gunnar de Frumerie* (b. 1908) has distinguished himself as a pianist as well as a composer. More "Frumerie" than "Gunnar" seems to kindle his Frenchified chamber music, often exceptionally attractive despite Gallic mannerisms. More of the Nordic poet may be found in de Frumerie's many piano pieces and songs; his ravishing Pär Lagerkvist settings, notably *När du sluter mina ögon* (When You Close My Eyes), belong to the cream of Scandinavian songcraft.

The picture of Swedish composition during the first half of the twentieth century, even as a hasty sketch, would be incomplete without mention of *Edvin Kallstenius* (1881–1967) and *Hilding Hallnäs* (b. 1903). Because of a highly personal tonal language based on what he called "harmonics" and singular ideas about tempo, Kallstenius' orchestral and chamber music carries a reputation of frightening difficulty. His transition into serialism during the 1950s seemed a natural event. A similar route has been followed by Hallnäs, long resident in Gothenberg. Hallnäs has always remained independent of any school or movement. In his earlier days Hallnäs devoted much time to song, but larger forms gradually took a central position in his production. Like Kallstenius, Hallnäs has written five symphonies and much instrumental music; his style, too, became internationalized upon his conversion to serialism.

End of an Era
Scandinavian fantasy about its shield of neutrality shattered at dawn, April 9, 1940, when German troops poured into Denmark and Norway. Both countries went under the iron heel of five years of Nazi occupation. Musical reaction was strongest in Norway. Difficult as things became in Denmark (especially after the Danes began to fight an underground war against their "guests"), the continuation of frank hostilities by a Norwegian government in London made the situation in the homeland more than grim. Immediately after the invasion Norway's cultural life lay paralyzed; attempts at restoration encountered hostility as people boycotted anything connected with the Quisling regime. Yet some composers, notably *Harald Saeverud* (q.v.) and his younger colleague *Klaus Egge* (q.v.) felt positively energized by these tragic and dangerous years. Saeverud, especially, vented his impotent fury and grief in a score of compositions; some of them he stuffed into desk drawers to await the day of liberation, but others actually saw wartime performance in spite of the Nazis.

Those not present in occupied Norway or Denmark own no experience from which to frame judgment. Enough to say that while art supposedly lies above politics, there were instances like the Flagstad affair when certain Norwegian artists lent varying degrees of alleged support to the Quislings. This led to some seriously damaged reputations when the German army departed in 1945.

On the other hand, the vast majority of Danes and Norwegians felt mutual solidarity within their countries for the first time in many years. National pride received fresh infusions of meaning as people gathered behind closed doors or stood resolutely in public parks to read their literature or hear their traditional songs. The war years, in effect, caused a rebirth of national romanticism which gave hope to many citizens during what otherwise seemed a night of endless darkness.

TOWARD THE NEW MUSICS

The downward slope of the twentieth century bristles with unresolved problems and conflicts, a time of ever-deepening cultural upheaval coupled with accelerating intellectual confusion. Anxiety has become a hallmark for the age, change the only certainty — fundamental change affecting every aspect of human endeavor, whether this take the form of science, technology, government, education or the arts. With the global spread of Western technology and a steady rise in world population compounded by urban congestion has come a gnawing sense of alienation; the individual feels a stranger in a depersonalized society, incapable of replacing discarded values with anything better than rank materialism or despotic collectivism. The speed and depth of these events have forced the artist to seek new, even unprecedented means of creative expression.

The indignant concert-goer can no longer blame the "agony" of modern music on a false turn taken at the close of the Wagnerian era. False or not, that turn was taken with far-reaching results, a flat refusal on the part of most composers to continue their art on a tonal basis. With the relationship and relevance of the artist's vision to his machine-conditioned fellow citizens vague at best, it should be no surprise to find composers withdrawing into private worlds, leaving the public to follow as best it can. During the 1950s and early 1960s virtually every major composer in the West increased his distance from the major/minor system of the "great masters" with replacement generally coming from some form of atonality, serialism or radical experimentation sometimes leading beyond the borders of traditional music into realms of noise and language. The introduction of electronic instruments and computer-based musical programming hastened this process.

Intense, self-conscious determination to "create the new" is typical of the arts in our time, a guiding principle simply taken for granted and predicated on total rejection of the past — itself a unique situation in the history of music. Obviously, the many forces contributing to new music (more rightly termed "new musics") imply changes far more basic than mere abandonment of tonality or reactionary anti-romanticism. Western music, to borrow from Alvin Toffler, has reached the state of "future shock."

One of the most significant factors characterizing music since Schoenberg has been the gradual parting of music from man. Fearsome complexity in contemporary pieces precludes amateur performance; increasing exclusivity of technique places the bulk of new scores beyond the reach of today's confused, ill-prepared listeners. (The ability of professional performers to master works their fathers would have declared unplayable, however, is remarkable.) Audience contact has not only been disjoined, but is seriously spoken of as superfluous. The corollary attitude arises: need a composer "compose" at all? John Cage arrived precisely at this point when he lucidly demonstrated that silence or adventitious, random sounds could make up the sum total of a given aural event. Clearly, Cage

42

took a position of anti-music where the artist rejects the definition of music as a game played with tones. At the other extreme, advocates of total control of musical production have turned to mathematics and automism, coded formalizations of musical structure which their influential advocate Iannis Xenakis refers to as "metamusic." All manner of modifications lie in between.

After 1945 — the year zero for the "new musics" — the Nordic sound was clearly venturing into strange, previously unknown territory.

New Music in Sweden

Although technologically and culturally advanced, no important aspect of the twentieth-century musical revolution originated in the Scandinavian countries. Strindberg, however, came to some interesting as well as prophetic conclusions in his 1894 essay "The New Arts, or the Role of Chance in Artistic Creation." Upon the cessation of global hostilities in 1945, Sweden for various reasons stood best prepared of the Nordic nations to receive the stimulus of new artistic directions. Subtle force, mainly from a school of native poets, had been gathering a head of steam for several years and helped condition the Swedish intelligentsia for events soon to come. The poets had raised awareness of modern life's dark tragedies, complete with mass-produced banalities and brutalities. Neutral Sweden's ringside seat through two World Wars gave ghastly support to this view, compounded by collective feelings of frustration and guilt. This highly sensitive, largely pessimistic doctrine of the plight of modern man permeated Sweden's postwar intellectual climate, perhaps most immediately demonstrable to foreigners through the mystical writings of Dag Hammarskjöld and the enigmatic films of Ingmar Bergman.

The message from Sweden's poets further included urgings to experiment with new, untried means of expression which fell right in line with postwar feelings in Continental Europe. In Swedish music, too, the soil had been prepared by a cadre of young composers trained outside ordinary academic channels by Hilding Rosenberg. During wartime isolation, a so-called Monday Group met weekly to study and dissect the classics of modern music — works from Hindemith, Bartók, Schoenberg and others. Curiosity within the "Monday Group" ranged wider, however, to include music of the distant past especially the Renaissance masters. Spearheading the group were *Karl-Birger Blomdahl* (q.v.), *Ingvar Lidholm* (q.v.) and *Sven-Erik Bäck* (q.v.); all three were destined for leadership in Swedish music of the 1950s and 1960s. Support also came from an impressive line-up of performing and scholarly talent eager to help further the cause of new music. Facilities for performance, therefore, lay readily at hand; Bäck, for instance, held the conductorship of an enthusiastic chamber orchestra. Assimilation of modern poetry (Swedish and foreign), close scrutiny of twelve-tone technique, refinement of orchestration and experiments with words and music became the daily bread of the "Monday Group."

One of the sharpest differences between contemporary music activity

43

in the United States and Europe lies in the field of radio; in general, European radio has proven a friend to today's composer, the exact opposite of the American experience. (Americans, however, have access to more and cheaper records.) For this reason much of the thrust behind the rapid advance of new music in Sweden has been the contribution of the Swedish Broadcasting Corporation, a public corporation in control of all (legal) radio and television broadcasting within the country. Swedish radio holds vast resources with musical policies set by some of the country's leading composers, a situation comparable to having Gunther Schuller or Elliott Carter in key staff positions at America's major networks. Merits or disadvantages of the two systems aside, Swedish radio is in the position to promote Swedish composers and to make propaganda for contemporary music.

Another factor accounting for the progressive attitude of recent Swedish music is the concert society *Fylkingen* founded in 1933. (The name refers to an advance formation of birds, the leading echelon.) For many years *Fylkingen* has brought the cream of contemporary music to Stockholm. In due time the organization felt the impact of John Cage and the pianist David Tudor, both exerting a profound effect on the Swedish avantgarde. As a result, *Fylkingen* has increasingly turned to "far out" activities such as "happenings" and other forms of paramusical activity. Mention must also be made of *Rikskonserter,* a younger and more conservative organization dedicated to giving nationwide concerts, but an active promotional direction with accent on contemporary music has become evident as well.

Well-organized and armed with modern means of communication, Swedish music since 1945 has not gone unnoticed by the world at large. Hilding Rosenberg's vision became reality: Swedish composers have been accepted as colleagues by their peers abroad. Composition within the country, despite a somewhat distorted foreign image, is by no means exclusively radical and/or correctly fashionable. Rosenberg's activists (Blomdahl, Lidholm and Bäck) hold center stage, but a more complete picture emerges from a glance at the list of pupils nurtured by Lars-Erik Larsson. Less attention has been paid to this loosely arrayed group, but they seem ünified by their determined resistance against the more dehumanizing aspects of musical abstractionism. What might be called "new humanism" provides the force behind such composers as *Jan Carlstedt* (q.v.), *Maurice Karkoff* (b. 1927), the short lived *Bo Linde* (1933–1970) and *Hans Eklund* (b. 1927).

Karkoff's symphonies have yet to free themselves from frenetic emotionalism; the composer's urgent aims seem better served when words lie at his disposal as in *Landscape of Screams* (1968), a chilling setting of Nelly Sach's concentration camp poetry, which might have come from Schoenberg himself. Formal clarity and clean, polyphonic lines mark the main works of Eklund, perhaps best represented by his three-movement symphony, *Music for Orchestra* (1960). Bo Linde left concertos and a handful of very beautiful songs suggesting an heir of Ture Rangström.

Alongside the sons of Lars-Erik Larsson, yet keeping his distance, stands *Allan Pettersson* (b. 1911), the lone wolf of Swedish music. Long an orchestral violist in Stockholm, Pettersson completed formal studies in composition at Paris. Slow maturation has marked his course as a composer. He groped forward with a series of long spun-out, melancholic symphonies remembering Mahler and Shostakovich, gloomy documents of personal anguish and proletarian suffering which earned Pettersson a reputation as a "bleeding heart." But in the stubborn, muttered protest of his Seventh Symphony (1967) the Nordic sound takes on renewed eloquence, a timely statement of grave concern honestly rendered without recourse to electronic gadgetry or "rock" beat.

Further variety in recent Swedish music has come from *Hans Holewa* (b. 1913), an Austrian in Stockholm since 1937 and among the first to consistently apply twelve-tone technique; *Eduard Tubin* (b. 1905), a symphonist originally from Estonia; *Sven-Eric Johanson* (b. 1919); *Björn Johansson* (b. 1913); the British-trained *Laci Boldemann* (1921–1969); the thoroughly cosmopolitan *Gunnar Bucht* (b. 1927); and *Sten Broman* (b. 1902).

A fresh group of younger composers came to the fore in Sweden during the 1960s. Academic backgrounds show differences, but most of them grew up in close contact with serialism and electronic sound. Leading the pack is *Bengt Hambraeus* (q.v.) who combines several talents (composer, musicologist, radio official, sonic experimenter, organist). At a comparatively early age Hambraeus found his way to the Darmstadt summer workshops and the electronic studios at Milan. While echoes from the Middle Ages sometimes enter Hambraeus' texturally complex music, he seems happiest as a tone scientist testing his ideas in clouds of futuristic sonority.

The dense, layered haze typically settling over a Hambraeus work finds marked contrast in the piercing crystalline lucidity of *Bo Nilsson* (q.v.), an aloof individualist who first sprang to prominence in Germany as a teen-age wonder boy. During the 1950s Nilsson received proper credit as one of the first composers anywhere to serialize "open form," employ aleatoric (chance) techniques and exploit microphones for sonorous effect.

Although both Hambraeus and Nilsson became familiar with electronic media (Hambraeus, in fact, delivered the first Swedish electronic piece), neither composer has committed himself entirely to this modality. More consistent cultivation of electronic music in Sweden has been shown by *Ralph Lundsten* (b. 1936) and his colleague *Leo Nilsson* (b. 1939). Starting out in the 1950s with so-called *musique concrète,* the team grew in sophistication with eventual establishment of their own studio "Andromeda." More advanced technical facilities, however, developed at the Swedish radio especially after the appointment of Karl Birger Dlomdahl as chief of the Music Department, a composer-director who had early taken the lead when he took the then-radical step of incorporating electronic effects into his opera *Aniara.*

General trends in European contemporary music found responses rather quickly in Sweden. *Lars Johan Werle* (q.v.) might be considered something of a counterpart to Hans Werner Henze. Werle has filed a sharply expressive edge to his music which can be used to telling effect in opera. On the other hand, the other-worldly sonorities and bold choral effects of György Ligeti, at one time a familiar face in Stockholm musical circles, found an echo in *Arne Mellnäs* (b. 1933). The term "pendulum dynamics" was coined by *Åke Hermanson* (b. 1923) and demonstrated in super-concentrated orchestral pieces like *In Nuce* (In a Nutshell) which seems to take a cue from the brevity of Webern. *Siegfried Naumann* (b. 1919), a dedicated conductor and promoter of new music, prefers a rigorous pointillism in his own works.

Radical approaches to compositions for the organ have reached the point where one can speak of a "Swedish school" of new organ music with linkages between Bengt Hambraeus, who had studied a while under Messiaen, and younger compatriots such as *Karl-Erik Welin* (b. 1934) and *Jan W. Morthenson* (b. 1940). Welin, considered a "phenomenal" organist by his peers, enjoys an international reputation as a persuasive spokesman for the new organ literature. Welin's contributions as a composer seem of lesser consequence. His chamber orchestra piece *Warum Nicht?* (Why Not?) seems an example of mere preciousness. Morthenson, on the other hand, takes a more intellectual turn with his writings on "non-associative music" and organ compositions illustrating what he calls " 'meta-music' — music on music." Electronic elements also play a major part in his various works. Mention of the Swedish school of new organ music brings up *Torsten Nilsson* (b. 1920), who stands somewhat apart from Hambraeus and the others as a "purer" organist and active church musician although there are secular works to his credit.

Perhaps the two "hottest" personalities in the Swedish vanguard during the explosive 1960s were *Jan Bark* (b. 1934) and *Folke Rabe* (b. 1935), both jazzmen but with solid academic backgrounds. Their famous co-composition *Bolos* (1962) for four trombones must be heard to be believed. Better still, it should be seen since *Bolos* belongs to the genre known as "instrumental theater" where visual elements become as important as produced sounds. *Bolos* amounts to a tone salad exhibiting just about every rasp, hoot, honk, sniffle and tinkle which men can milk from trombones whether assembled or disarticulated. Both composers have continued as experimentalists, with Rabe in particular gaining a name for himself in choral circles with his use of non-semantic word patterns, explosive speech accents and the phonetic color so frequently encountered in contemporary choral music. His *Rondes* for male or mixed choir has been widely performed.

Relationships between music and poetry have been the subject of renewed interest, especially in Stockholm, seat of much activity in the area of "text sound" or *poèsie sonore* with participants drawn here from several nations. This so-called "concrete" poetry is often projected over some sort of musical or electronic background. All languages and fragments of languages may be used. Whether such revived dadaism represents a potential art form or merely another coffeehouse "put on" remains to be seen.

New Music in Denmark

Danish accommodation to late twentieth-century music has not been easy. Accounts differ, but the immediate postwar period seems to have been characterized by lethargy. At least this was the conclusion reached by Virgil Thomson, who crossed the Danish border in the early 1950s as a visitor to unfamiliar territory; even the work of Carl Nielsen was scarcely known abroad at that time. Thomson recalled encountering an atmosphere laden with apathy, a marked contrast to postwar Germany where musicians and listeners encouraged all kinds of ideas and experiments in their haste to catch up with the march of progress. Thomson further observed scant desire to make contact with non-Danish composers, lack of harmonic technique and contentment with provincialism.

Despite these negative impressions, Denmark by no means lacked creative musicians of genuine ability. *Vagn Holmboe* (q.v.) and the younger *Niels Viggo Bentzon* (q.v.) proved the most forceful. Holmboe and Bentzon show entirely opposite personalities: the former is a soft-spoken thinker, the latter a manic dynamo. But during the 1950s both sought exit from contemporary dilemmas through a common tunnel — metamorphosis.

In music, metamorphosis means organization of a composition by a process of continual transformation of a single germinal starting point. Historically, this principle of form cannot be called innovative. Franz Liszt apparently first brought the concept into symphonic music and certain applications appear in the works of Carl Nielsen and Jan Sibelius among others. Holmboe saw here a rational aid to coherence, allowing the composer alternatives to the strict rules governing the Schoenbergian twelve-tone system. Much postwar Danish music steered by the star of metamorphosis; Niels Viggo Bentzon even went so far as to declare metamorphosis "The form of our times!" This enthusiastic war cry from the 1950s, however, has grown fainter.

Among Danish composers, Holmboe and Bentzon enjoy palpable foreign reputations; less can be said about their colleagues from the same generation. This diverse group includes *Herman David Koppel* (b. 1908), *Svend Schultz* (b. 1913), *Svend Erik Tarp* (b. 1908) and the prominent musicologist, sometime composer *Knud Jeppessen* (b. 1892). The French-trained *Jørgen Jersild* (b. 1913) might also be entered with them. Of the limited amount of music heard so far from these composers, this listener would rate Tarp as the strongest voice, an opinion based on his taut Symphony in E-flat (1948) and a stellar *Te Deum* from the war years. As a performer, Herman Koppel cut some memorable recordings of Carl Nielsen's piano music in the early days of the LP revolution. His own music suggests an eclectic mixture of Nielsen and Stravinsky, although in more recent works a Hebraic element has appeared much in evidence.

The premature death of *Ebbe Hamerik* (1898–1951) may have been a more significant loss than generally realized. Virtually alone in his generation, this scion of a prominent musical family received stimulus from the Viennese atonal school, notably Alban Berg. The spare, almost ascetic idiom cultivated by Ebbe Hamerik also lies close to the astringency of Fartein Valen. Greater opportunity to hear the symphonic works and operas of this offbeat composer should reveal some missing links in modern Danish music.

Despite the growth of radio and other means for mass communication, the Danes for many years seemed oblivious to what more alert Europeans considered musical modernism. For most Danish listeners little had taken place since the days of Mahler. This same audience, once confronted with mid-century realities, entered the postwar picture kicking and screaming. Live and televised appearances of such radicals as John Cage and Karlheinz Stockhausen brought bewilderment followed by anger. When the Korean clown Nam Yune Paik treated Danish audiences to one of his neo-dadaist routines complete with onstage demolition of a piano, reactions reached the state of a boiling volcano. With all degrees of avant-garde experimentation and perverse nonsense suddenly raining on their heads, the Danes went into months of furious and acrimonious debate accompanied by a flood of letters to the editor. Moderation finally took over to calm the furor. As one newspaperman diplomatically summed up: "It appears that Denmark's musical life is entering a new and lively period."

Not really. Since the 1960s the so-called new music has consolidated its position more firmly in Sweden and Norway than in the land of Carl Nielsen. Danish progressives seem feeble and uncoordinated despite the continued existence of the young composers league, DUT. Having settled accounts with serialism, Vagn Holmboe moved apart from the fray to deepen his own private means of expression. Niels Viggo Bentzon has apparently lost his compass and spins across the scene without evident direction, disgorging music like a machine, writing poetry, presenting "happenings." In the meantime, some of the younger composers are laboring under the uneasy feeling that the Establishment officially tolerates them but with the same benign indifference also shown toward pornographers. Press support for contemporary music comes rarely while the radio cannot truthfully be called a bastion for contemporary trends. As one of the more advanced composers put it: "New music here is in a ghetto . . . . We have money but are taken away."

But the younger men and their slightly older colleagues of the 1960s generation carry on with variable degrees of artistic success. Nearly all members of this group have made the inevitable break with the past although not always completely. Some have fallen into the trap of snatching at the latest fashion — a Schoenbergian twelve-tone phase, a Darmstadt serial phase, electronic music — but they have had to accept the fact that virtually all such impulses originated outside Denmark, making it difficult to shake a gnawing sense of provincialism. Not that Danish music from the 1960s onward is below standard; on the contrary, technical competence readily appears, but by erasing any conscious references to nation or folk-lore their music shows few differences from similar products coming out of Spain or Yugoslavia.

What once looked like a Danish radical front clustered for a while around *Jan Maegaard* (b. 1926), one of the first to pick up the twelve-tone cudgel in his country. A search for method and apologetics seem more typical of Maegaard than actual composition; his book *Musical Modernism* (1964) may be found in most Scandinavian bookshops and probably has done more than any of his compositions to soften northern audiences toward activity in contemporary music.

Some composers more or less identified with the Maegaard camp include: *Poul Rovsing Olsen* (b. 1922), *Peder Holm* (b. 1926), *Bernhard Lewkovitch* (b. 1927), *Aksel Borup-Jørgensen* (q.v.), *Ib Nørholm* (b. 1931) and *Tage Nielsen* (b. 1929). Two veterans who have jumped onto the same bandwagon are *Erik Jørgensen* (b. 1912) and the longtime expatriate *Gunnar Berg* (b. 1909).

Collectively, this roster of established Danish composers totals a great deal of talent; some of it has matured and moved on, some of it shows signs of stagnation. Typical of these composers is the short, compact, serially oriented instrumental statement, generally for orchestra but with Holm and Nørholm also expert manipulators of the string quartet. Vocal music has received a share of attention, especially from Lewkovitch, who has connections with Roman Càtholic church music. If his powerful Franciscan cantata *Il cantico delle creature* stands as an example, his is a highly individual voice. Olsen can also demonstrate refined personal expression, as in his early song cycle *Schicksalslieder* (Songs of Destiny, 1953) and the intriguing piano suite *Medardus* (1956).

Among their juniors, the "young lions" coming to the fore in the late 1960s, beards and sandals abound but a "superstar" has yet to arrive. New Danish music sorely lacks an aggressive idea man comparable, say, to Norway's Arne Nordheim. But *Bent Lorentzen* (b. 1935) shows a broader than usual grasp of the total situation since he views the scene not only as a composer, but also as a well-seasoned musical educator. Lorentzen has worked with the whole gamut of contemporary tools including electronic tape and loosely structured stage events. His orchestral work *The Unconscious* (1967) probes the creative spontaneity of the mind, while in the radio opera *Euridice* (1965), Lorentzen appears to attempt organization of the extraneous sounds of big city bustle, perhaps an act of homage to John Cage.

While the radical fringe seems more conspicuous in Denmark than elsewhere in Scandinavia, its impact and importance raise more questions than answers about the route of future music. If such composers as *Pelle Gudmundsen-Holmgreen* (b. 1932) or *Mogens Winkel Holm* (b. 1936) have a common denominator, this probably has its roots in a reaction against prescribed forms and anything even faintly resembling counterpoint. Winkel Holm, so far best known for a chamber opera *Sonate for Four Opera Singers* (1968), goes in for a simplified style which he calls "homecoming music." The studied cultivation of musical absurdity has captured the fancy of Gudmundsen-Holmgreen; in *Tricolore IV* this composer has striven (and evidently managed) to produce an orchestral trance state which he has described as "Immensely boring to play . . . and equally boring to listen to." This seems a reflection of the international urban subculture most likely by way of Terry Riley (his *In C* has deeply impressed the Danish juniors) with the ghost of Morton Feldman lurking in the background.

But all is not fun and games in new Danish music. *Ingolf Gabold* (b. 1942) speaks very seriously of bringing Jung's depth psychology to his (mostly vocal) pieces, whatever that may mean. If his harmonically subtle and gravely beautiful *Your Sister's Drown'd* (1968) for soprano and male chorus stands as any example, however, Gabold has given evidence of decidedly superior talent.

The fair-haired boy of Danish contemporary music, however, is unquestionably *Per Nørgård* (q.v.). His student record at the Royal Conservatory and under such teachers as Vagn Holmboe and Nadia Boulanger has been described as singularly brilliant. Lability has always been typical of Nørgård; he has steadfastly refused to step into any kind of a box for convenient labeling. Following a metamorphosis phase in the middle 1950s, he entered a zany period during which he showed interest both in serialism and, concurrently, with "Pop" culture. More recently he has transformed himself to an advocate of the "New Simplicity," a phrase on loan from Danish literary criticism which implies no "return" to anything, but rather means rejection of the new musical orthodoxy as perpetuated by the highly organized serialist "gurus" at Darmstadt. Both Ib Nørholm and Gudmundsen-Holmgreen also have leaned in this direction, but Nørgård has proceeded to take longer flights with his talk of "mystical religious philosophy" and audience "tune-ins." While music inviting audience participation no doubt can mean great fun, other "New Simplicity" offerings from Nørgård carry deliberate, calculated boredom to insane lengths. As one of the few Danish modernists to gain more than token international hearings, Nørgård and his future direction hold keen interest; he may represent a bellwether for his entire generation. Whether or not he ever settles down to a "style" means less than observing how he copes with evident overstimulation. Higher altitudes could mean vaporization in a cloud of mysticism like Scriabin (he too played with colored lights) or, perhaps, the numbing paralysis of an identity crisis.

New Music in Norway

In 1945 peace came to a ruined Norway. Most of her large prewar merchant fleet lay on the bottom and the retreating German army had systematically laid waste to large portions of the country. Yet wartime suffering and privation had taught Norwegians that a nation's most valuable heritage flows from its arts and culture. In the painful struggle to rebuild, music was not forgotten and for the first time began to receive substantial government support.

Norway's reborn national spirit rested on a considerably different and more realistic basis than the national romanticism of former years. New contacts formed between Norway and world music centers. Not only Paris and London, but New York as well began to receive recruits from the army of Norwegian musicians which once had marched lockstep to the Leipzig Conservatory. As German influence faded, foreign artists from many countries found their way north in increasing numbers to expose long-isolated audiences to the world. A few foreign musicians decided to settle in Norway, adding a touch of needed cosmopolitanism. Although some Norwegian composers, mainly from the older generation, continued their meditation on folk life, dangers of inbreeding were offset by the restless younger generation which began casting about for new means of expression.

At the end of the German occupation, Harald Saeverud stood out as the leading name in Norwegian music; he was soon joined by Klaus Egge who reached maturity during the 1950s. Egge quickly gained international recognition both as an organizer and creative talent. Belated interest in the music of Fartein Valen also belongs to this immediate postwar period, but death snatched Valen away before his singular brand of atonality could work itself out to logical conclusion. Although recognized as an important Norwegian composer since the 1930s, *Bjarne Brustad* (b. 1895) found renewed strength which he poured into a splendid, hard-hitting Second Symphony (1951). Brustad's four other symphonies, most representative chamber music and the opera *Atlantis* all appeared after the war.

Generally, Swedish composers swung into modern music as an organized band, the Danes arrived half-heartedly, while the Norwegians characteristically made the conversion as individuals. For a while ingrown conservatism held back progress with scant evidence of a truly active front. Each of Fartein Valen's pupils took to rowing his own boat in contrast to Sweden where the sons of Hilding Rosenberg locked arms and marched forward. Media support came slowly and only after a group of younger composers and performers publicly demanded that radio be brought to account for provincial and reactionary musical policies.

A few highly gifted composers who might have gotten things moving faster failed to sustain much of their initial promise for one reason or another. This listener has in mind *Edvard Fliflet Braein* (b. 1924) whose early works like *Concert Overture No. 2* (1949) and *Serenade for Orchestra* (1952) strike a witty, even impish stance, taking a cue from the Shostakovich First Symphony. Braein's beguiling blend of Norwegian openness and urbanity has always brought full acclamation from the public. Unfortunately, little was heard from Braein through the 1960s until he again

51

made contact with a Third Symphony (1968) and the well-received opera, *Anne Pedersdotter* (1971).

Similar disappointment might be registered in the case of *Edvard Hagerup Bull* (b. 1922). Despite his Norwegian name, Bull for all practical purposes chose to become a Frenchman; he continues to live in Paris where his music has become enthralled by the siren song of post-impressionism.

With the death of *Sverre Jordan* (1889–1972) the Norwegian "Old Guard" with clinging traces of national romanticism has just about faded away. Composers such as *Sparre Olsen* (b. 1903), *Karl Andersen* (1903–1970), *Conrad Baden* (b. 1903), *Erling Kjellsby* (b. 1901) and *Arne Dørumsgaard* (b. 1921) generally belong to this conservative circle with their works showing few evident modern influences beyond Hindemith. Kjellsby, however, must be singled out for the sheer excellence of his chamber music; his Fourth String Quartet, for instance, makes an exceptionally rewarding listening experience. Slight familiarity with music from Karl Andersen and Conrad Baden leaves an impression of solid academic stuff. A onetime protege of the late Kirsten Flagstad, Arne Dørumsgaard has tried to uphold a tired romantic song tradition.

Non-Norwegian listeners might readily confuse Sverre Jordan with Sparre Olsen; both were among the last to carry on traditions inherited from Grieg. Jordan long served as a conductor at the National Theater in Bergen; understandably, much incidental music and many songs have issued from his desk. A more formidable figure, Sparre Olsen went abroad during the 1920s, leading to early familiarity with composers like Hindemith and Bartók. But while he has absorbed much in the way of modern technique, Olsen's orientation as an artist has gone to the service of Norwegian folklore and poetry. His more important orchestral pieces and chamber music (mainly dating from the late 1940s and 1950s) show the influence of international polyphonic textures; Olsen hit the nationalist note hardest in his many choral pieces and songs.

As might be expected from a country where individualism takes high priority, current Norwegian music operates on several levels. Neither the conservatives nor the so-called avant-garde dominate the whole picture. This is why composers like *Johan Kvandal* (b. 1919) and *Finn Arnestad* (b. 1915) are difficult to pigeonhole.

Arnestad creates immediate interest because almost alone he has attempted to build on the rarified style of Fartein Valen, borne out by his dry piece for orchestra *Aria Appassionata* (1962). At the same time, Arnestad has maintained strong respect for the past with his refusal to hurry after the latest gimmick. *Cavatina cambiata,* a short orchestral piece from 1968, says nothing new, but with Arnestad that is not the point; this music holds the listener's attention through variations in instrumental timber and shrewd balance between atonal and chromatic harmony.

Kvandal (the son of David Monrad Johansen) takes a more extroverted position which sometimes admits an excess of rhetoric, at least in his drawn-out *Symphonic Epos* (1963). On the other hand, Kvandal's well-trimmed Concerto for Flute and String Orchestra from the same year sounds like the work of a different composer. One of his colleagues summarized Kvandal as "thoughtful — serious — conservative — solid." Both late-bloomers, Arnestad and Kvandal have gone their unspectacular way with strong personal convictions and disregard for fashionable "isms." Both leave an impression of integrity and elevated purpose although the question of distinctive style becomes debatable.

Composite influences have been reflected from the works of such composers as *Gunnar Sønstevold* (b. 1912); the prolific *Hallvard Johnsen* (b. 1916) whose symphonies seem to take a lead from Danish ideas about metamorphosis; *Øisten Sommerfeldt* (b. 1919); the Trondheim organist *Per Hjort Albertsen* (b. 1919); and *Tor Brevik* (b. 1932). None of these has managed to gain much of an international audience although their training has been anything but parochial. Sønstevold, for instance, has incorporated pops touches in his oratorio *Litany at Atlanta* (1972).

Edvard Grieg casts a long shadow, but by the late 1950s, it had become obvious that a generation with completely different orientation was going to speak for Norway. Most of the sparks in more recent Norwegian music have flown from a loosely allied, experimentally inclined coterie born about the 1930s and apparently the spiritual offspring of Pauline Hall. Starting as dissonant polyphonists, they sped through serialism, played the post-Webern game awhile and then picked up the challenge of electronic music. Chief members of this cosmopolitan group are: *Arne Nordheim* (q.v.), *Bjørn Fongaard* (b. 1919), *Alfred Janson* (b. 1937) and *Sigurd Berge* (b. 1929).

Forte of the oldest member, Fongaard, is microtonality, making him one of the few Nordic disciples of the veteran Czech modernist Alois Hába. Fongaard likes to place scrambled guitar micro-intervals on tape to get results which might astound the devotees of Andres Segovia or Julian Bream. A convert from jazz in his early twenties, Janson has joined the anti-serialist faction with realization of his creative ideas marked by decided lack of inhibition. In *Canon for Chamber Orchestra and Magnetic Tape* (1964), Janson exploits otherworldly sonorities, jazz riffs and howls from the performers. *Nocturne* (1967), a sort of cantata after Nietzsche, makes an even stronger case for this lively composer.

A few short electronic pieces have come from Sigurd Berge, but his main thrust has been into instrumental coloring and single-note construction under heavy influence from Hindu music. The hard surfaces and contrasting textures of a piece like *Chroma* (1966) for orchestra may not put many listeners in mind of the Hindu *raga,* but a common denominator is found in the use of one note as an organizing device.

The most aggressive talent among the young Norwegians dedicated to the "new musics," however, belongs to Arne Nordheim, particularly since his drift into electronic media. Hunched over tape spools, controlling ring modulators and twiddling the dials on assorted gadgetry, he can display remarkable directness and coherence not always found among workers in the electronic studio. But Nordheim's main interest focuses on refined nuances of tone, which has led him back to the orchestra. Repetitious tone clusters and sound clouds tend to dominate the thinking in his more recent compositions, some of which indicate sympathetic vibrations with Per Nørgård in Denmark.

Across the fjord, so to speak, the explorer catches sight of two stalwart atonalists and ISCM regulars, *Egil Hovland* (q.v.) and *Finn Mortensen* (q.v.). Neither has done much with electronic media, but their instrumental pieces since the mid-1950s increasingly bear the stamp of the international serialist avant-garde. Hovland, perhaps more free-wheeling and radical than Mortensen, sometimes brings indeterminancy to his work.

If modern music in Norway can claim a major transitional figure linking older styles to new, then *Knut Nystedt* (q.v.) stands as a good candidate. Like Klaus Egge, he also lines up as a "man in the middle." Nystedt, at one time a pupil of Aaron Copland, emerged after the war with a forward-looking image. He has maintained his international outlook, but has largely avoided radical experiments. Nystedt composes in all forms, apart from opera, with more recent years pointing up his exceptional qualities as a choral composer and conductor.

One of the fastest rising stars in Scandinavian music, *Antonio Bibalo* (b. 1922) has been settled in Norway since 1957, after having received training in his native Trieste and in England. The growth of Bibalo's reputation has become assured in international musical circles by such exciting compositions as *Autunale* (1968,) an exquisitely sensual chamber suite, and the *Sinfonia Notturna* from the same year. Diverse currents flow into Bibalo's work: his Italian-Slavic heritage, Japanese poetry, the prose of Henry Miller, a whiff of impressionism, the precise logic of Elizabeth Lutyens (perhaps his most influential teacher) and the crisp bite of northern air. Neither a radical modernist nor a conservative, Bibalo is definitely his own man and one to watch.

Among the younger crop of Norwegian composers of the postwar generation, attitudes vary widely, with greater emphasis placed on search for individual identity than alliance with any style of fashion, no matter how radical. In fact, some of the younger artists have expressed sharp criticism of so-called avant-garde music. Prediction about the immediate future becomes difficult except that it will most probably be characterized by pluralism. This listener can claim only scant familiarity with the music of Norway's younger composers, but looks forward with keen interest to the progress of *Kåre Kolberg* (b. 1936), *Bjørn Hallberg* (b. 1938), *Ketil Saeverud* (b. 1939, son of Harald Saeverud), *Folke Strømholm* (b. 1941) and *Ragnar Søderlind* (b. 1945).

Certainly, Norway's contemporary composers of whatever stripe have proven more than worthy of their noble musical heritage. But at least one development has become perfectly clear: the heirs of Edvard Grieg have decisively split from the "Song of Norway" past.

THE ROAD AHEAD

When this listener took his last journey to Scandinavia (Autumn 1972), there was a feeling that the "musical explosion" of the 1960s was over. Like the rest of Europe and the United States, the Scandinavians had reached the presumed limits of musical experimentation; with this last principle of composition on which men could agree gone, dissolution of the vanguard cult became a fact.

The younger composers, having grown up amid preachings and exhortations to discard the past, did precisely that, with a general rejection of systems whether based on serialism, John Cage's neo-dadaism or the vapid promises of electronic music. In Oslo, host city for the 1972 Nordic Music Days, both new and familiar names shared the programs as evidence that at least the will to compose still ran strong in the North. But at this particular get-together of the Scandinavian musical fraternity, the atmosphere seemed more open and relaxed. The hero of the hour was no wizard of electronic circuitry, or some determined barbarian smashing up instruments in the name of self-expression, but rather David Monrad Johansen, eighty-four years old, who reduced the generation gap with a straightforward string quartet.

With a world-wide cooling of experimentation, the up-and-coming generation in Sweden, Norway and Denmark finds itself seeking identity through a variety of means. They continue to hold world perspective, to travel abroad, but what they find often differs little from what they know at home — the same tools, the same problems, the same audience. The Scandinavians, after all, have used the past century to achieve a remarkable elevation in their standard of living to the highest in Europe, perhaps in the whole world. But advanced lifestyle carries a price. Some of the confusion encountered by northern artists derives from a self-conscious realization that outsiders are now looking more closely at them, sometimes with unrealistic expectations. This is an uncomfortable role, being thrust front stage center. But despite sketchy historical precedent these latitudes did give the world Ibsen, Strindberg, Grieg and Sibelius. They stand as worthy models. The Nordic voice, when it really has something to say, will be heard.

Guesses about the future of Scandinavian music come in all sizes and shapes. There is much handwringing, in and out of government, about musical education and the role of the arts in a welfare state. The Swedes, especially, have compiled a mass of data about the tastes and needs of their population. But this is of little immediate help to the composer who, having generally forsaken nationalism, feels as one with colleagues elsewhere in facing a confusing welter of possible choices, his own private "Hall of Mirrors." But by the same token, does he not enjoy ultimate freedom? To be able to maneuver, to hold options, to seize opportunity — this is the stuff of true liberty for the artist as for all men. In this the Scandinavian composer is blessed, even if life is no longer simple.

One promising field stands ready to absorb restless energies while things sort out — musical theater, opera or "neo-singspiel," whatever one cares to call it. A public which would not be caught dead at a contemporary music concert will assemble to share the experience of a good story wedded to music and theatrics, a milieu in which the Scandinavians excel. Some recent attempts at "total theater" like the Busotti-Welin production *La Passion selon Sade* in Stockholm may have encountered variable reception, but this observer can vouch for the electrifying impact of the Danish ballet *Dødens Triumf* (Triumph of Death) with its electronically-enhanced score by *Thomas Koppel* (b. 1944).

Regardless of the direction taken by future music in Scandinavia, no geographic, cultural or technical limitations shut the Nordic composer out of a forefront position in developments in Western music, if that is where he wants to be.

PART II

COMPOSERS GALLERY

HUGO ALFVÉN (1872–1960)

The usual image of Hugo Alfvén, Sweden's most effective musical champion of national romantic ideals, largely derives from his senior years, a long stretch from World War I until the Space Age, when Alfvén ripened as "grand old man" of Swedish music. A whole generation of his countrymen knew him mainly as a pipe-puffing sage at Uppsala, celebrated leader of choral societies, entrenched figurehead in The Establishment and man of many medals.

As time passed and honors rolled in, Alfvén's creative position grew increasingly static. He never swerved from his position as chief prop for Swedish national romanticism and he provides a strong reason for its delayed sunset. Alfvén displayed no shyness concerning his work or its importance to national life; his autobiography alone reaches the Wagnerian proportions of four thick, loquacious volumes.

But if Alfvén died an anachronism, historical amnesia should not dull the earlier years when he stood tall in the North as a forceful progressive. His unquestioned talent and thorough training (largely acquired in his native Stockholm) combined to project his individual voice far and wide, the first Swedish composer ever to see a substantial breakthrough beyond the Nordic circle.

As a captain of the modern orchestra, Alfvén bears comparison with the best; in him, students of choral music will find a past master. Full credit must be given him as a pioneer, the first truly successful translator of Swedish folk spirit into symphonic music as well as a father figure in the evolution of the male chorus. Although unrestrained sensuality sometimes flaws Alfvén's more ambitious works, redemption arrives with his striking ability to frame and color musical imagery as well as to plumb the recesses of the Swedish soul. No composer ever sang more lovingly of his native land than Hugo Alfvén.

Orchestral Music

SYMPHONY NO. 2 IN D (1898)   (50')

In his first pair of symphonies, young Alfvén had few models. He no doubt looked at Brahms and Svendsen for some bearings, possibly also at Sinding, but at the time he was running neck and neck with Carl Nielsen and a length ahead of Sibelius.

The sheer grasp of form and technique displayed by Alfvén in his Second Symphony should correct the false impression that he was strictly a lightweight. This is a real Nordic epic, pulsating with manly ideals developed with firm purpose. Flaws occur — the tendency for the slow movement to ramble; the fugal weightiness of the finale. But the first

59

movement belongs to the best in late-romantic Scandinavian symphonism, while the choice of a Swedish chorale for ultimate resolution proves more than apt. Perhaps not an unqualified masterpiece, but the Alfvén Second Symphony is music for anyone to reckon with.

SYMPHONY NO. 3 IN E (1905)   (34')

Conceived under the spell of a blissful Italian summer, the Third Symphony was intended by the composer as "A paean in praise of all the joys of life, sunshine and the joys of living." The gravity and darker textures of the Second Symphony move aside; high spirits abound. The music strives, perhaps too impetuously, for bubbling feelings and cloudless skies. Alfvén best measures up to his claim as a symphonist, however, in the more tranquil, melodically fertile Andante.

SYMPHONY NO. 4 IN C MINOR (1919)   (43')

What really went wrong? Why did Alfvén, after demonstrating such high promise, fail to mature as a symphonist in step with his two Nordic contemporaries, Carl Nielsen and Jan Sibelius? Maybe, like the Englishman Arnold Bax, he found himself an incorrigible romantic poet unable to adjust to the harsh artistic climate of postwar Europe. Whatever happened, Alfvén's fourth bid in his symphonic canon threatens to consume itself in bathos. Subtitled "From the Outskirts of the Archipelago," the work looks impressive on paper: orchestra of Strauss/Mahler proportions, the use of wordless soprano and tenor voices and vast, single movement ground plan. But this mammoth apparatus struggles in the grip of a hazy program, something about the love of man for woman expressed by children against nature symbols derived from the sea. Lush, emotive music, like any other, must rise or fall on its own merits. The Alfvén Fourth simply goes overboard: a film score without the pictures.

SYMPHONY NO. 5 IN A MINOR (1952)   (50')

Unless some amanuensis completes the revisions planned by Alfvén before his death, the Fifth Symphony as an entity seems headed for limbo. Alfvén finished the very long first movement in 1942, then mulled over the rest for ten more years. By this time Alfvén was living in the past. The first movement, sometimes played alone, strikes this listener as a muddled symphonic poem.

SWEDISH RHAPSODY NO. 1: MIDSOMMARVAKA (Midsummer Vigil) (1903)
                                                                        (13')

A classic — possibly Sweden's sole national romantic representation in the international repertoire. Compelled to capture the festive sights and sounds of St. John's Eve on the outer Stockholm archipelago, Alfvén organized his impressions as an ethnic dance rhapsody, translating them into glowing orchestral colors with bounce galore thanks to generous and knowing use of "walking tunes" and the *polska*. Few works from Scandinavia can boast such a wealth of irresistible melody.

SWEDISH RHAPSODY NO. 2: UPPSALA RHAPSODY (1901)   (10')

Just before Alfvén moved to Uppsala, campus elders approached him for appropriate musical trappings to help celebrate the 200th anniversary of Carl von Linnaeus, the university's most hallowed name. To oblige, Alfvén walked in the "Academic Festival" footsteps of Johannes Brahms, although substance for his piece drew from the venerable traditions of Uppsala itself — tunes and student songs bequeathed by Bellman, Gunnar Wennerberg, Prince Gustav and others. Alfvén laced these neatly together with the aid of jolly Germanic scoring.

SWEDISH RHAPSODY NO. 3: DALECARLIA RHAPSODY (1937)   (19')

Listeners familiar with the extroverted spirit of "Midsummer Vigil" will find no sequel here. Although dance moods are evoked, visceral excitement runs at low ebb. This is introspective music which gets below the surface of folk melodies, a sort of program piece telling of a herd girl's visions in lonely mountain pastures. Not easy music for foreigners to grasp, the Third Rhapsody speaks of deep-rooted Swedishness, not mere local color.

EN SKÄRGÅRDSSAGEN (A Tale of the Skerries) (1904)   (17')

Alfvén's cinematic seascape ably depicts rock-strewn beaches and slamming surf worthy of the painter's eye (Alfvén was, in fact, an expert watercolorist). Inspiration and form sustain his images, a full-blown tone poem ranking as typical but choice Alfvén.

FESTSPEL (Festival Piece) (1907)   (9')

Alfvén was something of a Swedish Elgar, a sort of "official" composer on call for patriotic songs and appropriate pomp and circumstance. *Festspel,* commissioned for the inauguration of the Royal Dramatic Theater, has become one of the most popular of Alfvén's many occasional pieces. Essentially a *grande polonaise* for full orchestra, *Festspel* is appropriately jubilant and noisy.

BERGAKUNGEN (The Mountain King) (1923)   (14')

Alfvén's unerring flair for folk tone admits no better example than his music for the ballet *Bergakungen* which he claimed to have written "with the blood of my heart." The staged version tells a typical Nordic story — an abducted maiden up for grabs in a fight between the "Mountain Trolls" and the "Forest Trolls." In the end, hero and heroine get buried by the "Snow Trolls."

Scored for large orchestra, the extracts usually presented in concert performance make an extremely effective dance suite full of authentic Swedish flavor and finding the composer in his element. The first three movements (Incantation, Troll Maiden's Dance and Summer Rain) prove utterly captivating; but the real excitement arrives with the justly-celebrated *Vallflickans dans* (Herdmaiden's Dance) based on a crisp, invigorating folk song.

DEN FÖRLORADE SONEN (The Prodigal Son) (1957)   (15')

This ballet suite should strike any listener as sheer delight, an amazingly fresh score from an ultra-conservative yet spry composer of eighty-five! Inspired by Dalecarlian folk paintings, this music comes on energetically and in full native dress. Here is found another of Alfvén's "greatest hits," the infectious polka *Roslagsvår* (Spring in Roslag) which, like the famous "walking dance" tune in "Midsummer Vigil," could stand as Hugo Alfvén's theme song.

GUSTAV II ADOLPH SUITE (1932) (36')

Alfvén shoulders a musket, breaks into Martin Luther's best-known hymn and marches off to the Thirty Years' War. Despite moments of pastiche, this revamped incidental music paints a reasonably valid tableau of Gustav Adolph's escalation of Continental politics. One movement, the noble Elegy, reveals Alfvén in one of his finest creative moments. Less can be said for the inflated finale depicting the Battle of Breitenfeld. Although Alfvén whips up enthusiasm in his battlepiece with sure command of the orchestra, he must take second place to such musical soldiers as Sergei Prokofiev (*Alexander Nevsky*) and William Walton (*Henry V*).

Chamber Music

SONATA IN C MINOR FOR VIOLIN AND PIANO (1896)

In his younger days, Alfvén found employment as a violinist at the Royal Opera with serious thoughts in his head about pursuing a career as a concert artist. At this point came his Opus 1 violin sonata, one of his rare excursions into chamber music, but by no means a frail or negligible effort. Gade and Sjögren come to mind as likely prototypes for this full-blooded sonata which falls into the broad Nordic-romantic tradition. Intense expressive feeling appears at almost every turn, perhaps best revealed in the third movement (Andante patetico), but the bold strokes and restless vigor of the outer movements also indicate a budding composer armed with strong ideas of his own.

Vocal Music

SOLO SONGS

Hugo Alfvén cannot be listed among the giants of Scandinavian art song, certainly not in the same category as contemporaries like Rangström or Sibelius. Yet his demonstrated capabilities in this area of composition command both affection and respect despite occasional lapses into excessive pathos and a fondness for less than front-rank poets. In the Alfvén songs, lyric elements predominate with literary correlation of subordinate importance. Folk elements are seldom in evidence, although some of Alfvén's arrangements of actual folk songs continue to win deserved popularity.

Most of Alfvén's songs fall into two creative periods: an early group from the 1898–1908 decade, then resurgent interest from the 1940s. Of the earlier songs, top honors go to *Ved Huset* (Toward Home), the melting *Sommardofter* (Summer Fragrances), *Skogen sover* (Sleeping Woods) and the well-known *Du är stilla ro* (You Are Still). *Gammalt kväde från Hälsingland* (Old Song from Helsingland) is a folk tone recreation of uncommon excellence. *Jag längtar dig* (I Long for You), however, seems saccharine.

The later Alfvén finds good representation in songs like *I stilla timmar* (In Quiet Hours) and the very beautiful *Så tag mit Hjerte* (So Take

62

My Heart) from 1946, which proves a Swede can write a superlative Danish song.

Of the folk-song settings, special attention goes to *Som stjärnan uppå himmelen så klar* (The Stars above Shine So Clear), which possesses such beauty and serenity that Alfvén requested it sung at his own funeral.

CHORAL SONGS

In Sweden, choral singing and the name Hugo Alfvén virtually became synonomous as the result of his long experience as a choral conductor, particularly of Uppsala's famed *Orphei Drängar* (The Servants of Orpheus) and other student groups which he often took on concert tours abroad. This intimate relationship with working choral groups gave him both stimulus and opportunity to turn out short, immediately engaging pieces in a cappella style.

The powerful *Gryning vid havet* (Down by the Sea) and *Aftonen* (Evening) have become Scandinavian choral warhorses, but the composer's subtle use of chromatic harmony for atmospheric effects has not become stale. Of several choral folk-song settings, pride of place must be given to *Och jungfrun hon går i ringen* (The Girl in the Dance Ring), a merry tune from *Västergötland* which serves beautifully as a Christmas carol. In *Tjuv och tjuv, det ska du heta* (Thief, That Is Your Name Now) Alfvén carries on the bucolic tradition of August Söderman.

The serenade *Lindagull, Lindagull lilla* (Linda with the Golden Hair), a piece for tenor solo and male choir, has gained widespread popularity in the Nordic countries. During the First World War, Alfvén came up with the patriotic hit song *Sveriges flagga* (Sweden's Flag) which has become a semi-official national anthem. Neither piece impresses this listener as belonging to Alfvén's best.

For Further Exploration

Symphony No. 1; Incidental music for *Synnøve Solbakken; Drapa; En bygdesaga* (A Country Tale); Four Tunes from Leksand; Romance for violin and piano; piano pieces; cantatas; songs; choral pieces.

KURT ATTERBERG (1887–1974)

Regrettably, Kurt Atterberg must be listed among the casualties buried beneath the avalanche of non-tonal music engulfing the world since 1950. But tides of fad and fashion, even radical change itself, did not erase what Atterberg managed to accomplish nor quench his impulse to keep working at an age when most men sit rocking on the porch. This vigorous octogenarian presided over the premiere of his Ninth Symphony ("Sinfonia visionaria") as late as 1967.

Once widely performed and discussed, Atterberg's music has always reflected outspoken Swedish spirit but in a very personal, supremely lyrical manner. Like Alfvén, Atterberg can be considered a national romanticist, but his preference for large forms like the symphony and opera demanded that he concern himself with matters beyond mere local color. Doubtless some would consider the prolonged presence of Atterberg in modern Swedish music as antediluvian, yet fair evaluation must grant his position as the strongest symphonist in Sweden's late romantic group, the equal of Stenhammar and a cut above Alfvén and Rangström.

Though less common today when radio and public education have somewhat broadened the job market in Scandinavia, composers of Atterberg's generation frequently pursued double careers, one to feed the body, the other to feed the soul. But even under this necessity Atterberg displayed uncommon energy: civil engineer, patent office official, authority on radio, journalist and music critic, conductor, musical organizer, and composer all belong to his busy lifetime. But behind all these activities stands a steady, dedicated artist; discovering his creative work always brings pleasure.

Orchestral Music

SYMPHONY NO. 2 IN F (1913)   (41')

Although the Second Symphony is nakedly romantic by today's esthetic and flawed by occasional constructional miscalculation, the lofty purpose and high-minded lyricism sweeping through it still hold up as one of the truest expressions of Swedish feeling in symphonic form. Magnificent pages occur in the first movement with its balance between agitation and pastoral serenity; unfortunately, the finale is less cohesive and less inspired. But the center core of this bold symphony, bedrock, emerges in the second movement (Adagio-Presto) where Atterberg manages to keep the lines of slow movement and scherzo separate yet flowing together. His recapitulation of the hymnal adagio theme in a blaze of grandeur remains unforgettable. Throughout the piece Atterberg controls the richness of his ideas and curbs excess sentiment.

SYMPHONY NO. 4 IN G MINOR: SINFONIA PICCOLA (1918)   (22')

Parental favoritism for certain offspring as against others may not always be admired, but must be respected. Atterberg, at least on occasion, looks upon his "little" G minor symphony as a lesser flight compared to his "big" G minor symphony (the Eighth, composed in 1944), his personal favorite. Without disputing the composer's own pecking order, the Fourth Symphony can be safely placed near the top of Atterberg's works list. Here is lithe, splendidly coherent music making liberal use of native thematic material. The drive of movement one recalls Carl Nielsen while in the slow movement Atterberg evokes the rose-tinted glow of a northern summer's night. Folkishness increases in the scherzo with dancing continuing right on through the rondo finale.

SYMPHONY NO. 6 IN C (1928)   (29')

Once the center of international scandal, Atterberg's infamous Sixth Symphony was initially entered in a silly contest cooked up by a record company on the occasion of the Schubert Centennial. After taking the $10,000 first prize, Atterberg rocked the music world with a flurry of press statements stating, in effect, that the jury could not tell their Schubert from *smörgåsbord*. He revealed that his last movement contained, "A rather true citation of a famous Schubert theme," along with snippets from other famous composers. The "Schubert connoisseurs" (Atterberg's words) on the jury were scarcely amused.

Actually, Atterberg's symphony is anything but a jerry-built hoax. Much of it had been completed before announcement of the contest and the work fits comfortably into the line of Atterberg's development. Polished eloquence and a firm grasp of symphonic logic are plainly evident. Impudence does occur in the "plagiarized" finale. But why must a symphony, even one from Sweden, necessarily be "elevated" or "serious"? Perhaps that was Atterberg's point all along.

DE FÄVITSKA JUNGFRURNA (The Wise and Foolish Virgins) (1920)   (17')

Originally composed for Les Ballets Suédois in Paris, the concert version of *The Wise and Foolish Virgins* takes the form of a free-flowing dance rhapsody rather than a compartmentalized suite. Variations on the old Dalecarlian folk chorale *The Kingdom of Heaven Is Like Ten Virgins* gives the piece unity, and the cool, restrained serenity of rural Sweden. The overall effect of this exquisitely lyrical score is that of a stately sarabande.

SUITE NO. 3 FOR VIOLIN, VIOLA AND STRINGS (1922)   (15')

Note for note and bar for bar, Atterberg's Third Suite may well be the single most beautiful work to issue from his hand. Conceived as an unpretentious double concertino, the suite's three sections (Prelude, Pantomime, Vision) derive from an initial function as incidental music for Maeterlinck's miracle play, *Sister Beatrice*. On this spiritual note the composer has created an atmosphere of sublime poetic tenderness.

SUITE NO. 5; SUITE BAROCCO (1923)   (17')

Originally, this was music for a revival of Shakespeare's *The Winter's*

Tale, a play with a mood that has much in common with the Swedish musical temperament. Atterberg chose six baroque dance forms adding up to music in "ye olden style," yet the languid melancholy and wistfulness of the North rises to the surface. Scored for modest forces of woodwinds and strings, *Suite Barocco* provides a set of tuneful, sometimes moving miniatures which rise well above mere pastiche.

SUITE NO. 8: SUITE PASTORALE (1931)   (21')

Music styled much like *Suite Barocco,* but as sometimes happens in the case of sequels, the earlier inspiration eludes recapture.

ALADDIN OVERTURE (1941)   (6')

Atterberg's opener for an opera based on Oehlenschläger's *Aladdin* proves deft, direct and dashingly theatrical with a topping of pseudo-orientalism. This pleasant overture should find its way to more "Pops" programs.

Vocal Music

FANAL (1932)

Of Atterberg's five operas, *Fanal* seems to have generated the most interest from critics and the public. Available accounts suggest sufficient merit for occasional revival. The libretto, of Austrian origin, relates the story of a sixteenth-century hangman, feared and despised by the community, who saves a princess from a bloodthirsty mob. Because his occupation has made him an outcast, he must renounce his love. But the heroine's father brings a happy conclusion, an ending for the opera which one critic found "cheap" and "contrived." The same commentator, however, felt that Atterberg's orchestral palette was "full of bright colors" and that the opera was "very cleverly and firmly built up." Jussi Björling starred in the premier performance. Collectors of vocal recordings may be familiar with Björling's rendition of *I männer över lag och rätt* (Man Stands over Law and Justice) from *Fanal.* Hopefully, the future will enable listeners to learn more of Atterberg's work in the field of music drama.

For Further Exploration

Symphonies Nos. 5, 7, 8 and 9; *Ballad and Passacaglia;* Horn Concerto; Cello Concerto; *Älven* (The River); *Värmland Rhapsody; Sinfonia per Archi; Härvard Harpolekare* (Herverd the Bard); *Per Svinaherde* (Peter Swineherd).

SVEN-ERIK BÄCK (b. 1919)

A forefront modernist, Bäck developed within the seminal Stockholm "Monday Group" of the 1940s along with Blomdahl and Lidholm, but less foreign attention has been paid to his music compared to his two colleagues. Generally speaking, Bäck has remained more consistent than Blomdahl and more versatile than Lidholm. An early convert to serial procedure, Bäck has striven to refine and humanize his creative work. He thinks nothing of enriching his complex technical vocabulary by reaching back as far as Gregorian chant for some needed musical tool. Intricate rhythmic patterns are a hallmark of his style, imparting both dazzling brilliance and constant agitation to his instrumental pieces and chamber operas. But there is another side to this composer. Deep religious feeling lies at the heart of Bäck's artistic creed and is spelled out most clearly in his superior choral writing. So far Bäck has not shown himself a particularly prolific composer (teaching responsibilities and work with the state radio have increasingly encroached on his composing time), but whatever this forceful and energetic composer delivers carries a firmly inscribed and distinctive signature.

Orchestral Music

SINFONIA PER ARCHI (1951)   (18')

The astringent tone of Bäck's early string symphony reflects a once-fashionable neo-classical dissonant style. All components of the piece proceed in a deeply serious, well-disciplined manner with occasional release of bleak poetry. But concessions to lyricism fail to outweigh stiffness and inhibition; a dash of contrasting playfulness might have proven welcome. Documentation of Bäck's growth as a composer seems the work's chief asset.

SINFONIA DA CAMERA (1955)   (13')

Initially received as a pathbreaking piece during the turbulent days when atonality began descending on the Swedish scene, Bäck's pocket symphony sounds entirely tame a decade or so later. At this point the composer freed himself from the grip of linear polyphony typical of his earlier work in favor of the twelve-tone row and thinner textures. Manipulation of the new material was not yet expert, however, and Bäck's abrupt, declarative ideas suffer from occasional congestion. Yet the seeds of his more mature style stand in plain evidence: a feeling for rhythmic freedom, concise form and forward motion achieved by repeated regrouping of motivic fragments.

A GAME AROUND A GAME (1959)   (15')

Taut and scintillating, this three-movement concert piece takes title and inspiration from a welded sculpture group by Björn Evenson showing

67

an elongate metallic mother furiously at play with leaping offspring. Bäck's music reduplicates the same enormous energy: steely string resonances stretched over hair-trigger responses from a battery of fifteen separate types of percussion instruments. The composer's results end up as elegant as they are breathtaking, surely one of the outstanding works in Sweden's musical showcase.

CONCERTO FOR VIOLIN AND ORCHESTRA (1957, 1960)   (17')

A professional stringman himself, Bäck wisely understands that a violin sounds best when singing, not sawing. Serially conceived, the concerto's ambiant, ornamental solo line unwinds against an orchestra with greatly expanded percussion section — almost an habitual feature of Bäck compositions. Overall design retains the classic three movements with much given to discrete "point music" arrayed against a full spectrum of percussion color and comment. But the solo violin stays well forward, fully coming into its own during an exceptionally lyrical middle movement.

Chamber Music

SONATA FOR SOLO FLUTE (1949)

Bäck's three-movement sonata offers any flutist an interesting challenge — music in a modern style yet with ample expressive content. Neobaroque ornamentation is elaborate, the sharply accented melodic line embroidered with supple rhythmic lacework. Swedish origin might explain the sonata's very serious mood and business-like efficiency.

STRING QUARTET NO. 3 (1962)

Lucid structural coherence joined to rhythmic plasticity form the principal attractions of Bäck's orchestral work, but in his Third String Quartet the composer seems to shift ground; he becomes very difficult to grasp. Single unit construction effaces orientation by division lines while contrasts between sections blur in a tangle of slithering glissandi and grinding dissonance. Knotty, intellectualized abstractionism in this instance seems to indicate that Bäck is seeking escape from the strictures of applied serial technique.

FAVOLA FOR CLARINET AND PERCUSSION (1962)

Not exactly "chamber music" in the traditional sense, but the small forces required and the intimate nature of this piece relate more to a "little theater" atmosphere than the concert hall. Although set up as three short movements, *Favola* essentially amounts to on-going dialogue between narrator (clarinet) and a circle of contributing listeners (drums, gongs, triangle, piano and whatnot). The ensuing conversation seems more structured than profound, but the exchange between the more lyrical clarinet and the assertiveness of five meticulous percussionists sticks to the point. The clear texture and intelligence found in *Favola* have helped make this one of Bäck's most often-performed works.

Vocal Music

KATTRESAN (Cat Journey) (1952)

Bäck has worked closely with young musicians and student orchestras for several years, giving him special insight into the place and function of educational music. *Kattresan* could fall into that category, a cantata for the under-ten generation after the amusing storybook poems of Ivar Arosenius. Subtitled "Concerto per bambini," the score calls for assorted percussion instruments as might be found in any schoolroom in addition to a children's choir. Unavoidably, music of this type bears similarity to the *Schulwerk* of Carl Orff, but Bäck displays a real flair for neatly presented humorous material enjoyable at any age.

TRANFJÄDRARNA (The Crane Feathers) (1956)

Play with something long enough and you are certain to break it — that is the moral behind the old Japanese legend underlying this intriguing chamber opera. Urged on by nosy neighbors, farmer Yohyo breaks a promise to his wife Tsu out of pure greed. She then reveals herself as a crane no longer able to weave gorgeous cloth for him from crane plumage. Instead she must fly off to the faraway clouds. Bäck manages this inscrutable plot with rare skill. Two contrasting twelve-note series make up the infrastructure of the opera, one serious representing the love bond between Tsu and Yohyo, the other the counterforce of the neighbors' meddling. A children's choir and deft employment of percussion further enhance this brilliant score.

FÅGELN (The Bird) (1960)

The meaning and significance of Bäck's third opera, a one-act work similar in scope and style to *The Crane Feathers,* eludes this listener. Even Swedes become lost in the symbolism and imagery of *The Bird* which is taken from a radio play by the Yugoslavian writer Aleksander Obrenovic. Bäck invests his "moral fable" with fastidious musical detail as laconic as the text.

MOTETS

Bäck's intimate knowledge of Gregorian chant and Palestrina's pure style found comparatively early outlet in his set of "St. John Motets" composed in the middle 1940s. About 1959 he embarked on a major project to supply two dozen new motets for the Church, one for each important feast day of the liturgical year. Much comment has arisen about Bäck's spiritual motivation and strong religious anchorage; in a very true sense his numerous a cappella motets stand as sermons in music. In them Bäck displays consummate mastery of his linear-polyphonic choral idioms along with varied feeling and different degrees of intensity.

SECULAR CHORAL PIECES

Even when not composing for the Church, Bäck brings austere dignity and deep sensitivity to his choral writing. *Visa* (Song) and *Våren* (Spring), two brief a cappella pieces, amply convey the essentials of his choral style.

For Further Exploration

Intrada; Movimento II; O Altitudo II; String Quartet No. 2; *Ett spel om Maria* (A Play about Mary); *Gästabudet* (The Banquet); *Ikaros;* Incidental music for Strindberg's *A Dream Play.*

CARL MICHAEL BELLMAN (1740–1795)

Bellman must be regarded as a Swedish specialty, a troubadour cutting across lines of eighteenth-century taste through his genius as a poet and magnetism as a performer. Bellman's work was created to be sung by the poet himself, cittern in hand. He sang neither ballads nor folk songs, only his own poetry with tunes either invented or plucked from the court dances and operas of Gustavian Stockholm. The informality of Bellman's singular art and his predilection for gin-soaked companions created the image of an extemporizing bohemian, but Bellman devoted much time and care to the preparation of his material, which ranges from the simple ditties of his youth to the masterful song-poems of his tragic old age where form and balance unify with dazzling mastery of the Swedish language. This special kind of "musical poetry" had no definite antecedents and but the paltriest of imitative successors.

Can Bellman's art be appreciated without intimate knowledge of the Swedish language? Categorically, no — at least not to the degree his countrymen have taken these songs to heart over the past two hundred years. Translations prove helpful, but only provide approximate shadows of Bellman's artistic impact. Also problems of interpretation loom large because of the intense personal nature of a Bellman performance, which requires the poet's own uncanny ability to mimic people and musical instruments. Lack of such nuances too often results in renditions which are stilted, precious or both.

Laughter and tears lie close together in Bellman's art; the irony of his lines still comes through, but what might have sounded uproariously funny in an eighteenth-century Stockholm tavern may have a contrary tinge of gallows humor today. A serious undertone lurks beneath the devil-may-care bravado of Bellman's lines, allusions to the finality of death as it conveys almost desperate sympathy for the inhabitants of his debauched world. Although a genuine humanitarian, Bellman took life at the top and the bottom of the social scale as he saw it; unlike Hogarth, Bellman the moralist never appears.

Vocal Music

SONGS

Some two thousand surviving poems have been attributed to Bellman; most of these are classifiable as songs. The essential Bellman, the work upon which his fame rests, saw publication just before he died in the form of two collections: *Fredmans epistlar* (Fredman's Epistles, 1790) with 82 songs and *Fredmans sånger* (Fredman's Songs, 1791) containing 65.

70

Both words and music were printed together, confirming their insepara-bility.

In these two volumes the unique world of Carl Michael Bellman springs to life, song after song immortalizing a gallery of tipplers and tap-room types from a Stockholm long past. The title figure and the poet's alter ego, Fredman, actually existed, a former royal watchmaker fallen on evil days and now stumbling in rags through the crooked alleys of "Old Town" with his last watch long since pawned and ironically annihilating time in his "little green hourglass of booze." Constable Movitz, Father Berg, Corporal Mollberg and others join poor Fredman's revels and hang-overs. Of the girls, Bellman lavishes some of his choicest lines on Ulla Winblad (modelled after a real life demimondaine), an uninhibited tavern nymph whom the poet equates to a "priestess in the Temple of Bacchus."

Even for the casual listener some of Bellman's best-known songs can become treasured gems. *Haga* (Butterflys at Haga, FS 64) may represent Bellman's supreme moment as a songwriter, a perfectly crafted little prism sighting "the misty park of Haga in the frosty morning air." Its tune, of Bellman's own making, might have won the envy of Mozart. The popu-larity of *Ulla, min Ulla* (Ulla, My Ulla, FE 71) is well-deserved, a lover's serenade combined with pastoral rapture. In the drinking song *Joachim uti Babylon* (Joachim of Babylon, FS 41) the song-poet presents one of his sharpest Biblical parodies. The imitative aspect of Bellman's art reaches clear focus in songs like *Blåsen nu alla* (Blow One and All, FE 25) where the singer mimics a posthorn for an imaginary ride out to Stockholm's *Djurgården* (Deer Park). In the delectable *Opp, Amaryllis* (Up, Amaryl-lis, FS 31) Bellman gives us a cunning glimpse of rococo dalliance.

But to think of Bellman solely for his songs dwelling on the simple joys of life overlooks the full reach of his genius. The Fredman songs also show a darker side, the world seen through tired and disillusioned eyes. Sometimes Bellman gives his depressing views with startling accuracy as in *Undan ur vägen!* (Out of the Way! FE 38), which depicts the raggle-taggle funeral procession of Corporal Boman's grave: this song reaches a pitch of wild intensity almost unknown in eighteenth-century music. The innocent-sounding minuet for *Ack, du min moder* (Oh, Mother of Mine, FE 23) plays ironic counterpoint to the befuddled Fredman awakening in a gutter, cursing the carnality of his parents whose seed brought him to this wretched earth, then staggering back into a nearby gin shop for another round with his beloved bottle. No remorse, only sober acceptance of death frames the mood of *Gubben är gammal* (Old Men Honor the Aged, FE 27), which represents Fredman's last thoughts.

FISKARENA (The Fishermen) (1773)

Bellman's occasional stage pieces have only peripheral importance and owe their chief motivation to efforts to ingratiate himself with Gustav III. One or two of Bellman's feathery playlets saw performance before courtiers, and he provided the composer Wikmanson with a libretto for the little operetta *Häckningen* (Bird-breeding).

71

Sometimes a Bellman "opera" called *Fiskarena* receives performance at the Drottningholm Theater. Actually, this is second-hand reconstruction of fragments of a pastoral operetta which Bellman slaved over in 1773; no evidence exists to indicate this work reached the stage during his lifetime. Original text and music have all but vanished; however the celebrated *Opp, Amaryllis* (FS 31) has fortunately survived.

JØRGEN BENTZON (1897–1951)

Like several other Scandinavian composers, Jørgen Bentzon proved adept at dual careers, in his case, law and music. As one of Carl Nielsen's rare private pupils, an intimate relationship naturally sprang up between them, but Bentzon was no mere carbon copy. He developed a style which set him apart as the first true modernist in Danish music, for his deep delving into technical problems led him away from traditional major/minor tonality. Bentzon's more characteristic music remains rarified, knotty even to seasoned listeners. During his later years, however, Bentzon favored populist cultural causes, and he helped found a people's music school in Copenhagen. Without decrying Bentzon's democratic idealism, this shift in his direction blunted the original thrust of his radical style; he began "writing down" to the man-in-the-street as exemplified by comparatively weak pieces like his *Dickens Symphony* (1939) and the opera *Saturnalia* (1944). The more interesting Bentzon belongs to the 1920s and 1930s, yet his many songs for student and amateur choral groups indicate "popular" music of reasonably high quality.

Orchestral Music

SYMPHONIC TRIO (1929)   (25′)

About 1925 Bentzon took leave of conventional tonality to move into a compressed technique built on freely organized counterpoint which he referred to as "character polyphony." Evidently, he extended Nielsen's keen perception of the intrinsic character of specific instruments — an idea foreshadowing such constructivist composers of a later generation as Elliott Carter. The timbre and registration of a given group of instruments actually help decide the flow of a given musical idea.

Symphonic Trio gives a sampling of Bentzon's theories in action; it is a rigorously cerebral concerto grosso with each of the soloists (violin, cello, horn) leading his own small orchestra. These modules, in effect, play against each other. The violin's "character" seems derived from rapid scale passages, the cello serves as a lyrical foil, while the horn plays "straightman," punctuating the activities with curt fanfares. Bentzon's "character polyphony" adds up to complex, very "un-Danish" music, but obviously the work of a powerful individualist.

MIKROFONI NO. 1 (1939)   (16′)

A curious piece for small orchestra and baritone voice, *Mikrofoni No. 1* again points up the singular, experimentalist path once followed by Jørgen Bentzon. The players are grouped for maximal exploitation of the microphone as known in the 1930s. But apart from gimmicks, Bentzon's "microphony" demonstrates sound musical values, a type of vocal suite in

73

three related movements employing medieval Latin verse. The cool objectivity of much of this music recalls Ravel. A disquieting note at the very end alludes to the gathering of war clouds then looming over Europe.

RACCONTO NO. 1 (1935)

Between 1935 and 1951 Bentzon produced six *Racconti* (Narratives) for diverse instrumental groupings as an extension of his "character polyphony" ideas. He placed emphasis on terse, single-movement layout, supple thematic material and sharp instrumental profiling. *Racconto No. 1* calls for the unusual combination of flute, saxophone, bassoon and double bass.

RACCONTO NO. 3 (1937)

Bentzon's third application of the *racconto* concept finds him exploiting the resources of the wind trio (oboe, clarinet, bassoon). The results are wry but approachable.

RACCONTO NO. 5 (1945)

Musical gamesmanship using instruments of the standard wind quintet; play occurs within a concentrated single movement marked by astringency plus a dash of impudence perhaps as an echo from Carl Nielsen.

For Further Exploration

Fotomontage Overture; Symphony No. 1 in D (On Dickens' Themes); Sinfonietta for Strings; Variations for Small Orchestra; *Sinfonia seria;* String Quartets (5); *Saturnalia;* choral music.

NIELS VIGGO BENTZON (b. 1919)

What makes Bentzon run? Heredity? Genetic fallout from great-grand-father J.P.E. Hartmann or cousin Jørgen Bentzon? Perhaps merely the ferment of the times fuels his restless flame. But whatever the reason, Bentzon grew from a child prodigy into a jovian figure possessed with a demonic lust to write music. His opus list (well on the way to four hundred items) shows no sign of diminished fertility at the time of this writing.

Niels Viggo Bentzon has rarely paused long enough to formulate a truly personal style or attach himself to any particular school, but despite much dabbling in modernism his eclectic speech draws much from neo-classicism. He might be likened to a diner with voracious appetite rattling through a smörgåsbord of styles, heaping his plate with slices of Hindemith, gobs of Bach, spoonsful of Schoenberg with a scoop of Thelonious Monk for dessert. Much of his music sounds rugged, impetuous and improvisatory; this in no way prevents the occasional emergence of almost romantic feeling. If Bentzon has an earlier counterpart, that composer might be Bohuslav Martinů.

Historically, Bentzon moved with the earliest Danish twelve-tone enthusiasts, but eventually the concept of metamorphosis won him over. Gradually, Bentzon began moving in two main directions: a tonally oriented orchestral idiom coexistent with a liberal variant of serialism in his operatic experiments. He has also published his own poetry and flings himself into "happenings" with equal gusto.

Orchestral Music

SYMPHONIC VARIATIONS (1953)   (18')

With *Symphonic Variations* the composer advances deep into metamorphosis country. A seminal idea, first heard lurking in the orchestra's lower registers, becomes less a transfigured "theme" than a color complex passed through ten closely connected, largely vigorous sections to reach a sonorously extended culmination. While considerable musical intelligence is needed to follow all ramifications of the initial idea from Bentzon's starting point, or "pattern" as he calls it, frequent tempo changes and the composer's talent for swift improvisation hold interest and command admiration.

PEZZI SINFONICI (1956)   (14')

The frightening fluency of the Bentzon composing "machine" (he has the ability to crank out symphonies with the speed of a Mozart) does not presume slipshod results. *Pezzi sinfonici* (Symphonic Pieces) comes smartly tailored; no buttons are missing and all seams stay out of sight. In this piece Bentzon aimed to refine and simplify the polyphonic expression-

75

ism as practiced in works like *Symphonic Variations*. In a sense *Pezzi sinfonici* exhibits a strong neo-classical bent with its slow, lyrical introduction followed by integrated fast-slow-fast pattern. Events resolve into a firmly stated chorale-like climax. Closely argued, logical and decisive, *Pezzi sinfonici* shows Bentzon in a highly flattering light.

Chamber Music

CHAMBER CONCERTO FOR 11 INSTRUMENTS (1948)

Dedication to Copenhagen's Collegium Musicum helps explain the energetic neo-baroque contrasts of this restyled concerto grosso, although a classical streak generally runs through Bentzon's music from this period. Scoring is interesting and unusual: winds, double bass, percussion and three pianos. With triplicate keyboards at his disposal, Bentzon found evident delight; he used them as a driving force not only in the busy end movements, but in the more reflective Adagio as well. But the rest of the band, particularly a pair of trumpets, more than hold their own amid Bentzon's amiable chatter. No serious message here, merely solid music making overlaid with a touch of jovial good humor.

MOSAIQUE MUSICALE (1949)

Although in *Mosaïque Musicale* the composer sends a terse germinal motive through metamorphic change, no special problems should face the general listener. Development comes logically within a type of cyclical pattern cast as a single, unified movement — a musical "mosaic." Four instruments participate (flute, violin, cello and piano); Bentzon exhibits restraint in the smooth blending of their respective timbres.

STRING QUARTET NO. 6 (1960)

The later Bentzon sounds much like the earlier Bentzon. He repeats himself with talent. Busy and concentrated music, the Sixth Quartet suggests excursions into free atonality, urged on by the composer's customary pep. The brief Andante provides some nice touches, neo-baroque melody over pedal-point.

Keyboard Music

SONATA NO. 3 (1946)

A redoubtable concert pianist himself and champion of contemporary keyboard music, Bentzon considers the piano an essential tool brought to bear in perhaps half of his enormous output. Compared to his work in other areas, his solo piano pieces exhibit greater freedom and waywardness because they often catch, camera-like, his inspiration at white heat. One of Bentzon's better known sonatas, the Third at times recalls Prokofiev in its energetic propulsiveness, although Bentzon's piano style shows less steely brilliance. For all his furious determination, however, Bentzon holds firmly to the discipline of four compact movements.

SONATA NO. 4 (1949)

The exhausting Fourth Sonata typifies Bentzon's restless muse, a torrent of notes and accidentals carrying along a broad range of introverted and extroverted ideas. But Bentzon does more than merely splash around with black and white keys; the neat order of six contrasting episodes linked in pairs governs flow. Sometimes sheer opulence threatens to clog forward motion, but tension gives way to unabashed, almost romantic lyricism as in the paired movements designated 3/4; here the composer produces a sensation describable as "melodic shock."

SONATA NO. 5 (1951)

Bentzon's Fifth Sonata for pianoforte is shorter, more buoyant and decidedly more classical than its predecessor. Sheer love for kinetic energy lessens in favor of studied angularity and percussive, jazzy rhythms. Referring to this sonata, the composer mentioned his admiration for Prokofiev; no doubt he agrees with the Russian's view that "I want nothing better than sonata form, which contains everything necessary for my purpose." In truth, Bentzon's keyboard sonatas find parentage in those from Prokofiev. The last movement of the Fifth Sonata, however, might startle American ears — shades of George Gershwin.

TOCCATA (1940)

Although probably considered heady stuff in Denmark at the time of composition, Bentzon's early, exuberant *Toccata* has become one of his best-known piano pieces. The composer's craggy determination and tough dialectic had already formed. Musically, *Toccata* takes the route of theme with transformation, a process in which the composer allows his fantasy free rein.

TRAESNIT (Woodcuts) (1951)

The title *Woodcuts* might imply a set of miniatures, but the composer probably intended to convey the idea of a piece that is clear, simple and easy to grasp. Clear, yes; simple, no. Another study in metamorphosis (austere thematic motive in minor thirds taken through eleven stages of growth), much of this music appears strained, hesitant, overthoughtful. Bentzon spends too much time gingerly picking his way from note to note; however some arresting moments appear in the work's dream-like, almost romantic resolution.

PAGANINI-VARIATIONS (1968)

When it comes to a new angle on the celebrated, but tired, Paganini theme this listener still prefers the duo-piano contribution from Lutoslawski. In stripping his material down to bare essentials, Bentzon only becomes baffling. According to Danish record jacket notes in English: "In the 'Paganini-Variations' the composer has thought of the old Paganini-caprice, but cut away the theme's slur. All that is left is just the empty violin fifth which slides up and down the keyboard." Amen.

DET TEMPEREREDE KLAVER (The Tempered Piano) (1964)

The idea to cross swords with J.S. Bach (and Hindemith) in this series of twenty-four preludes and fugues came, Bentzon once explained, when he felt half-formed chunks of music raining down on his head: "It was always a case of staggering home and going into desperate battle with the piano keys where . . . I realized approximately eighty minutes of piano material . . . a sort of gigantic metamorphosis . . ."

To recall an old saying, when a composer runs out of ideas he writes a fugue. Bentzon, however, has turned things around; he runs out of fugues before exhaustion overtakes his teeming imagination. Presumably, the music of *The Tempered Piano* might flow on forever. Of course, not all Bentzon's thoughts are stimulating. Dry spots certainly appear, but interesting music does float down this stream of notes with reasonable dependability.

Yet when the eighty minutes are up at the end of the twenty-fourth prelude-fugue combination, and the listener in turn finds himself "staggering home," he may remain skeptical of whether he has heard a meaningful synthesis of Bentzon's ideals or merely been exposed to a clinical experience.

Vocal Music

SAGN (Legend) (1964)

Bentzon's most talked-about vocal works to date remain the cantata *Bonjour Max Ernst* (1962) and the opera *Faust III* (1963). Both carry vanguard modernist reputations and have been spoken of as "surrealistic." Similar feelings for experimentation and unconventionality belong to *Legend,* composed for the 100th anniversary of the Copenhagen Student Song Society. Besides male choir with tenor soloist, the scoring includes brass and timpani used with considerable effect in pointing up the text which is sung, shouted and whispered over emphatic instrumental timbres. This expressive hunting scene (from the poem *Sagn* by Erik Knudsen) shows determination to get the lines across to the listener, but the choral idiom employed is not always handled with finesse, sometimes becoming studied and drab.

For Further Exploration

Symphonies (13); *Five Mobiles*; *Mutationen*; *Variozioni breve*; *Intrada*; Piano Concertos (5); Violin Concerto; Cello Concerto; Flute Concerto; Oboe Concerto; Accordion Concerto; *Sinfonia Concertante; Concerto per Archi; Concerto for Six Percussion Players;* Triple Concerto (flute, oboe, bassoon); Copenhagen Concertos (6); *Chamber Symphony for 17 Instruments*; String Quartets (9); Violin/Piano Sonatas (5); Sonata for Solo Cello; Variations for Solo Flute; Sonata for Horn and Piano; several trios for diverse instruments; piano music; Variations for Organ; *Faust III* (opera); Shelley Songs; *Metaphor, The Courtesan, The Door* (ballets); *Bonjour Max Ernst*.

FRANZ ADOLPH BERWALD (1796–1868)

Only in his final year of life could the elderly Franz Berwald see positive signs that more than token recognition had been given him by his countrymen after years of composing. But even then, election to the prestigious Academy of Music passed by a close vote of seven to four; too little, too late and begrudgingly given at that. Some may judge Sweden's indifferent treatment of her finest nineteenth-century composer a blot on her cultural history, but latter-day judgment must be tempered by the realization that Franz Berwald was not exactly a lovable person. Although he sometimes extended great kindness to younger artists, his abrupt and flinty manner of dealing with others made him numerous enemies.

Berwald's distinctive style matured when public interest in serious music lay at low ebb in Stockholm. Splendors of the Gustavian era had gone and the full stimulus of national romanticism had yet to arrive. Public favor went toward salon music and imported vogues in opera. The lack of sentiment in Berwald's music precisely indicates a major reason for cool reception by the Swedish public of those days. Berwald fully realized the barrier of provincialism he faced at home, causing him to spend much time abroad, first in Berlin, then Paris and Vienna where his creative energies hit full stride in the 1840s.

Classic, not German romantic roots nourished Berwald's music; he also derived much from the early nineteenth-century theater overture particularly as developed in France. But Berwald was no mere reflection of Continental schools. His originality is noteworthy. As he once carefully explained, his music was conceived "in an entirely personal manner" without reliance on current fashions.

Only a few musicians of his time appreciated Berwald's originality. Liszt and Hans von Bülow both registered admiration; Mendelssohn, sometimes cited as Berwald's "friend," only met the Swedish composer on a few occasions and cared little for him personally. Breakthrough for Berwald had to await the coming of the twentieth century, long after his death, when such countrymen as Tor Aulin and Wilhelm Stenhammar took up the baton on his behalf.

Orchestral Music

SYMPHONY IN G MINOR: SINFONIE SÉRIEUSE (1842)   (30′)

In theory there are six Berwald symphonies, in practice four. Numerical ordering is confused. A youthful First Symphony (1820) exists only as fragments; besides, Berwald disowned most of his early work. Whereabouts of a "Fourth" Symphony remains a mystery. Enough evidence exists, however, to reasonably assume that Berwald considered "Sinfonie sérieuse" his first real work in this form. It initiates a period in the composer's development when his real genius began to burn brightest. The symphony's lack of striking melody finds compensation in malleable themes capable of true development. Berwald fit them into a classic-romantic pattern rich in organizational detail without being fussy. Much of the "sérieuse" asserts itself in high-strung discourse so typical of the mature composer. The scherzo (marked *stretto*) is particularly commendable.

SYMPHONY IN D: SINFONIE CAPRICIEUSE (1842)   (26')

Although the "capricieuse" as presently known is a reconstruction from the composer's own short score (the original manuscript mysteriously vanished just after Berwald's death), the first two movements of this symphony should dispel all doubts that Franz Berwald was a true master of the nineteenth-century symphony. A more relaxed work compared to its predecessor, "capricieuse" opens with some of Berwald's most ingratiating and compelling ideas. These enlarge in a context of firm logic and restrained lyricism, at times with a captivating "swing" to the melodic contour. The tranquil Andante presents an exalted song-like theme of Nordic character. A slight sag in inspiration becomes detectable during the last movement, however, despite promising introduction by means of an elfin scherzo.

SYMPHONY IN C: SINFONIE SINGULIÈRE (1845)   (25')

During Berwald's lifetime only the disowned First and the "sérieuse" actually reached performance; the "singulière," his finest work in symphonic form, had to await a more understanding generation. Much about the "singulière" shows the composer well in the forefront of his contemporaries when it came to ideas about structure. Among the symphony's novel features is a split slow movement flanking the scherzo, a practice Berwald also carried to some of his chamber music. Tight control, sharp dynamic contrasts and lucid, meticulous scoring all operate to vitalize the "singulière," one of the first truly great works of its type born in the North.

SYMPHONY IN E-FLAT: SYMPHONY NO. 4 (1845)   (25')

Composed the same year as the "singulière," Berwald's last symphony will probably continue to be identified as his Fourth although most likely his Sixth in actual order of production. In any event, he delivered another masterpiece. Unlike the independent spirit of the "singulière," the E-flat Symphony finds Berwald reverting to convention by casting his ideas into four distinct movements. But the content, sheer melodic inspiration and orchestral mastery brought to this final symphony runs exceptionally high even for Berwald. A new warmth comes from these pages especially in the slow movement and superb scherzo. Even though Berwald had many creative years left when he completed the E-flat Symphony, he began his descent from the summit when obviously in command of his fullest powers.

PIANO CONCERTO IN D (1855)   (21')

"If I had to deliver an opinion of your work," Liszt wrote to Berwald, "I would say that its most striking characteristic seems to be a lively invention, superbly disciplined by long experience, and an engaging spirit and treatment of the instruments. Thus you satisfy the demands of Art without ever offending good sense." The same perceptive words well apply to Berwald's sole piano concerto, by no means the most original of his compositions, but a better one than long neglect would imply. Musically, the concerto lies somewhere between the glitter of Dussek and the romanticism of Schumann, a work in three continuous movements, each constructed on the basis of full technical assurance.

ALVALEK (Play of Elves) (1841) (8')

Unlike Berlioz or Liszt, full-blown romanticism with its literary trappings failed to attract Berwald the orchestral composer. Instead, his six extant *Tongemälde* ("tone paintings") deal with picturesque imagery in only a modest way. *Alvalek* is a pleasant pixie piece, a delicately scored introduction and scherzo of gentle playfulness but minor consequence.

MINNEN FRÄN NORSKA FJÄLLEN (Memories of the Norwegian Alps)
(1842) (10')

This engaging musical picture postcard became the most often-played of Berwald's works during his lifetime and hails from the composer's productive Vienna period. In the opening Andante, Berwald introduces what sounds like an authentic Norwegian folk tune, but despite much headscratching on the part of experts, this has defied precise identification. In the summer of 1827 Berwald toured Norway with Jan van Boom (a piano teacher at the Stockholm Conservatory) giving concerts both at Christiania and Bergen. Perhaps the mysterious melody entered Berwald's subconscious then. His first use of the tune, however, occurred in one of his earlier operas without intentional reference to anything Norwegian. But when dusted off several years later and fitted into his tone poem the melody adds the perfect atmospheric touch.

BAJÄDARFESTEN (Festival of the Indian Dancers) (1842) (11')

Although typically Berwaldian in pitting nervous orchestral agitation against smooth counter melody, this essay into exotica finds the composer unable to free himself from his own mannerisms.

Chamber Music

STRING QUARTET IN G MINOR (1818)

In 1818 young Berwald had begun to spread his wings; he left the nest of the Court Orchestra and was yet to be soured by the rebuffs of fortune. He had been composing steadily and had attained new assurance in a pair of string quartets (the present work and a lost companion in B-flat) which rank among the finest products of his early period. The composer's skill as a violinist and studies under Edouard Du Puy began to pay off in the superior quality and harmonic imagination displayed in this forward-looking quartet. Interesting here are Berwald's novel ideas about modulation which were well in advance of their time.

STRING QUARTET IN E-FLAT (1849)

Berwald's pair of quartets from 1849 belong to the cream of his output. Both show absolute supremacy over form and contrapuntal balance. As in the symphonies, the composer exhibits harmonic and structural audacity. In the E-flat Quartet he places his scherzo centrally, within an adagio which is in turn bracketed by animated end movements sharing the same thematic material. The result is one of the most ingenious and warmly lyrical works from Berwald's hand.

STRING QUARTET IN A MINOR (1849)

Sometimes listed as "Quartet No. 2," the A minor returns to a standard four-movement sonata plan; the work also exhibits deeper seriousness and stronger chromatic character than its mate in E-flat. Something close to Beethoven-like authority appears. Berwald's last two quartets came in response to a growing interest in chamber music from the Stockholm public, but Berwald never compromised his exploratory position. After a performance of one of these new quartets, he asked the opinion of A.F. Lindblad, who politely replied that a particular passage had struck him as quite charming. Berwald snapped back in his usual testy manner: "Really? I shall have to change it then."

STOR SEPTETT (Grand Septet) (1828)

The earliest of Berwald's works to win general acceptance, this piece for clarinet, flute, horn, violin, viola, cello and double bass may well have taken the Beethoven Septet as its model. About the same time Berwald may have essayed a second work in this form, but the whereabouts of this rumored companion piece is unknown.

Cohesive and generally easy-going, Berwald's Grand Septet offers little of a startling or revolutionary nature; his themes tend toward dryness while handling of harmonic material seldom rises above the ordinary. The jocular finale, however, gives this music a lift when most needed.

PIANO TRIO NO. 1 IN E-FLAT (1849)

In response to public demand for ensembles for home use, Berwald produced four Piano Trios between 1849 and 1851. They enjoyed modest but definite success giving the composer the rare experience of seeing his music favorably received in Sweden. The E-flat Trio pretends to nothing except pleasantness; Berwald's more radical traits lie subordinate to mild, unobtrusive romanticism. Yet, writing about one of these piano trios, a German critic attacked violently what he considered "the most terrible music of the future." For Berwald, even his smaller victories contained flaws.

PIANO TRIO NO. 3 IN D MINOR (1851)

The first movement (Allegro non molto) offers a mood of refined intimacy, but the rest of this trio seldom suggests more than amiable competence.

PIANO QUINTET IN C MINOR (1853)

Considering the elan and vitality of Berwald's symphonies and string quartets, the more subdued proceedings of the piano trios and quintets may disappoint new converts to his cause. Heavy criticism has been heaped on Berwald's ensemble piano writing with some degree of justification. Mere decoration substitutes too often for substance; passage work can rarely be called gripping or exciting. Yet the two piano quintets offer a great deal of charm. Romantic warmth glows quietly within the C minor Quintet which also shows Berwald's own ideas about form in a complex of telescoped movements.

PIANO QUINTET IN A (c. 1856)

Berwald's second entry in the piano quintet field shows more of a classic profile than its predecessor. Emotional feelings are more controlled as well. This chaste, easy-to-take music spins out along sinewy lines, bright and airy textures punctuated by crisp keyboard accents.

Keyboard Music

FROM THE MUSICAL JOURNAL (1818–1820)

Berwald's handful of piano pieces and a single work for organ are of slight importance compared to his work in other areas. He considered himself by training a violinist, although this in no way prevented him from teaching piano, with apparent success, in later years. During youth, however, Berwald ventured into musical publication, joining others in a Stockholm publication called *Journal de Musique*. The first and third volumes of the journal were given over entirely to piano pieces by Berwald, adding up to a list of ten. Of these one critic observed: "We do not know if Herr Berwald is a pianist, but his compositions would suggest this is not the case." A reasonable comment. Pieces like *Echo,* the *Rondeau-Bagatelle* in B-flat and *Tempo di Marcia* in E-flat hardly presage another Chopin. But Berwald must be allowed more than a crumb of credit for *Theme and Variations* in G minor, also from the journal, which may not be from the hand of a virtuoso pianist, but does show a well-organized musical mind at work.

THREE PIANOFORTE PIECES (1859–1860)

Familiarity with *Presto feroce,* the second member of this small collection, should set to rights the false notion that in pianistic matters Berwald was an inveterate bumbler. Almost every note of this wholly effective scherzo is stamped with his characteristic profile which cannot be mistaken for the music of another. This listener hopes the wait will not be too long for a hearing of the two companion pieces: *Romanza e scherzo* and *Une plaisanterie.*

Vocal Music

ESTRELLA DI SORIA (1848)

On April 9, 1862, Berwald's three-act grand opera *Estrella di Soria* (libretto by Otto Prechtler) opened at the Royal Opera in Stockholm. A cool reception from public and critics, however, nudged it off the boards after only four performances. Subsequent revivals, while uncommon, have occasionally taken place in Sweden.

Estrella di Soria boasts a splendid overture introducing dramatic and lyrical material appearing later in the opera. Despite occasional shades of Mendelssohn, this overture has won a place alongside the symphonies to represent Berwald at his best.

The less interesting music drama as a whole revolves around a triangle situation in fifteenth-century Spain. A Castillian countess marked for love's tragedy, the heroine Estrella di Soria loses the game of hearts to a Moorish princess named Zulma. Although Estrella has a few soaring moments, notably her Act I aria "By dark thoughts eternally tormented," most of the story plods along over hundrum music.

Act II, however, becomes enlivened by an incongruous *Polonaise*. Berwald frugally inserted into his opera this piece which he had composed a few years previously as a *pièce d'occasion* honoring Charles XIV.

DROTTNINGEN AV GOLCONDA (The Queen of Golconda) (1864)

To nineteenth-century composers, operatic success meant the swiftest path to fame. But too often the lure of the musical stage proved a siren song for composers whose talents really moved in other directions. Like many others, Berwald spent countless hours laboring over works of a musico-dramatic nature only to end with a dismal record: eleven starts with four abortions, two total disappearances and five survivors; only two of his stage works got as far as feeble acclaim. Of course, some of Berwald's operatic ventures fell into the singspiel category, but even here his lack of imagination and sure nose for third-rate librettos proved extraordinary.

The Queen of Golconda was the last shot in Berwald's locker, his final attempt to scale the heights of the opera world and, in fact, his final work of any type. Written with Christina Nilsson in mind, the world premier was long in coming — April 3, 1968, a full century after the composer's death.

The overture can stand alone as a decent concert piece, but it lacks the fire of the stunning curtain-raiser for *Estrella di Soria*. For plot, Berwald chose a blood-and-thunder French romance relating the adventures of one Aline, a captive lady of quality elevated to the throne of the mythical land of Golconda in India. Her lost love turns up as the French ambassador, helps her put down a revolt and stays on as King of an exotic paradise.

This listener has yet to hear the entire *Queen of Golconda,* but doubts if the opera will produce any startling musical or dramatic revelations.

For Further Exploration

Allvarsamma och Muntra Hugskott (Serious and Joyful Fancies); *Wettlauf* (Tournament); Concerto for Two Violins and Orchestra; Duo for Violin and Piano; Piano Trio No. 3; *En lantlig Bröllopsfest* (A Rustic Wedding) for organ or duo-piano; cantatas; selections from operettas and operas; songs.

AXEL BORUP-JØRGENSEN (b. 1924)

Borup-Jørgensen grew up in Sweden, but Hjørring in North Jutland was his birthplace, and he took most of his training under Jersild and Schierbeck at the Royal Conservatory, qualifying him as a Danish composer, but definitely one of the new breed. His more representative pieces so far owe something to Webern — perhaps more to Luigi Nono — but he softens jagged pointillistic lines and abruptness so typical of run-of-the-mill serial music. Instead, refined sonority and expressive imagination take priority in this composer's carefully structured music. Borup-Jørgensen avoids strenuous, self-conscious efforts to prove his individuality; when he does it seems effortless.

Orchestral Music

MUSIK FOR SLAGTØJ + BRATSCH (Music for Percussion + Viola) (1956)
(10′)

Characterized by the composer as "symphonic chamber music," this cohesive demonstration of rhythmic vitality vibrates to the sound of deftly employed hardware. The viola serves more as a coordinator than a traditional foil and furnishes lyric balance to the crisp chatter of its percussive partners. While hardly revolutionary, the piece remains stimulating despite obvious "1950s" sound.

NORDISK SOMMER PASTORALE (Nordic Summer Pastorale) (1964) (10′)

The judges awarded first prize to *Nordic Summer Pastorale,* an entry in a contest sponsored by the Danish State Radio. Doubtless the composer's shrewd sense of "prizemanship" told him to produce a comparatively conservative piece of immediate appeal scored for modest forces. This modernized version of the traditional Scandinavian pastoral suite compresses its neo-impressionistic communication into one movement, a shimmering canvas painted in microtonal brushstrokes, a haze of sound barely in motion.

Chamber Music

STRING QUARTET NO. 5: TORSO (1965)

A study in confrontation, "Torso" requires the string quartet to face itself "on line" against material previously played onto tape. Borup-Jørgensen splits his tones up into tiny fragments to the point where parts of the resultant "octet" sound like a mass attack by mosquitoes. However, most open-minded listeners should find the piece fascinating if only out of respect for the composer's craftsmanship, which puts all the parts together with the precision of a Swiss watch.

For Further Exploration

Cretaufoni for orchestra; *Microorganisms* for string quartet; *Mobiles* for viola, marimba, and piano; *Pocket Oratorium; Winterpieces* for piano; *Im Volkston* for female choir.

KARL-BIRGER BLOMDAHL (1916–1968)

When heart disease finally conquered Blomdahl, he stood at the peak of his career, an internationally recognized and respected leader in contemporary music. Two opposed views on Blomdahl remain: hero worship exemplified by blurbs on record jackets proclaiming him "Sweden's leading musical revolutionary" (a half-truth at best) versus sour grapes, critics' mumblings that he traded integrity for whatever fad happened to come over the hill. Admitting a streak of eclecticism, even opportunism, in Blomdahl's work, just as much attention should be paid to the man's own forceful, energetic personality which entered into everything he wrote. In one way or another Blomdahl was ever on the move. He was last to deny admiration for Hindemith's linearity, the pointillism of Webern and Boulez, or the stimulating ideas of John Cage at various stages of his own development. But the sum of outside influences equals one found closer to home which did just as much to channel Blomdahl's creative direction: his close friendship with the poet Erik Lindegren. When asked about influences, Blomdahl replied with typical frankness: "It's about the same thing as when one works on a scientific project and consults various publications for solutions to problems that others have come up with, and then evaluates them in the light of one's own experience. The sources of reference vary according to the nature of the task."

The word "task" held significance for Blomdahl; each new work represented a whole or partial solution to a given problem. How to cope with serialism, how to equilibrate music with dance, how to write Space Age opera. And what about electronic music? Computer music? These were the complex challenges on which Blomdahl fed. He worked at an exciting time in Swedish music, first appreciating the value of intellectual curiosity with the "Monday Group," then on his own way with sharpened skills, confidence, and an always open mind.

Orchestral Music

PASTORAL SUITE (1948)   (19′)

A work for strings inspired by the "Suites" of Erik Lindegren, fragmentary poems about love and memory combined with cinematic glimpses of nature. These bittersweet reflections, not memories of Beethoven's romp in the country, animate the work. The composer brings a single theme through a series of contrasting variations, a balanced, organic continuity even though formal requirements for a suite (divided movements) are met. Although Blomdahl had composed several orchestral pieces previously, *Pastoral Suite* marks his coming of age with new emphasis on energizing and imaginative rhythmic patterns.

PRELUDE AND ALLEGRO FOR STRINGS (1949)   (6')
A grimly determined little piece, *Prelude and Allegro* began as a movement for string quartet, then fattened into a version for full string complement which seems to make sense; these dark-tinged rumblings and growling sonorities could swallow four players.

SYMPHONY NO. 3: FACETTER (Facets) (1950)   (22')
The Swedes consider "Facets" their first important composition incorporating serial technique. Initial performance took place in 1951 at the Frankfurt ISCM Festival and gave Blomdahl the wings he needed to soar toward general European recognition.

Serial procedure may be at work, but human emotion insinuates in passages marked "appassionato" and in the nature of employed motives which possess vital, searching character. The symphony unfolds without pause, a generally concise statement proceeding from a mysterious opening section on through a deft "prestissimo" to a climax of full organic growth; the music then unwinds to close the circle as things began with sighs from solo flute. In Blomdahl's view this title "Facets" refers to different sides of the same germinal idea, further demonstration of the adaptability and unifying function of symphonic form.

CHAMBER CONCERTO FOR PIANO, WOODWINDS, AND PERCUSSION (1953)
(15')
One of the most immediately appealing items on Blomdahl's works list, *Chamber Concerto* follows much the same plan as *Pastoral Suite,* four compact movements linked as variations on a single thematic idea. Instrumentally, however, *Chamber Concerto* shows greater freedom and flexibility as it maneuvers through angular, peppery rhythmic material. Blomdahl's impulse to forge ahead with extroverted, almost primitive vigor keeps within reasonable bounds, thanks to clear design and the composer's sense of proportion.

FORMA FERRITONANS (1961)   (12')
Blomdahl's industrial tone poem descends in direct line from such previous onomatopoetic replies to the Machine Age as Mossolov's infamous symphonic movement "Steel Foundry" and Honegger's *Pacific 231.* However Blomdahl's realization is less crude; pictorial realism takes a back seat to what he called "scientific imagery" projected as seething, shifting layers of orchestral sound. To fulfill a commission from the Oxelösund Iron Works for the opening of a new plant, Blomdahl researched the formation of steel all the way from underground ore deposits through the man-controlled processes of smelting and conversion to the finished product. Blomdahl ingeniously matched tone intervals with the Atomic Table, atomic weight and number, determining progressions and tone relationships. His ample rhythmic imagination was stirred by the actual sights and sounds of a steel mill at work. Somehow this unusual concoction finds authentic outlet in musical terms, a stunning, fully coherent study in orchestral sonority.

DANCE SUITE NO. 2 (1951) (8′)

Several important Blomdahl scores derived from three-way collaboration between himself, Erik Lindegren, and Birgit Åkesson, the latter one of Sweden's most controversial exponents of "free dance." *Dance Suite No. 2,* for clarinet, cello, and augmented percussion, amounts to overgrown chamber music. Consisting of a few episodic miniatures, this music is easy to take with its intimate instrumental dialogue and patches of lazy jazz rhythms.

SISYFOS (1954) (25′)

The music for *Sisyfos* first appeared as an independent dance suite three years before reaching the stage with Birgit Åkesson's choreography. Literary foundation for the enterprise, a Lindegren poem, places most emphasis on events leading to the fall of Sisyphus, mythical ruler of Corinth, rather than his better-known fate as the frustrated boulder-pusher in Hades. Laid out as six closely connected movements, the suite gathers momentum slowly, but with pace achieved, it strains relentlessly toward eruptive culmination in a Dance of Life sounding for all the world like a complex of mambo rhythms. As with much of Blomdahl's eclectic music, the outcome is extremely effective as a listening experience.

SPEL FOR ÅTTA (Game for Eight) (1962) (25′)

In the composer's words, "a personal milestone," a comprehensive summation of artistic growth within the orchestral medium. *Game for Eight* is dance-derived, yet symphonic in scope and content. The numeral "8" not only refers to the complement of dancers required, but carries further into the score's eight-movement format. All Blomdahl's previous exploration into rhythm, timbre, and sonority jell in this new mold. His opening pages bring utter fascination, a suddenly activated mechanism which snaps, rings, and jingles. Sharply articulated tone-rhythm complexes generate the rest of the piece, but spice comes from a light sprinkling of borrowed melodic snatches (as from *The Marriage of Figaro*). Blomdahl usually builds his choreographic suites up to smash conclusions, but *Game for Eight* closes with a soft, almost ghostly elegy.

Chamber Music

SUITE FOR CELLO AND PIANO (1944)

Most of Blomdahl's formal chamber music came from his formative years. He produced little in this area after 1945, although examples of pseudo-chamber music, such as the two Dance Suites, must be taken into account. In a sense, Blomdahl's extroverted personality tugged against the more intimate forms of composition. But the well-fashioned *Suite for Cello and Piano* indicates better-than-average understanding of the instrumental resources involved, a concise, almost hurried, four-movement piece of some substance written for friends in the "Monday Group."

TRIO FOR CLARINET, CELLO AND PIANO (1955)

A rare example of chamber music from the mature Blomdahl, his own statement about the piece seems perfectly clear: "A piece of uncomplicated chamber music of mainly lyrical character." So long as the listener bears in mind that by "lyrical" Blomdahl means "atonal," no one should be disappointed. Both astringent and dark-hued, the trio supplies interesting material at all points with a bonus in enjoyment from the impish scherzo (Allegro giocoso).

Vocal Music

I SPEGLARNAS SAL (In the Hall of Mirrors) (1952)

The "Facets" Symphony and this cantata put Blomdahl on the map; both have been singled out as his real masterpieces. The text, almost a blueprint for musical realization, comes from the so-called "sonnets" of Erik Lindegren's *The Man Without a Way*. This is explosive, fragmentary verse, radically different from anything previous in Swedish literature, which comments pessimistically on the plight of modern man.

Blomdahl responded with a setting for soloists, chorus, speaker and orchestra; he cemented things together by means of twelve-tone block structure braced by an imaginative array of coloristic effects. The textual material preserves "word-melody" inherent in Swedish speech. The whole cantata is arranged as a single "curve of expression" with the listener thrust at once into a literal Hall of Mirrors lit by glass-cold reflection of what sound like myriad tinkling chandeliers. The work moves on to passages exploiting contemporary references (slow blues, boogie-woogie) with contrasting interludes of quiet writing for soloists and small instrumental groups, or, as in the sixth movement, massed forces in a convulsive outburst almost blowing the whole piece apart. The concluding *tranquillo* returns to opening glassy atmosphere, the lost soul seeing endless reflections of himself and unable to decide anything.

FIVE ITALIAN SONGS (1954)

Minor Blomdahl, grouping one song on a text by Salvatore Quasimodo with four from Giulio Arcangioli. Each song is so short as to be epigrammatic. Blomdahl displayed only slight interest in art song as the brevity shown here might imply.

ANABASE (1956)

Direct address to the audience is a salient feature of Blomdahl's music; this almost "populist" attitude accounts for both his success and the critical sniping aimed at his work. Departure from this line, a step sideways to recondite material occurs in the present work. *Anabase* by St.-John Perse (Aléxis Léger), the so-called Mandarin of French poetry, has been called one of the key poems of our age, a vast allegory of a poet-conqueror coming out of Asia. The sweep and majesty of Perse's lines present a formidable challenge to any musician daring to set them. A hearing of Blomdahl's attempt suggests to this listener that the composer has waded out beyond his depth. His serialistic mosaic sounds pretentious, irritatingly neurotic and like a poor copy of Honegger's "Old Testament" style.

ANIARA (1959)

Blomdahl's Space Age opera has become his most famous, if not necessarily most representative, work. The libretto comes from an epic poem by Harry Martinson containing elements of science fiction, allegory, and prophecy all touching the depths of pessimism. The year is 2038, the earth ("Douris") a cauldron of molten cities and radioactive fallout as the result of man's final folly. With all life doomed, huge spaceships shuttle between Douris and another planet in a massive resettlement program. One of these craft, the "Aniara" with 8,000 souls aboard, suffers a damaged rudder, swerves off course, and hurtles permanently out of control toward galaxies beyond the beyond. The opera reviews the collective tragedy of all on board as they try coping with their hopeless fate.

Life, of sorts, goes on aboard "Aniara" under the harsh ship's captain. The passengers cling pathetically to earthly ways as in their Midsummer Festival when there are no more seasons. Daisi Doody, a pop singer, still belts out the "old songs" but everyone has forgotten what the words used to mean. Last link to home, a semi-animate electronic wonder called Mima, not only entertains but tries to soften news reports of the cataclysm back on earth; these eventually become so horrible that Mima ceases function, a machine literally dying of grief. Finally the survivors of twenty years' wandering come to realize their aimless drifting through the cold, meaningless emptiness of space has an inner counterpart in the hollowness of their own souls.

Blomdahl avoids both fuss and complexity in his presentation; *Aniara* simply moves along as a sequence of tableaux rather than a musico-dramatic unity. Without specific hero or heroine, personal identification cannot exist; with the possible exception of the colorful Daisi Doody and the saintly "Blind Poetess," most of the opera's bulging cast comes on like so many Buck Rogers stereotypes. Onstage, however, the work jells thanks to swift action and dramatic punch. Musically, *Aniara* relies on a hodgepodge of contemporary clichés, but the score never loses contact with theatrical justification. High spots appear in the jazzy Midsummer Festival and with the souped-up electronic chaos accompanying the collapse of Mima. The joyless, touching hymn sung during the release of the "Urn of Rescue" also sticks in the memory.

At its Stockholm premier on May 31, 1959, *Aniara* seized world attention — the first Scandinavian opera to reach a broad foreign audience and enjoy the benefits of modern publicity. If anything, this chilling account of arrogant modern man's *Paradise Lost* gains urgency as time goes on. The message reads: Do better than place blind faith in technological progress or face the consequences. The green hills of earth make up the only home mankind will ever know.

Electronic Music

ALTISONANS (1966)

During his last years, Blomdahl fell more and more under the spell of pure science. Among his friends was the Polish physicist Ludwig Wikliska, who kindled the composer's interest in the musical possibilities of cosmic signals. *Altisonans* followed accordingly, a taped sound collage of interminable duration based on recorded sunspots and signals from orbiting satellites. The piece contains no "composed" music; the results are indistinguishable from ordinary birdsong.

For Further Exploration

Minotaurus; Fioriture; — resan i denna natt (— Voyage of This Night); *Herr von Hancken.*

JAN CARLSTEDT (b. 1926)

At a time when other Nordic composers of his generation went scurrying off after the latest atonal shibboleth, the freshly graduated Carlstedt sat down to write a formal, full-length symphony. His independence of mind has persisted. But any observer of Swedish music in the 1960s might have formed the wrong impression of Carlstedt's indolence — a mere handful of works produced between 1955 and 1965, most of them in small form and respectful of tradition.

Actually, these years found Carlstedt biding his time, "hibernating," to repeat his own expression. His Dalecarlian heritage required full digestion, so Carlstedt pondered long over folk chorale and fiddlers' tunes. His intent was not to become a second Alfvén, but rather, as he has stated, to seek "a fresher tonal language, more outwardly directed and closer to life, more in harmony with man and nature." In addition, the years of slow maturation brought a strong humanistic element to Carlstedt's artistic creed while renewed interest in classical forms has muted obvious folkloric coloration.

Carlstedt is by no means alone in believing that music today should convey more than a scramble for new tools or constant crisis in method, and his various performing and organizational activities as well as his compositions have acted as a growing counterweight to the boundless experimentation in Swedish music. With signs looming that abstractionism for its own sake has reached a state of exhaustion, a reasonable assumption might be made that Carlstedt's time has come.

Orchestral Music

SYMPHONY NO. 2 (1968)   (34')

Impetus for Carlstedt's Second Symphony appears plainly on the fly-leaf of the manuscript: "A Symphony of Brotherhood in Honor of Martin Luther King, Jr." Yet judgment should not rush to label the symphony an example of so-called music of commitment, for this music aims instead to carry forward the spirit of King's own metaphor when in a speech he voiced hope for a "symphony of brotherhood" among all men. Beethoven, of course, projected a similar vision in the summary pages of his Ninth Symphony, but Carlstedt takes a less grandiose view of his artistic responsibilities.

Generally allied to the Sibelius/Shostakovitch school, the Second Symphony opens with a solemn motive from the bells followed by dark-hued discourse, at times lightened by rays of hope (Moderato). The struggle reaches greater intensity and passion in the second movement

92

(Allegro-Adagio) linked directly to the epical finale (Largo) where proud, hymnic resolution soars from the concluding pages. When, as here, a composer has truly something to say, the symphony as an art form is far from moribund.

Chamber Music

EIGHT DUETS FOR TWO VIOLINS (c. 1958)

In contrast to the folk-fiddling traditions in Norway and the rest of Sweden, which is basically solo music, two or more players working with spontaneous counterpoint is a hallmark of the Dalecarlian style. Nothing could be more natural, then, for a composer like Carlstedt to use dual, mutually supportive violin lines for these free transcriptions of Swedish folk tunes. The upshot is chamber music well off the beaten track but highly interesting.

SONATA FOR SOLO VIOLIN (1959)

Carlstedt's Sonata places severe demands on both listener and performer. Music which lies somewhere between the contrapuntal determination of Reger and the motoric harshness of Bartók, the Sonata's extended thoughts at times approach the monumental. Helpful clarification of this deeply involved piece comes from three separate, well-paced movements: Preludio, Scherzo, Romanze e Finale.

STRING QUARTET NO. 2 (1966)

Carlstedt's Second Quartet builds upon a series of cumulative dramatic and dialectic contrasts organized into five closely connected movements. The basic core material starts off dry and sober, but dialogue gathers animation by half-time. The final movement peaks on vigorous four-way conversation of sufficient rugged disposition to recall Charles Ives (a purely coincidental relationship, of course, as far as Carlstedt is concerned). The composer remains one of the few Swedes from his generation to uphold the quartet heritage.

Vocal Music

SEX VISOR FRÅN OVANSILJAN (Six Songs from Ovansiljan)
FEM KORALER FRÅN ORSA (Five Chorales from Orsa)

In these two sets of early pieces for women's and mixed choir respectively, Carlstedt dwells softly and lovingly on folk memories from his home country.

For Further Exploration

Symphony No. 1; Sonata for Strings; Sonata for Two Violins; String Quartets 1 and 3; Divertimento for oboe and string trio; *Pentastomos* for woodwind.

KLAUS EGGE (b. 1906)

As warrior-at-large for Norwegian music, energetic Klaus Egge plunged into myriad activities during the 1950s and 1960s, placing him among the leading cultural spokesmen from the North. But devotion to promotional and organizational duties have run parallel to Egge's steady development as a composer. Three phases of his creative life can be defined: first his intense Norwegianism of the early 1930s, exemplified by his often-mentioned *Draumkvede* sonata for piano (1934) based on the old Norwegian "Dream Ballad"; next a period of growing interest in polyphonic textures; then postwar emergence as a symphonist moving toward greater depth of expression and refinement of orchestration. Although long committed to free tonality, Egge has brought stricter serial technique into some of his more recent offerings, indicating a possible fourth phase in his career.

Norwegians unhesitatingly consider Egge their "man in the middle." His artistic position rests on compromise between Norwegian musical traditions and the demands of modernism; he has fought to bridge the gap between native ethos (he was born in Telemark) and developments since Schoenberg. Care and concern have gone toward weaving Norwegian folk music elements such as block chords, *slåtter* rhythms, ecclesiastical modes and tetrachord construction into textures born of sinewy, dissonant counterpoint. Although a pupil of Fartein Valen, Egge's approach to the full implications of atonality has been circumspect and never at the expense of his own individuality. Egge produces forcefully persuasive music sometimes difficult to swallow on first hearing; like the man himself, it can be tough and assertive. But Egge's first principle is quality and a sustained level of common sense runs through his work like a ramrod.

Orchestral Music

SYMPHONY NO. 1: LAGNADSTONAR (Sounds of Destiny) (1942)   (41')

Egge's five symphonies and Saeverud's nine form the cornerstone of twentieth-century Norwegian symphonism. Wartime catharsis seems the basis for Egge's First Symphony, a work dedicated to Norway's merchant seamen "who took part in the Great World War." Although the composer pondered mightily over this symphony's structure, the piece conveys an impression of a sprawling, loose-limbed giant. Written in epic-romantic style with long polyphonic strands and hints of Sibelian color, Egge's burly symphony, its drama and dedicated purpose, seem best realized in the noble Adagio. The drawn-out first movement (Andante espressivo/Allegro assai e decisio), however, comes up with some equally fine moments. Less enthusiasm can be claimed for the murky Finale where the strain begins to tell.

SYMPHONY NO. 2: SINFONIA GIOCOSA (1947)   (19')

Egge's second entry in the symphonic field wins on all counts. The grammar might suggest Bartók or even Stravinsky in places, but accent and inflection are plainly Norwegian. In the Second Symphony Egge has trimmed his sails: thematic material is trenchant, rhythms varied and driving with derivation from native folk sources. Structurally, movement one relies on straightforward sonata form; the evocative "mountain air" atmosphere of the ensuing Adagio dolcissimo comes as a song without words. Egge winds up with a forceful rondo which rings changes on ethnic dance rhythms. Full of brusque, "jocose" humor, the Second Symphony has a tendency to sound disturbingly aggressive, but repeated hearings bring their rewards.

SYMPHONY NO. 3: LOUISVILLE (1957)   (19')

Repetition of proven formulas does not suffice for a composer like Egge who seldom covers the same ground twice. The challenge of preparing a new symphony for an American orchestra brought Egge to explore the possibilities in metamorphic organization, the fresh approach taken in his Third Symphony. The tightly bundled themes of the Second Symphony were sidestepped, with Egge now taking time to dwell longer on his ideas, some of which were born during the "suspended animation" of his transatlantic flight to the U.S.A. Cast in one movement, but with well-defined fast-slow-fast ground plan, the Third Symphony beautifully balances elongated material against dramatic contrasts. New orchestral transparency also marks this fine work as a milestone in Egge's development.

SYMPHONY NO. 4: SINFONIA SOPRA B.A.C.H – E.G.G.E. (1967)

Klaus Egge can never be accused of being a faddist, but like several musical elder statesmen, he has felt the urge to narrow the generation gap. The single-movement Fourth Symphony finds Egge turned serialist using letters of his and Bach's name as the first eight notes in a twelve-note motive. This involved puzzle unfolds logically and attractively, but does nothing to change this listener's feeling that the essence of Egge's art lives elsewhere.

PIANO CONCERTO NO. 2 (1944)   (20')

Rightly regarded in Norway as one of Egge's top achievements, the Second Piano Concerto sustains interest by means of seven interlocking variations on the old Telemark air "Sunfair and the Dragon King." Scoring is kept to bare essentials (piano and strings) but the sound wells out robust and full-bodied. Romantic lushness or keyboard exhibitionism finds no place in Egge's thinking. His concerto flows naturally in long polyphonic lines, a continual weaving in and out of almost improvisatory impulses analogous to the intricate tracework on Viking Period jewelry or the ornate woodcarvings adorning Norway's medieval stave churches.

CONCERTO FOR VIOLIN AND ORCHESTRA (1952)   (29')

Some of the composer's countrymen have gone on record in their declaration that the Violin Concerto belongs in the masterwork class. Certainly the slow movement (Grave) represents an example of Egge's loftiest writing, but there is something too cool and aloof about much of this music, setting it somewhat apart from the usual vigor and animation so typical of Egge. Almost no excitement ruffles the surface; apart from a touch of faster action in the short finale, the concerto breathes the calmness of a mountain lake.

CONCERTO FOR CELLO AND ORCHESTRA (1966)   (29')

Concerning his only cello concerto, the composer has said that he has "First and foremost tried to consider the cello as a song instrument." More varied than the Violin Concerto, the Cello Concerto builds on four movements: an introductory set of variations, a knotty Allegro presenting the main argument, a relaxed interlude, then a cheerful conclusion Allegro energico.

Chamber Music

SONATA FOR VIOLIN AND PIANO (1932)

Early in his career Egge made the decision to write for the larger forms and build upon a polyphonic scaffold rooted in the soil of Bach. The present work (Op. 3) marked Egge's first plunge into sonata form but carries out his intentions with marvelous clarity as well as determination. This is deeply felt, almost passionate music abounding in rich, malleable themes but direct and assertive. Young Egge was very much his own man.

STRING QUARTET NO. 1 (1933, rev. 1963)

An act of homage upon the death of a close friend (the poet Hans Reynolds), the whole quartet grows out of the mood expressed in the opening movement (Largo funèbre) where serenity overcomes outpoured grief. But the most interesting portion of the quartet arrives with the third movement (Andantino fugato), where Egge's brisk polyphony works toward an authentic Greenland Eskimo lament (marked Lento monotono), which serves as a dramatically hushed bridge to the last movement. This holds special significance within the work's context because Reynolds had been an ardent student of Eskimo life. How much touching up Egge felt necessary when revising his early string quartet is difficult to judge, but, emphatically, the piece as it now stands shows no trace of the novice.

QUINTET FOR WINDS (1939)

Based on modally conceived themes, Egge's non-discursive wind piece recalls the archaic flavor of Old Norse music. More attention seems paid to workmanlike but dry fugal sonority than to wit or adventure.

Keyboard Music

SONATA NO. 1 FOR PIANO: DRAUMKVEDE-SONATE (1934)

The *Draumkvede* (Dream Vision) is one of the oldest known Norwegian folk ballads, a sort of miniature *Divine Comedy* handed down by word of mouth from an anonymous Norwegian master of about the year 1300. The poem relates the visions of Heaven and Hell during the long sleep of Olav Asteson (probably St. Olav). Three melodies with a fourth variant for the chanting of the *Draumkvede* have survived; they are strongly modal and suggest the character of medieval music. Egge, in this sonata, both quotes and uses fragments of the *Draumkvede* melodies. But for all the vividness of the poem's imagery, Egge's sonata has a curiously restrained, almost studious quality. At times his play with modal elements brings the piece close to the sound of Debussy, but Grieg remains at considerable distance since the basis of Egge's sonata is polyphonic rather than harmonic.

FANTASY IN HALLING RHYTHM
FANTASY IN SPRINGAR RHYTHM (1939)

Egge's fantasies for piano belong to a set of three, but for some reason a companion *Fantasy in Gangar Rhythm* has become overshadowed. These pieces amount to two-part inventions built upon folkloric tetrachord structure (free tonality using four-note modal "rows"). This crisp, pungent use of native brick and mortar not only gives the composer a type of atonal tool, but also renews the spirit of the Grieg-Halvorsen *Slåtter*.

PIANO SONATA NO. 2: SONATA PATETICA (1955)

Although public concertizing lies outside Egge's broad range of activities, his personal mastery of the instrument is complete and the keyboard lies close to the heart of his creative work. Besides two piano concertos and the "Draumkvede" sonata of 1934 which launched Egge as a force in Norwegian music, his major statement for piano to date rests with "Sonata patetica." Strong emotions are obviously involved in this typically Eggean no-nonsense piece which sets much of its discourse in spiky, animated language all the more rugged for its free tonality. Just how a "pathetic" or plaintive element enters into this music, however, is difficult to explain.

Vocal Music

DEN DAG KJEM ALDRI (That Day Will Never Come) (1944)

Well-known in Scandinavia, the present Vinje song for mixed chorus begins with restrained feelings later expanded to great beauty when Egge adds telling high-voiced melisma.

For Further Exploration

Symphony No. 5; Duo-concertante; Trio for violin, cello and piano; *Fjell-Norig* (Mountainous Norway); *Sveinung Vreim* (dramatic symphony); *Fanitullen* (ballet); *Star-Snow Dreams* (song cycle); choral pieces.

NIELS WILHELM GADE (1817–1890)

"Niels Wilhelm Gade!" exclaimed one biographer, "— there is for us Danes a singularly broad and joyous ring to that name." To Danes, no doubt, but to others Gade came to personify the prime fossil of the romantic era, the academically dessicated "Mrs. Mendelssohn" pouring forth pernicious vapors of what some wag termed "Mendelssohnacidic Schumannoxide."

Actually, much of the abusive criticism heaped upon Gade's memory can be taken as secondhand nonsense parrotted by writers apparently unfamiliar with any of his music. True enough, Gade's symphonies and oratorios, once widely performed, have long ago fallen by the wayside. But when seen in proper perspective, the "Old Lion" of Scandinavian music comes into focus as an exceptionally gifted and conscientious artist, the first native composer from the North (Buxtehude possibly excepted) to win international attention and acclaim.

A poetic melodist and skilled technician, Gade felt at home in both the large and small forms of musical expression, but he seems to have watered down his original promise as a Danish nationalist in preference for routine, though palatable, cosmopolitanism. Gade doubtless shared the antipathy of his mentor Mendelssohn against exaggerated local color, the fervent nationalist's insistence on *my* rivers, *my* folk songs, *my* dancing peasants. Instead Gade turned more toward classic ideals, although a true Danish fragrance never entirely left his music. Sometimes Gade could fall victim to his own facility, but he always wrote well and usually had something interesting to say. On at least a few occasions, Gade produced strong, characteristic music of lasting value. On the basis of these works the much-maligned Gade deserves an honorable position among the second echelon figures of the romantic era.

Orchestral Music

EFTERKLANGE AF OSSIAN (Echoes of Ossian) (1840)   (14′)

Gade's Opus 1 (but not his first orchestral piece) lit the fuse for his skyrocket leap to fame and remains a touchstone of Danish romantic music. Lines by Uhland gave the young composer a motto for this concert overture and indicate his feelings at the time: "We are not bound by any formula; our art is called poetry." The overture takes its cue from the fraudulent *Ossian* poems published by James MacPherson which made an enormous impression on Continental romanticism. The overture contains passages of bardic eloquence and heroic splendor alongside others displaying poetic glow. These more than compensate for the work's somewhat wobbly form.

SYMPHONY NO. 1 IN C MINOR: ON ZEALAND'S FAIR PLAINS (1842)   (36')

In a letter to his sister dated January 13, 1843, Mendelssohn wrote: "Yesterday we went through a new symphony by a Dane by the name of Gade and we are to perform it in the course of the ensuing month. It has given me more pleasure than any work I have seen for a long time." Mendelssohn's delight was no doubt heightened by the second movement, a wispy scherzo so close in spirit to his own music. But the sweet-sounding Danish flavor of the remainder belongs entirely to Gade's fresh and authentic nationalist inspiration. The symphony's subtitle refers to an early patriotic song by Gade, a hearty tune worked into the first movement (Moderato; Allegro energico). Other folk-song elements can be felt throughout the symphony with particular beauty arising from the slow movement (Andante grazioso). Gade's enthusiasm, however, becomes loose-jointed in the rambling finale where he seems hell-bent to conquer the world for Danish national music at one stroke.

NAPOLI (1842)

During the nineteenth-century salad days of the Royal Ballet, new productions could involve almost the whole Copenhagen musical community. *Napoli* was one of Bournonville's most lavish undertakings, a ballet still in the active repertoire. Gade did not supply the entire musical score (H.C. Lumbye, Holger Paulli and E. Helsted also took a hand in these proceedings), but his serene and luminous music for the celebrated Blue Grotto Scene represents one of the highlights of the entire extravaganza.

BRUDVALS AF "EN FOLKSAGN" (Bridal Waltz from "A Folk Tale") (1842)
(4')

Because it is still played at most Danish weddings, Gade's *Bridal Waltz* can be taken as one of his "greatest hits," but originally this was ballet music. While Gade's infectious waltz definitely fits into the lollipop category, this music sounds as inherently Danish as anything by Lumbye and should help bury the mistaken notion of Gade the stuffy pedant.

Chamber Music

SONATA NO. 2 IN D MINOR FOR VIOLIN AND PIANO (1849)

Of Gade's three violin/pianoforte sonatas, the D minor (Op. 21) carries the best reputation. Gade's pithy themes may not sweep the listener away in awe, but he has produced virile, well-constructed and communicative music in the high romantic manner. The end movements begin with slow introductions while a passing scherzo interrupts the poetic middle movement (Larghetto), a sonata plan anticipating Brahms.

STRING QUARTET IN F MINOR (1851)

Gade seemed shy about string quartets, although he was adept in all branches of his art. Of his three works in quartet form, two were tucked away unpublished (the present work and another, undated, in E minor). Only a year before he died his third attempt appeared but was published as "String Quartet No. 1." The composer's reservations about his F minor quartet, at any rate, seem justified: this music is weak and shows pallor.

99

Neither Schumann's passion nor Mendelssohn's live-wire intensity disturbs the unruffled blandness of this Gade opus.

STRING QUARTET NO. 1 IN D MAJOR (1888)

Far superior to the F minor quartet, the D major proceeds with well-ordered flow under a sure and cultivated hand. Nothing profound emerges, but suave and mellifluous string writing brings its own rewards. The ingratiating slow movement (Andante poco lento) sounds particularly attractive, indicating the "Old Lion" still handy with an unfailing supply of warm melody at the ripe age of seventy-one.

NOVELLETTER (Novelettes) (1853)

The designation *novellette* for a musical composition was apparently introduced by Schumann to indicate a group of short contrasting pieces vaguely suggesting a narrative. His disciple Gade used the form on at least two occasions, the present work for piano trio (Op. 29) and again in 1874 for a more famous set of Novellettes for string orchestra. The influence of Schumann runs very deep in the first set with certain thematic similarities almost startling. Drawing-room music, of course, but just the sort of thing to enjoy after a heavy Danish lunch.

FANTASY PIECES FOR CLARINET AND PIANO (1864)

Gade does not usually leap to mind as a composer of display pieces, yet his works list contains all manner of pleasant surprises. In his *Fantasy Pieces* the composer offers four short, contrasting movements, hardly music of great moment but entirely agreeable and well suited to the mellow middle registers of the featured instrument.

Keyboard Music

FORAARSTONER (Sounds of Spring) (1841)

Piano pieces sprouted at all stages in Gade's career. While few of them pretend to weighty substance, their technical assurance, genuine romantic outlook and spots of Nordic coloration combine to make their presence welcome in another age. The three light and airy etudes designated *Foraarstoner* make a thoroughly appropriate and charming salute to Spring. Gade's stylistic influence on young Edvard Grieg was probably not very strong, but the similarity between the first of the *Foraarstoner* (Allegretto grazioso) and Morning Mood from the *Peer Gynt* music is remarkable.

AKVARELLER (Watercolors) (1850)

In all, Gade published three volumes of *Watercolors,* the present two volumes (Op. 19) with a third (Op. 57) following many years later. Gade chose generic titles like Scherzo, Romanza, Humoresque instead of more suggestive designations, even though musically these little piano sketches derive from the Mendelssohn-Schumann school.

ARABESKE IN F MAJOR (1884)

Gade departed from miniaturism in this splendid study consisting essentially of four sections knitted together by transitional passages of improvisatory character. Throughout Gade displays rich pianistic imagination; seldom does he show himself more openly expressive than in this music.

PIANO SONATA IN E MINOR (1840, rev. 1854)

Gade's only solo sonata required several years to reach final shape, evidently an opus taken most seriously by the composer if only to justify its dedication to the great Franz Liszt. Neither Lisztian penetration nor bravura appears, however. Content and structure suggest instead a keyboard counterpart to the Danish master's series of eight symphonies, works gradually keeping more to the general European classic-romantic outlook than to specifically Nordic latitudes. But Gade was no mere epigone. His Piano Sonata shows independence of mind both in motivic material and form, a type of cyclical construction. The romantic feeling displayed keeps to the reserved side, although more overt lyrical feeling shines through in the central movement (Andante). There is nothing stuffy or pedantic about this well-planned sonata; its logic and solidity are superior.

TRE TONESTYKKER (Three Sounding Pieces) (1851)

Gade's era was not heavily endowed with masterworks for the King of Instruments, but as both composer and player Gade more than upheld the Danish tradition of excellence in the organ loft. From 1858 until the very day of his death, Gade sat before the manuals and pedals in the old Navy Church (Holmens Kirke), Copenhagen. His *Three Sounding Pieces* display solid professionalism without the least trace of mawkishness or misplaced sentiment. The F major opener wells forth as a grandly sonorous toccata. Reflective meditation settles over its much shorter C major companion. The set concludes with a substantial fantasia in A minor.

FANTASY ON THE HYMN "LOVER DEN HERRE" (1873)

The sturdy old hymn tune "Praise to the Lord" gets spectacular treatment from Gade, a brilliant festival prelude with trumpet obbligato. This extroverted showpiece for organ gives still another glimpse of Gade's range as a musician.

SØRGEMUSIK FOR ORGEL (Funeral Music for Organ) (1887)

Softspoken, workmanlike music intended for an admiral's funeral; this is minor, routine Gade.

ORGAN CHORALES (Posthumous discoveries; composition dates uncertain)

Unless more of them come to light, Gade composed only three chorale preludes for organ, obvious acts of homage to J.S. Bach. These brief works include two settings of *Hvo ikkun lader Herren raade* (In God's Hands Only Is Our Life) and one of *Al Højeden oprunden er* (How Brightly Shines the Morning Star). They make worthy tributes.

Vocal Music

ELVERSKUD (The Erl King's Daughter) (1853)

The cantata *Elverskud* rightly stands as Gade's unequivocal masterpiece. The title literally translates as "elf struck," the critical moment in a venerable ballad when Sir Oluf, out riding on the eve of his wedding, encounters the elfin princess and her court dancing on a misty moor. Oluf refuses her invitation to join in, and her angered curse is reinforced by a

101

blow on the knight's back — elf struck! The shaken Oluf returns to his castle to be found dead the next morning by his mother.

Gade exerted complete control of both words and music in *Elverskud,* for he helped put the text together himself from the old balladic material. Words and music form a perfect marriage, and the composer's judicious balance of solo, choral and orchestral numbers could not be bettered. What elevates *Elverskud,* however, is Gade's gorgeous yet understated romantic tone painting. Memorable high points include the magical Prologue, the horns-and-strings Camelot-like vision at the beginning of Part I, the hymnal "Morning Song" bridging Parts II and III, and Sir Oluf's ravishing ballad "Så tit jeg rider mig under ø" (When Through the Meadows) — here Gade reaches one of the supreme peaks of Danish musical romanticism. In fact, not to know *Elverskud* is to have no knowledge of Danish music at all.

SOLO SONGS

Like his mentor Mendelssohn, Gade wrote some fine art songs, yet both composers generally fared better in other areas. In his youth, Gade came into close understanding of Danish poetry and folk song largely under the influence of his teacher A.P. Bergreen. His reputedly best songs, therefore, have strong national flavor as in the *Holger Danske Songs* from 1863.

Of the smattering of Gade song material so far heard by this listener, the "Church arias" make the most rewarding discovery. These unpretentious, devout settings of the 130th Psalm as well as Danish verse touch upon tender lyricism of a type not often associated with this composer. *Princesse Gloriant* is a charming song, possibly Gade's most famous, which sets the lines of B.S. Ingemann in the best romantic manner. *På Sjølands fagre sletter* (On Zealand's Fair Plains) is an old Gade favorite, incorporated for over a hundred years in most Danish school songbooks as well as in his First Symphony. Gade wrote this song in 1838 for one of Bergreen's patriotic collections. Gade took a more "arty" approach when he tackled such through-composed songs as the weighty *Knud Lavard* and *Hvorfor svulmer Weichselfloden?* (Why Is the Vistula in Flood?) to words by Carsten Hauch. A third Hauch song, the gentle *Birken* (Birches), seems less memorable, but in the H.C. Andersen song, *Sig himlen hvaelver så ren og klar* (The Sky Is Clear and Pure), Gade turned out a little gem.

For Further Exploration

Symphonies, Nos. 2 to 8; *Michel Angelo Overture; In the Highlands;* Overture No. 3; *Hamlet Overture;* Violin Concerto; *Holbergiana;* String Quintet; String Octet; *Novelettes* for strings; Violin/Piano Sonatas Nos. 1 and 3; Piano Trio in F; *Mariotta; Comala; The Crusaders; Spring Fantasy; Zion; Psyche;* songs.

EDVARD HAGERUP GRIEG (1843–1907)

The idolatry shown toward Grieg's memory in Norway is understandable; the whittling away at his fame elsewhere is not. Continual harping on his "miniaturism" and sneering condescension about "salon music" ("pink bonbons stuffed with snow" to repeat Debussy's flip opinion) shred the patience of any music lover taking care to learn something about Grieg's total output and his aims as an artist.

By no means Europe's first or strongest nationalist composer of the romantic period, Grieg made no pretensions of classing himself with Mozart or Beethoven either. Yet his music has captured the attention of listeners around the world as none other; despite every conceivable distortion and type of arrangement, some of his melodies continue year after year among the most widely known from all "classical" composers — a fact galling to his detractors.

Quality, not popularity, however, governs the relevance of Grieg's music today. Most of what he wrote shows freedom from banality and cloying sentiment. At times he succumbed to his own mannerisms, but he seldom struck a false or insincere note. The mastery of harmonic coloration of this decided original and his ability to synthesize the essence of Norwegian musical folklore not only pointed toward impressionism, but also gave a foretaste of such formidable nationalists as Mahler, Bartók and Vaughan Williams. Grieg's music also conveys special magic all its own, some sort of mysterious preservative guarding its freshness no matter what the tides in musical fashion.

Orchestral Music

IN AUTUMN OVERTURE (1866, rev. 1887)

This early concert piece, expanding a previous song *The Autumn Storm,* did not mark Grieg's debut as an orchestral composer. At Gade's suggestion, he completed a Symphony in C minor in 1864 which received a few performances but was soon withdrawn (although Grieg later issued the two middle movements for duo-piano as *Deux pièces symphoniques,* Opus 14).

The *In Autumn Overture,* byproduct of Grieg's first trip to Rome although later revamped, shows some wobbly form in places and gives way to feelings of excess melodrama at times, but the whole adds up to a creditable job still viable as music. The introductory pages find Grieg in a poetic frame of mind, but gusty winds and the nip of Fall air dominate the more tumultuous passages.

CONCERTO IN A MINOR FOR PIANO AND ORCHESTRA (1868)

Miniaturists ordinarily do not write masterful concertos. "The Grieg"

103

still holds its position as one of the half-dozen best-loved piano concertos of all time, fulfilling Brahms' postulate that a piece of music alive after fifty years is immortal. People who pretend to hate "popular" masterworks are doomed to live with it.

The Opus 16 listing might be deceptive since Grieg was at work on the orchestration almost to the end of his life. But the solo part retains all the composer's youthful spontaneity and drive. The Piano Concerto wound up Grieg's early "sonata" period in grand summary fashion. Although he made some fitful starts at a second concerto years later, the project failed to budge. Grieg never passed this way again.

SIGURD JORSALFAR SUITE (Sigurd the Crusader) (1872, rev. 1892) (14')

Originally, the *Sigurd Jorsalfar* music was hurled together for one of Bjørnson's stage-crammed historical pageants, this one dramatizing events in *Heimskringla* (the chronicles of ancient Norway) relating Sigurd's homecoming from the Holy Land to vie with his brother for the throne. For the theater version Grieg summoned manifold forces of soloists, chorus and orchestra; many years later he rearranged some of this music as a concert suite for orchestra only. There are three movements: a chivalric Prelude entitled "In the King's Hall," a restless intermezzo "Borghild's Dream" and a finale coming as "Homage March," a world-renowned warhorse. While the *Sigurd Jorsalfar Suite* may be no great epic, the piece does convey honest Norse conviction.

PEER GYNT: INCIDENTAL MUSIC (1875, rev. 1886)

Both Ibsen and Grieg wrongly assumed that their stage version of *Peer Gynt,* an outrageous poetic satire on Norwegian foibles, would arouse no more than slight interest outside the North. This proved untrue. *Peer Gynt* with Grieg's music played long runs in various European cities not to mention periodic revivals. In many respects, however, Grieg's music broadcast the name *Peer Gynt* far more widely than the play, especially through the vehicle of the two *Peer Gynt Suites* (1888, 1891) which made Grieg one of the most widely-known composers of his day. But these two suites by no means exhausted all the worthwhile music in the original score which, incidentally, remained unpublished until after the composer's death.

Subsequent revivals of *Peer Gynt* have increasingly called Grieg's incidental music into question; purist directors would just as soon toss it out of the theater. New *Peer Gynt* music is now available (see Saeverud) and German composer Werner Egk has turned the work into an opera. For these and other reasons Ibsen's play and Grieg's music have become separated.

The full musical score for *Peer Gynt* presents a paradox — some of Grieg's most familiar music side by side with esoterica. In all, the original contains twenty-three numbers, teaching new respect for Grieg the resourceful theater composer. Leaving the two suites aside, further evidence for Grieg's mastery may be found in the ultra-Norwegian Act I Prelude, the bizarre Dance of the Troll King's Daughter, the melodramatic conclusion of Act II, the vivacious scene with the teasing *seter* girls, the antiphonal

104

horn writing in the Act III Prelude, and the impressive Heath Scene in Act V. As concert fare, the *Peer Gynt* Suites 1 and 2 have been played to death, but some new performing edition using remaining portions of the score could give this amazing music a new lease on life.

NORWEGIAN DANCES (1881) (14′)

Grieg's creative life suffered from fits and starts; during dry spells he would reshuffle his manuscripts to make arrangements of arrangements. But in *Norwegian Dances* the conductor Hans Sitt beat him to the draw with an impeccable version for orchestra. Grieg's four-hand piano treatment of these folk melodies from the Lindeman collection, however, is equally enjoyable. All four movements of this suite present the quintessence of Grieg in their abundant harmonic color, sprightly rhythms and concise form.

HOLBERG SUITE: FROM HOLBERG'S TIME (1884) (20′)

The great eighteenth-century dramatist Ludvig Holberg spent most of his life in Copenhagen, but Norwegians let no one forget that Bergen was his birthplace. In 1884 the whole town turned out to honor Holberg's 200th anniversary which included unveiling of a statue down by the waterfront. These ceremonies called for music from another famous native son, so Edvard Grieg wrote a small cantata to help present the statue, but the festive atmosphere spawned a more durable work, a "suite in olden style" for piano; then, almost immediately, the happy thought occurred to recast the whole piece for strings. The results proved glorious, easily some of the finest music for string orchestra from the entire nineteenth century. The Grieg melodic magic operates freely in these antique dance forms; he is no miniaturist dabbling in baroque pastiche, but a knowing composer engaged in a process of musical renewal. There are five movements, each of high quality: Prelude, Sarabande, Gavotte, Air and Rigaudon.

TWO ELEGIAC MELODIES (1881) (9′)

These are two continuously popular string orchestra arrangements of songs from the Opus 33 Vinje set: *Heart Wounds* and *Våren* (The Last Spring). The first carries more sentimentality than usual for Grieg and verges on salon music, but the poignant *Våren* represents Grieg of the highest order.

TWO MELODIES (1891) (8′)

Exceptionally fine craftsmanship appears in this less-known pair of transcriptions for strings from Grieg's world of song. *Norsk* (Norwegian) starts as a pleasant bit of folk color but surprises when brisk pace slackens for an ardent middle section. *Det första Möde* (The First Meeting) unfolds on a chromatic melodic line showing more than a hint of eroticism.

TWO NORWEGIAN MELODIES (1895) (11′)

Actual folk music, not previous songs, supplies the material for this idyllic string piece which comes close to qualifying as a pastoral suite. *In Folk Style,* the first number, sings a long-spun melody with touches of Griegian bitter-sweetness. Sunrays chase off the dark clouds, however, when time comes for the jaunty rusticity of *Cowkeeper's Tune and Coun-*

105

try Dance, based on a herding call and *Stabbe-Låtten* (comic "stumping dance") from Valders. In Grieg's knowing hands these earthy tunes sprout vigorously.

OLD NORWEGIAN MELODY WITH VARIATIONS (1891, orchestrated 1900)
(17')

Keeping track of Grieg's retreads can pose a problem. The present piece for orchestra was taken from a set of duo-piano variations based on the ancient ballad *Sigurd and the Troll Bride;* another setting, for solo piano, may be found in *Six Norwegian Mountain Melodies* put together by Grieg around 1875. Wistful charm clings to the pristine ballad air, but most folk melodies balk at symphonic adaption, this one not excepted. His theme is superb but Grieg's usual lyrical buoyancy deserts him; when his variations are not ordinary they run to flaccidity. But the smoothness and clarity of Grieg's orchestration commands respect.

SYMPHONIC DANCES (1898)   (27')

Next to the Piano Concerto, the *Symphonic Dances* on Norwegian themes marks the only mature, large-scale Grieg composition expressly conceived for orchestra. Wondrous melody invests all four movements, with particular praise going to the gilt-edged *halling* opening the work and also to the gentler Allegretto starting the second movement. In *Symphonic Dances* Grieg deploys his orchestra with customary imagination and discernment, yet the piece cannot escape criticism for inherent structural weakness; all the fine Norwegian melodies in the world cannot compensate for lack of genuine symphonic growth in an extended work of this type. In the hands of an astute conductor, one able to stitch the seams more tightly, *Symphonic Dances* can become an invigorating listening experience; otherwise this music may simply run out of gas.

LYRIC SUITE   (15')

The so-called *Lyric Suite* is a hybrid, orchestral dressing-up of selections from Book V of the *Lyric Pieces* for piano. First thought to orchestrate this music occurred not to Grieg, but to the conductor Anton Seidl who presented his arrangement at concerts in New York during the 1890s. Informed of this flattering act of piracy, Grieg tracked Seidl's arrangement down, expressed admiration for the idea but felt the orchestration "too heavy for my intentions." Then he set about his own arrangement including some changes in content (*Bell Ringing* swapped for *Shepherd Boy* in the first movement). The other movements were retained: *Peasant March,* the beautiful *Nocturne* and *March of the Dwarfs.* In any event the wonderfully realized Grieg-Seidl-Grieg *Lyric Suite* has deservedly grown in popularity to rival the First Suite from *Peer Gynt.*

Chamber Music

SONATA NO. 1 IN F FOR VIOLIN AND PIANO (1865)

A product of youthful Danish days, Grieg's delightful F major Sonata combines classical balance, drive and irrepressible melody. While not particularly "Norwegian" in feeling, the national flag does begin to flutter in the middle movement (Allegretto quasi andantino) which throws off strong hints of Hardanger fiddle tunes.

SONATA NO. 2 IN G MINOR FOR VIOLIN AND PIANO (1867)

Written in Christiania when Grieg was twenty-four, the Second Sonata reputedly marks the start of his plunge into folklore. Many years later Grieg remarked about his violin sonatas: "The first naive, rich in models; the second, national, and the third with the wider horizons." Both Gade and Liszt went on record as finding this piece full of obvious Norwegian character. But if Grieg actually worked genuine ethnic material into his Second Sonata, his exact sources remain to be demonstrated. Already the dividing line between true Norwegian folk music and Grieg's own creative imagination are impossible to draw. Certainly, this fresh, amiable sonata lies close to folk music with dance rhythms entering the picture at several points.

SONATA IN A MINOR FOR CELLO AND PIANO (1883)

Although this Sonata is dedicated to Grieg's cello-playing brother John, the composer began to think less of the work with passing years and some listeners might agree that here Grieg took a long step sideways. All three movements contain a fair percentage of warmed-over material, traces of other works like the Piano Concerto, Homage March from *Sigurd Jorsalfar* and Solveig's Song from *Peer Gynt* keep popping up. Yet Grieg managed smooth integration of his self-borrowings. Essentially dramatic in concept, the Cello Sonata offers overlong, yet tuneful and idiomatic writing for the featured instrument's warm, throaty timbre.

SONATA NO. 3 IN C MINOR FOR VIOLIN AND PIANO (1887)

Several years before he wrote the present sonata, Grieg issued a fateful statement: "I will fight my way through to the great forms, cost what it may." His C minor Sonata (along with the G minor String Quartet) stands as his supreme effort to win that fight. If Grieg failed to free himself completely from encircling limitations of style and mannerism, he acquitted himself well in the attempt. Stressful urgency dominates the Third Sonata; even the slow movement (alla Romanza), containing one of Grieg's most beautifully shaped melodies, suffers agitated interruption. Both end movements toss with stormy drama leading to closure of the piece on a note of grim determination. Seen from any angle, the C minor Sonata crowns all of Grieg's chamber music.

STRING QUARTET IN G MINOR (1878)

Deep in the reaches of Hardanger Fjord, during a winter's respite in the hamlet of Lofthus, Grieg faced one of the most serious crises of his career — evidence of faltering creative power. If his G minor Quartet composed during that winter strikes the ear as an impassioned, almost desperate testament of faith, it is — much like Smetana's "From My Life" Quartet. The work departs entirely from traditional polyphonic quartet writing in favor of a strict melodic-harmonic technique unified by a "motto theme" introduced at the outset and carried through in one guise or another to unify the whole piece. This is also one of the first quartets in the standard repertoire to employ cyclical construction. Dedication reads to Robert Heckman, a Cologne string player who gave Grieg advice while he was putting this exciting, trail-blazing quartet together.

STRING QUARTET IN F: UNFINISHED (1891)

Apparently Grieg considered his G minor Quartet but a prelude for greater instrumental works to come, a key to his creative future. "I believe I shall find myself again this way," he said. Fate decided otherwise. As Grieg could not complete another piano concerto, so the powers needed for a second quartet were denied him. Yet Grieg left hiṣ F major Quartet no mere torso; he essentially finished two full movements which his friend Julius Röntgen prepared for posthumous publication. The obscure status of Grieg's "Unfinished" Quartet is not difficult to understand once the work is heard. The opening Allegro vivace enjoys lucid instrumentation but fusses and frets over almost every bar; the ensuing Allegro scherzando sounds like a pallid, bloodless mockery of Grieg's usually rich and songful idiom.

Keyboard Music

EARLY PIANO PIECES: FOUR PIECES (OP. 1); POETIC TONE PICTURES (OP. 3); HUMORESKER (OP. 6) (1861–1865)

Grieg played three of his *Four Pieces* before an appreciative Leipzig audience just before he graduated from the Conservatory; appropriately, they reflect deep admiration for Schumann. But the fresh-baked Leipzig graduate began to light the sparks for his mature idiom in the *Poetic Tone Pictures* and particularly in the four splendid *Humoresques*. Anyone acquainted with romantic piano literature hearing these unfamiliar pieces for the first time would unhesitatingly say, "Grieg."

SONATA IN E MINOR (1865)

Lucid, clean-limbed and concise, Grieg's early (and only) piano sonata belongs with the best of his output. Classical guidelines are observed but place no restriction on the composer's fertile harmonic and rhythmic imagination. Grieg appropriates the Chopin-Schumann dialect, partly by way of Gade, as a housing for his drive and drama, yet many details of harmonic coloration and progression proclaim a young master in his own right.

FUNERAL MARCH FOR RIKARD NORDRAAK (1866)

When Nordraak lay dying alone in Berlin, his supposed friend and boon companion Grieg only replied with stony silence to Nordraak's repeated entreaties to come to his deathbed. Whatever Grieg's reasons for such apparent callousness, he felt genuine grief at Nordraak's passing which he poured into this funeral march for piano, later rescored for band and brass ensemble. As somber accompaniment down rain-splattered cobblestones on the way to the grave the piece is most appropriate and effective (Grieg even wanted it played at his own funeral). Musically, it sounds like a curious mixture of the Piano Concerto and the opening movement of Mahler's Fifth Symphony.

BALLADE (1875)

Chopin stands in the background, but this narration belongs entirely to Grieg's private world. Conceivably Grieg's keyboard masterpiece, this intense, even nervous music, refuses to yield its secrets easily, a confession wrapped in veils difficult to penetrate. In his wide-ranging concert tours Grieg avoided placing the *Ballade* on his programs, a clue to his depth of personal involvement. Structurally, the *Ballade* takes the form of fourteen closely interlocked variations on an old ballad tune from Valders.

LYRISKE STYKKER (Lyric Pieces) (1867–1901)

Book I (Op. 12, 1867): *Arietta, Waltz, Watchman's Song, Fairy Dance, Folk Song, Norwegian Melody, Album Leaf, National Song.*

Book II (Op. 38, 1883): *Berceuse, Folk Song, Melody, Halling, Springdans, Elegie, Waltz, Canon.*

Book III (Op. 43, 1886): *Butterfly, Lonely Wanderer, In My Native Land, Little Bird, Erotic, To Spring.*

Book IV (Op. 47, 1888): *Waltz Impromptu, Album Leaf, Melody, Halling, Melancholy, Springdans, Elegy.*

Book V (Op. 54, 1891): *Shepherd Boy, Norwegian March, March of the Dwarfs, Nocturne, Scherzo, Bell Ringing.*

Book VI (Op. 57, 1893): *Vanished Days, Gade, Illusion, Secret, She Dances, Homesickness.*

Book VII (Op. 62, 1896): *Sylph, Gratitude, French Serenade, The Brook, Phantom, Homeward.*

Book VIII (Op. 65, 1896): *From Early Years, Peasant's Song, Melancholy, In Ballad Vein, Wedding Day at Troldhaugen.*

Book IX (Op. 68, 1898): *Sailor's Song, Grandmother's Minuet, At Your Feet, Evening in the Mountains, At the Cradle, Valse Melancholique.*

Book X (Op. 71, 1901): *Once Upon a Time, Summer Evening, Puck, Peace of the Woods, Halling, Gone, Remembrances.*

In his *Lyric Pieces* Grieg invites the music-lover into his intimate world more simply, if less revealingly, than in his songs. These little mood pictures form a veritable tonal diary of Grieg's creative development, his growing mastery of harmonic color, delicate shading and the native ethos. The picturesque titles given to the *Lyric Pieces* harken back to the practice of Schumann, but the music includes some of the most distinctive Grieg ever wrote. Many of the *Lyric Pieces* have become thrice familiar thanks to long use by piano teachers and amateur pianists; others have circulated less widely.

The range of moods is wide, from quaint drawing room morsels like *At the Cradle* or *Grandmother's Minuet,* through warm personal tributes (to Niels Gade and wife Nina), cameo studies in Norwegian fantasy, impressionistic essays like *Bell Ringing* or *Summer Evening* and on to myriad examples of just plain Griegishness.

Critics today commonly dismiss keyboard pieces from the past century almost contemptuously as "salon music." Yes, the *Lyric Pieces* are examples of salon music, works intended for use in the home, not the concert hall. But this has nothing to do with quality. Grieg's good taste and critical responsibility assured an unusually large proportion of high-class pieces in these collections. The banal, the trivial and the commonplace simply fail to appear.

STEMMNINGER (Moods) (1905)

Gathered together toward the end of the composer's life, this collection of essentially more "lyric pieces" is not notably distinguished. Titles are: *Resignation, Sherzo Impromptu, Night Ride, Folk Tune, Study, Student's Serenade* and *Mountaineer's Song.*

ALBUMBLADE (Album Leaves)

Usually known by the German designation *Albumblatt,* these four pieces display uneven merit. Number 1 in A-flat comes from the composer's early days (1864); the more important numbers were written a decade later, between 1874 and 1878. The popular Number 2 in F makes much use of elaborate chromatic writing. Local color appears in the third and fourth *Album Leaves.* The last member of this set, in C minor, amounts to a short piano work of considerable substance.

NORSKE DANSER OG VÌSER (Norwegian Dances and Songs) (Op. 17, 1870)

The *Lyric Pieces* may stand as Grieg's daybook, but this seven sets of piano pieces in frank folk style form a dictionary of his art. The long hours Grieg spent evaluating the source material going into his Opus 17, 66 and 72 collections alone must have seemed endless, but a task undertaken with genuine love. Grieg could hardly have intended such "uncouth" music for popular consumption, and no doubt caused his business-minded publishers to wince.

Twenty-five separate songs and dances, mostly drawn from the Lindeman collection, found their way into Opus 17. Sometimes mistakenly considered "folk song transcriptions," these almost epigrammatic ethnic studies are better considered "folk tune recreations" newly harmonized and freely rendered. Hearing them in continuous series is like perusing a specialist's catalogue, but for anyone caring about Grieg's total production these pieces come as a real find — the "missing link" between Grieg's personal world and folklore.

FOLKELIVSBILLEDER (Pictures of Folk Life) (1872)

A group of three pieces in folk style with some thematic interchange, this set contains one outstanding number: *Bridal Procession Passing By,* Grieg at his purest and a tonal version of the romantically inspired rustic canvasses of Adolph Tidemand. As orchestrated by Halvorsen, "Bridal Procession" has been grafted onto the Act I wedding scene in the *Peer Gynt* music. The two companion pieces have been overshadowed in popular esteem, but *On the Mountains* sounds appropriately fresh and virile, if a trifle repetitious. *From the Carnival,* the concluding number seems comparatively pallid.

NORSK FOLKEVISER (Norwegian Folk Tunes) (Op. 66, 1896)

These masterful realizations of the Norwegian rural spirit belong with Grieg's best works in any category. Basically an armchair student of peasant life, Grieg took much of his source material off the library shelf, but not here; most of these nineteen numbers were collected by the composer himself. In refining these tunes, Grieg summoned some of his craftiest keyboard secrets, bringing a new glow to the simplest lullaby or rawest cow call. Opus 66 contains many wonderful moments including *I Ola-Dalom, i Ola-Kjonn* (In Ola Valley, By Ola Lake) later taken by Delius for his *On Hearing the First Cuckoo in Spring.*

SLÅTTER (Norwegian Peasant Dances) (Op. 72, 1902)

If nothing else, *Slåtter* should bury the weary contention that Grieg was a mere drawing room tinkler. Here he assembled seventeen Hardanger fiddle tunes taken directly from the old Telemark player Knut Dale. Standard violin transcriptions were first taken down by Johan Halvorsen, who passed these on to Grieg for final realization in keyboard form. Although both Halvorsen and Grieg had standard European musical educations and found much of this country music perplexing, they attempted no misguided "corrections" which might disturb the wild nature of these *Gangar* and *Springdans* tunes. Some of the fiddler's embellishments, however, admittedly escaped capture. What came out was strange music of surprising modern character, at times indistinguishable from Bela Bartók, with unexpected rhythms and jarring tonal clashes, especially evident when Grieg brings the percussive quality of the keyboard into play.

IMPROVISATIONS ON NORWEGIAN FOLKSONGS (Op. 29, 1878)

This little-known Grieg opus suggests music that the composer might have played for his friends in private — relaxed and fanciful folk tune elaborations with hints of very personal lyricism. The first improvisation is based on the dialogue song *Guten å Gjenta på fjöshjellen* (Boy and Girl in the Cow Barn), the second the Valders air *Dae va eigong en Kungje* (There Once Was a King).

VALSES-CAPRICES (1883)

A pair of duo-piano pieces, the *Valses-Caprices* deserve favorable mention. Minor Grieg, but still warmly expressive music spiced with some unusual harmonic progressions.

Note on Grieg's Piano Style

The pianoforte lies at the heart of Grieg's music; he sat at the keyboard from childhood through his final days. Just before Grieg died the reproducing piano came to technical perfection enabling companies like Welte-Mignon to capture all nuances of a player's technique directly. Grieg was among the many celebrated concert artists of his day to leave a personal signature to posterity via piano rolls. Now, with some of this priceless documentation transferred to commercial LP records, the sound of Edvard Grieg literally playing his own music may be heard in any living room.

Taking Grieg's advanced years into account when he made his "recordings," this listener admits being greatly disturbed, then bemused at Grieg performing Grieg. Details like note values, tempo markings and so forth scarcely bothered him at all; exaggerations of rhythm and an almost offhand attitude toward phrasing stand in startling contrast to the

111

virtuoso pianist of today. Actually Grieg's relaxed, "all heart" approach belongs entirely within the circle of the romantic school. This exact style was carried on by Percy Grainger, a Grieg protege, who for years performed the Piano Concerto and other Grieg pieces according to what must be accepted as the composer's own performing conception. But authentic or not, this style of playing may prove unacceptable to later generations.

Vocal Music

Grieg composed about 150 art songs for solo voice and piano. Practically none of them incorporate folk song, rather Grieg the song writer aimed primarily to enhance the literature of his age with texts drawn from four languages: Danish, German and the two forms of Norwegian, *Riksmal* and *Landsmal*. Ethnic interests and explorations down new tone roads were reserved for the piano and chamber music.

In terms of emotional range, Grieg's songs seldom stray beyond the conventions of romanticism. Most of them look backward to models supplied by Kjerulf, Schumann and Heise in their typical nineteenth-century subject matter. Longing for home, nature pictures, patriotism, happy and unhappy love and the death of children are recurrent themes, but despite the dangers surrounding such material Grieg steered clear of mawkish sentiment. He brought instead economy of expression and his gift for exquisite melody to the bulk of his songs. In more than a few his genius shone brightly, and small masterpieces are by no means exceptional.

Despite an occasional essay into "through-composed" song, Grieg stuck mainly to strophic form, the familiar *romanser* so typical in Scandinavian music. Unfortunately, grave misunderstanding of Grieg's song style has arisen thanks to uncritical publishers of his day who shipped his songs to eager customers all over the world in often wretched, sometimes even senseless, German translations creating the distorted view that Grieg wrote "lieder." Today, little excuse exists not to hear these many gems rendered in their original languages.

HJERTETS MELODIER (Heart's Melodies) (1864)

Grieg started writing songs when still a student at the Leipzig Conservatory. More came within a year of graduation, notably this collection setting H.C. Andersen lyrics. One of them became the most popular song Grieg ever composed, known everywhere as "Ich liebe dich" but originally saying *Jeg elsker Dig* (I Love You) in perfectly clear Danish, a song written under the spell of his cousin Nina Hagerup whom he was courting at the time. Three companion songs in this album show less sentimentality, but only *To brune Øjne* (Two Brown Eyes) has gained much favor.

ROMANCER OG BALLADER (Romances and Ballads) (1863–1869)

These are settings from Norwegian poet Andreas Munch composed at various times in various places — Copenhagen, Rome, Christiania. Here too is Grieg's first solo song with Norwegian words, *Solnedgang* (Sunset), a quiet mood of utmost simplicity. Others in the collection display ballad character and rank with the best from Grieg's formative period: *Harpen* (The Harp), *Udfarten* (Departure or Outward Bound), and *Vuggesang*

(Lullaby). Despite its title, *Vuggesang* is properly rendered by male voice: a sorrowful goodnight from a father to his motherless child.

ROMANCER (1865–1866)

Most of these eight songs adopt a soothing manner recalling Kjerulf. They draw on assorted Danish poets plus one song from Bjørnson. Oddly, the best-known song here stands stylistically apart from the others — the burly *Efteraarstormen* (The Autumn Storm).

FIRE SANGER (Four Songs) (1870–1872)

In this superb collection Grieg really sinks his spade into native soil, capturing the optimism of the lyrics which Bjørnson sprinkled liberally through the pages of his novelette *The Fisher Maiden*. All four of these beautiful songs deserve greater recognition: *Det förste möde* (The First Meeting), *God Morgen* (Good Morning), *Tak for dit råde* (Thanks for Your Warning) and *Jeg giver mit digt til våren* (I Give My Poem to Spring).

SEKS DIGTE (Six Poems) (1876)

Fame as an incisive, protesting dramatist has obscured Ibsen's power as a poet, a master at conveying elusive sadness and veiled resignation. Nina and Edvard Grieg performed these settings privately for their author; after the final notes had died away the greatly moved Ibsen embraced the couple whispering the single word, "Understood." *En Svane* (A Swan) ranks among Grieg's most celebrated songs, but the remaining five are also believed to reflect the same delicate experience which Ibsen had with a certain Thea Brunn; a case of the married man missing another woman's earnest signals of love. The other titles: *Spillemaend* (The Minstrel), which Grieg also incorporated into his G minor String Quartet; *Med en vandlije* (With a Waterlily); *Borte* (Departed); *Stambogsrim* (Album Verse); and *En fugelvise* (A Bird's Song).

FEM DIGTE (Five Poems) (1876)

A minor poet, but personal friend of the composer, John Paulsen furnished Grieg with material for three song collections. In this first collaboration only *Med en Primula veris* (The First Primrose) has gained much currency, a springtime evocation of fragile loveliness. However the companion songs also contain enchantment: *Et hab* (A Hope), *Jeg reste en deilig sommerkvaeld* (I Wandered One Lonely Summer Evening), *Den aergjerrige* (Ambition), and *Pa skogstien* (On a Woodland Path).

MELODIER (Melodies) (1873–1880)

Aasmund Vinje possessed one of the most complex personalities in nineteenth-century Norway, a strange combination of bursting patriotism and cold cynicism. But Grieg, like many others, found his poetry fascinating especially when he rhapsodized on the beauties of Telemark. The immortal melody Grieg conceived for *Våren* (Spring) well exemplifies the depth of his empathy. *Fyremal* (The Goal) makes propaganda for the *Landsmal* language cause (one of Vinje's pet projects), the reason for Grieg's stirring melody (later arranged for strings as *Norsk*). Other fine songs in these two folios include: *Et syn* (A Vision), *Ved Rundarne* (Return to Rundarne), and *Gamle mor* (Old Mother).

FRA MONTE PINCIO (From Mount Pincio) (1870)

One of Grieg's grandest songs written with great sweep and understanding of Bjørnson's hilltop meditation high above the Eternal City of Rome. This time Grieg uses extended form, much enhanced by subsequent orchestration, to help capture the golden tints of sunset as the poet muses over Rome's vanished glory.

PRINCESSEN (The Princess) (1871)

Another of Bjørnson's sunset moods, this time in the form of a one-sided dialogue between the princess in her bower and a shepherd boy's horn. The same text also attracted Kjerulf and Delius.

SEKS SANGE (Six Songs) (1889)

With this collection Grieg returns to German poetry and shifts from Norwegian to more generalized romanticism. Outstanding songs occur here: The Goethe setting *Zur Rosenheit* (Time of Roses), Geibel's *Dereinst, Gedanke mein* (Ere Long, O Heart of Mine), and Uhland's lively, carefree *Lauf der Welt* (Way of the World), a song worthy of any good tenor. Although belonging among Grieg's better-known songs, *Ein Traum* (A Dream) runs a saccharometer reading close to "Ich liebe dich."

SEKS DIGTE (Six Poems) (1889)

Grieg and the colorful Danish man-of-letters Holger Drachmann cemented their friendship during the summer of 1886 while roaming the mountains of Norway in search of adventure and fresh inspiration. Their resultant musico-poetic sketch book (*From Mountain and Fjord,* Opus 44) verges on mediocrity; Grieg served his friend much better in this later collection which includes such gems as *Julesne* (Christmas Snow) and *Forårsregne* (Spring Rain).

ELEGISKE DIGTE (Elegiac Poems) (1894)

Altogether Grieg turned out three albums of Paulsen songs — a charming first collection, a weak second (Op. 58), and the present set of five songs. Top honors here go to the double setting of *Til En* (To One) and the deeply moving *Farvel* (Farewell).

FEM SANGE (Five Songs) (1894)

During the 1890s Scandinavian literature experienced a strong neo-romantic revival which owed much to Vilhelm Krag. His most meaningful volume of poems appeared in 1891 to immediately capture a sympathetic audience including veteran songwriters like Grieg and Sinding; both did justice to *Der skreg en fugl* (Scream of a Bird), in Grieg's hands a stark and graphic snapshot of a wounded gull far out at sea, a pitiful white dot against the gray sky symbolizing vanished dreams of youth. The piercing first notes of the song have been traced to an actual gull's cry jotted down by Grieg one day on the Hardanger Fjord. Of the other Krag songs, *Mens jeg venter* (While I Wait, or In the Boat) has become better known than its companions: the gentle spinning song *Linden Kirsten* (Little Kirsten), the high-spirited *Og jeg vil ha mig en hjertensjaer* (And I Will Take a Sweetheart) and the grief-stricken song by the empty crib *Moderen synger* (Mother Sings).

BENZON SONGS (1900)

Grieg's last will and testament as a songwriter ended as he began, in Danish. Quality of the last ten songs, on texts by Otto Benzon (Op. 69 and 70), varies, with this listener's preference going to *Der gynger en baad paa Bolge* (A Boat Rocks on the Waves), *Eros, Lys Nat* (Radiant Night) and *Ved Moders Grav* (By Mother's Grave).

HAUGTUSSA (1898)

Scandinavian music offers fewer treasures greater than Grieg's *Haugtussa* song cycle. To hear these songs performed in a language other than Arne Garborg's *Landsmal* verges on frank criminality as Grieg implied when reacting to a German critic's verbose review: "He understood these songs about as well as a bull understands a red rag!"

Grieg spent two years laboring over *Haugtussa;* he envisaged a larger work but, perhaps for the best, failed to get it into shape. In any event, the work sent to his publishers forms a unified, coherent cycle of eight songs. *Haugtussa* means "Hill Maid," the nickname for the *seter* girl Veslemøy whose simple mind can no longer distinguish the "real" world from her troll-haunted mountains. The poems selected by Grieg tell of Veslemøy's first love and inevitable heartbreak. The core of *Haugtussa,* however, lies in the ravishing nature poetry brought to each little scene with understated emotion. The very essence of West Norway's spectacular landscape flashes from these songs with remarkable clarity.

Sometimes one or two of the *Haugtussa* set are programmed or recorded apart from the others, a terrible disservice to Grieg's intentions. Only when heard in uninterrupted form can this penetrating musical experience be truly appreciated.

LANDKJAENNING (Landsighting) (1872)

Grieg's most popular choral piece (originally written as a benefit for the Trondheim Cathedral's restoration) saw revision some years later in a version for baritone solo, male chorus and orchestra. Text comes from Bjørnson's poem *Olav Trygvason* depicting the stern-faced Olav full of missionary zeal "Steering o'er the North Sea cold" at the moment when he sights the shores of Vikingland. Grieg's piece smacks of synthetic religiosity, yet he musters sufficient hearty Nordic tunefulness to save the day.

ALBUM FOR MALE VOICES (1878)

More should be heard of these dozen folk-song settings for unaccompanied choir: Grieg considered them among his more important works. Unfortunately the best-known number *Den store, hvide Flok* (The Great White Host) is the least interesting of the lot and conveys the erroneous impression that these are religious songs. Actually, contents show variety: folk dance arrangements, humorous pieces, a drinking song and others arranged with considerable rhythmic verve and opportunities for solo voices. Not exactly *Carmina Burana,* but here is a side of Grieg's art too often overlooked.

FOUR PSALMS (1906)

These free transcriptions of four old Norwegian hymns for mixed choir and baritone solo can be placed without hesitation among Grieg's finest works. Grieg was not a particularly religious person (he once admitted to a vague interest in Unitarianism), but in taking up the venerable hymns of Brorson, Tomissön, and Laurentius he showed how an inspired musician could revitalize a whole tradition. In *Hvad est du dog skjøn* (How Fair Is Thy Face) his mood is devoutly serious. *Guds Søn har gjort meg fri* (God's Son Has Set Me Free) rolls forward on a militant tune with pause for a meditative middle section. Further contrast appears with the pronounced liturgical feeling enveloping *Jesus Kristus er opfaren* (Jesus Christ Is Risen) in which Grieg provides a memorable setting of the *Kyrie eleison*. With sublime final Psalm *I Himmelin* (In Heaven Above), the creative life of Edvard Grieg drew to a close.

For Further Exploration

Symphony in C Minor; *Bergljot; Den Bergtekne* (The Mountain Thrall); *Foran Sydens Kloster* (At a Southern Convent Gate); *Scenes from Olav Trygvason; Barnlige Sanger* (Children's Songs).

116

EIVIND GROVEN (b. 1901)

Groven has always stood at the extreme wingtip of Norwegian ultra-nationalism, a diehard son of Telemark with musical pipeline driven straight into regional soil. Although Groven took some early training in Oslo and Berlin, he taught composition to himself mainly to avoid outside "contamination" as he systematically mastered all native folk instruments. Everything about Norwegian folk music has concerned Groven. Besides folk-song collecting and co-editing a fat anthology of Hardanger fiddle tunes, Groven has delved into theoretical problems of folk music tonality even to the point of constructing his own instruments, like his Just Intonation Organ, to further assist his research.

As a composer Groven cannot be glibly classified as a primitive or tardy romanticist; unlike other ethnically oriented composers (Bartók, Villa-Lobos) he attempts no synthesis of his country's music with the outside "mainstream." To him folklore constitutes living experience; he borrows only what he needs from the Western tradition to exalt the grass-roots sound of Norway. Sometimes his orchestra sounds like a huge Hardanger fiddle. Predictably, form has been Groven's stumbling block; his attempts to build symphonically by means of "chain development" found in native dances have proven too frail. Yet the joyful outdoor freshness of Groven's best pages can bring keen delight, and he may be cited as one of the most original purveyors of elemental Nordic sound.

Orchestral Music

BRUDGOMMEN (The Bridegroom) (1933)   (80')

Inspiration for this sprawling dramatic symphony came from a short story by the regional author Refling Hagen, a theme of transcendental love by the farm girl Elsie for an unseen fiddler in a distant valley set against the grim backdrop of the Black Death. Music of great beauty and serenity emerges from *The Bridegroom,* but serious drawbacks appear as well. What amounts to three long tone poems for orchestra precede the entry of voices for a final cantata-like section; so much attention is paid to setting the mood, evoking symbolism and eerie forest imagery that the involved plot and character profiles have become fuzzy well before the composer really comes to grips with his text. As musical evocation of folkloric mysticism, *The Bridegroom* can claim moments of rare distinction, but Groven's discursive preoccupation with atmosphere fails to make a convincing case for such a long stretch of music.

HJALARLJOD OVERTURE (1950)   (7')

A difficult title to translate. "Ringing sound" aptly describes general impact of this splendid overture, but misses the intended effect — the musical recreation of Old Norway. The expression "to hjala" refers to tone

117

signals passed between mountains or across fjords usually by herdsmen of bygone days. Groven has worked an old Gudbrandsal Valley cattle call into his overture, and in this instance his folk-based formula clicks. He drenches the listener with modal cadences and insistent *Gangar* rhythms to conjure up a four-star Technicolor soundscape of the Norse heartland. Composed to help honor Oslo's 900th anniversary, Groven's festive overture rightly took a prize.

Vocal Music

MOT BALLADE (Towards the Ballad) (1931)

Groven seems most at home when writing free-form music for chorus and orchestra. *Mot Ballade,* based on a Hans Kinck story, finds the composer at his very best. Set up as a three-movement lyric suite, *Mot Ballade* relates a farm girl's amorous adventures with the local troll. But the work's dramatic details hold less interest in themselves than as a thread on which Groven strung a row of bright and captivating melodic episodes. Here is music to simply sit back and revel in, straightforward Norwegian lyricism of the purest quality.

MARGJIT HJUKSE (1963)

The 1930s, the 1960s — it makes no difference to Groven; his style has been insulated against all intervening changes in the outside world of music. But the years have taught the composer how better to condense his never-ending fantasy, as in this short "mini-cantata." Down in Telemark, it seems, they tell of Margjit Hjukse, another unfortunate troll bride. She gets a two-hour reprieve to visit her sorrowful father, but when time is up and the Troll King comes to carry her back to his mountain lair the poor girl sheds "more tears than a horse has hairs."

The eager folklorist can encounter the Margjit Hjukse legend in three forms: a folk tale, a folk song and a fiddle tune. Groven combines all three in one of his neatest offerings. Scoring calls for chorus, three vocal soloists and Hardanger fiddle.

PA HOSPITALET OM NATTEN (In the Hospital at Night) (1946)

This touching choral piece (also arranged for soprano with orchestra) pays musical tribute to the pages fallen from the deathbed of Henrik Wergland, Norway's greatest patriotic poet. Groven expresses these lines with simple sincerity.

For Further Exploration

Symphonies Nos. 1 and 2; Piano Concerto; *Norwegian Folk Dances; Tunes from the Hills; Draumkvaee; Ivar Aasen Suite; The Story of a Town.*

BENGT HAMBRAEUS (b. 1928)

One of the most diversified figures on the northland musical scene, Bengt Hambraeus commands deep knowledge of several highly specialized areas; he can, for example, discourse authoritatively on the intricacies of medieval notation, then almost in the same breath report the latest movements of Karlheinz Stockhausen. In a sense, Hambraeus belongs to two worlds: the distant past and the immediate future. Trained initially as a musicologist and organist, he stepped to the forefront of Scandinavian modernism after several summers of Darmstadt exposure. He gets credit as the first from Sweden to produce electronic music (the mid-1950s found him active in studios at Milan and Cologne). In 1957 Hambraeus joined the staff of the Swedish Broadcasting Corporation where the atmosphere and availability of equipment further stimulated his desire to explore the new frontiers of music. In 1972 he moved to Canada.

Hambraeus' work, often employing mixed electronic and instrumental means, can make difficult listening. It fits no mold or standardized formula, but seems to digest conglomerate ideas from Cage, Messiaen and Varèse with the Middle Ages thrown in. Few of his works settle anything, rather they represent a continuum of possible responses to an initial idea. The experimental direction is paramount, often dealing with fundamental issues like sonority for its own sake. Fragments of sound alone do not readily adapt to extended structure, but Hambraeus has exerted control over form by timbral mixtures, with progress measured by a process analogous to organ registration.

Reference to composers like Hambraeus, Sweden's leading experimentalist, is less helpful to learn where music is at, but rather where it may be going.

Orchestral Music

TRANSFIGURATION (1963)   (15')

A scrabbling and volcanically eruptive piece for full orchestra, *Transfiguration* moves with relentless deliberation, a harsh yet transparent series of events disclosing admirable inner workings. Some passages show affinity for Xenakis or the leading edge of the new Polish school, further proof that what an electronic synthesizer can do a standard symphony orchestra might do better.

ROTA II (1963)   (15')

In *Rota I* (1962), Hambraeus created a work for three orchestras, or, in alternate version, for one orchestra plus prerecorded tape. *Rota II* follows the same inspiration into the more restricted medium of organ and bell sounds subjected to electronic transformation. (Strictly speaking, the work may not qualify as "orchestral" music, but with composers like Ham-

119

braeus such distinctions become fuzzed.) "Rota" means what it says, a repetitive ritual making much of bright-sounding, incantatory bell effects.

TRANSIT II (1963) (5')

Really an instrumental quartet (horn, trombone, piano and electric guitar), *Transit II* packs much into a small space; the combined effect of Hambraeus' ensemble can sound almost massive and shattering. Here the composer exploits echoes, timbre and block sonority.

TETRAGON (1965) (15')

The unexpected sometimes lies behind Hambraeus' recondite titles. The name of the game in *Tetragon* seems a type of *musique concrète* based on timbres of ancient instruments borrowed from Stockholm's Music History Museum. Repetitive trumpet flourishes announce a heraldic beginning, perhaps Hambraeus the medievalist rising to the surface. Soon his beloved bells arrive to join with organ and harpsichord sounds in the formation of dense layers; these lead to cumulative commotion brought to a wilder pitch than usual for Hambraeus by the sudden entry of a soprano voice. This listener feels *Tetragon* makes the grade as one of Hambraeus' more fascinating realizations.

FRESQUE SONORE (1966) (25')

A beautifully organized if complex piece, *Fresque Sonore* was expressly conceived as a fresco for loudspeakers. Each of several instruments including organ and percussion along with a solo soprano received individual recording, some musicians playing several parts. Synchronization and modulation then became the task of the composer seated at the control panel. A "live" performance of *Fresque Sonore,* therefore, cannot occur. The work's rotational construction and plan of motion give a carousel effect, a slowly revolving, continuously changing pattern of sonorous effects with attention focused first on one group or combination of instruments, then on another. The full ensemble never plays at once.

RENCONTRES POUR ORCHESTRE (1971) (23')

The idea to pick up scraps from other sources and paste them into a sort of orchestral collage goes back a long way in modern music, at least to Charles Ives, but with more recent application at the hands of Stockhausen (*Opus 1970*) and Berio (*Sinfonia*). In what he considers a series of "encounters" or "confrontations," with fragments from Reger, Wagner, Scriabin and other composers including himself, Hambraeus uses a large orchestra with obvious skill and refinement of textures. But he seems reluctant to state the clue material with anything like clarity, giving the listener only the faintest hint that at a given moment he may be working, say, with the "Tristan chord." Of course all the borrowings may be deliberately scrambled and unrecognizably juxtaposed, but this takes the fun out of things. But the main problem with *Rencontres,* from a listener's point of view, is that heavy emphasis on timbre over motion reduces the pace to unvaried sameness.

Keyboard Music

CONSTELLATIONS FOR ORGAN SOUNDS (1959)

Organ sounds placed on two-track tape emerge from four speakers.

The effect is largely coloristic as the listener gets bathed in swirls and layers of organ timbre devoid of perceptible forward motion. Perhaps this hovering sense of timelessness reflects the influence of Messiaen.

INTERFERENCES FOR THE ORGAN (1962)

Music suggesting a continuation of *Constellations,* but here preparations have become simplified; the performer can proceed directly to the organ loft without having first to wire the church or hall for sound.

Hambraeus' stated aim in *Interferences* is, nevertheless, realization of electrico-acoustical tone qualities, but only within the sphere of the organ's own resources. Much is made of the organ's ability to hold sustained tones; these are subjected to pitch fluctuations, overtones in combination and the "switch-off" effect executed by shutting off the organ's motor and letting a tone decay naturally.

Vocal Music

RESPONSORIER (Responses) (1964)

Ceremonial instead of exploratory purpose lies behind *Responses,* a type of church cantata written to help celebrate the 800th anniversary of the Uppsala Archdiocese. The occasion aroused the composer's "Gothic" sensibilities, leading him to portray the wildness and extravagance of Gothic architecture in sounds instead of stone. This music is homophonic, concentrated and evocative of the imagery sought. The "responses" relate to extended organ-choral dialogues. Climax of the work appears when Hambraeus the cathedral builder gets to the belfry and cuts loose with real church bells which invest his piece with an intriguing and joyous carillon-like substrate, an effect in music previously unknown to this listener.

MOTETUM ARCHANGELI MICHAELIS (1967)

Music honoring St. Michael, first and foremost of the angels, is uncommon; Hambraeus helps correct this situation with a powerfully effective motet for mixed choir and organ based on Latin prayers from the saint's feast day. In a style which might pass description as a panoply of rich modal sonority punctuated by broken rhythms, Hambraeus offers a succinct and starkly forceful work. Dedication reads to Edgard Varèse.

For Further Exploration

Rota I; *Giuoco del cambio*; *Spectrogram*; *Introduzione — Sequenze — Coda*; Concerto for Organ and Harpsichord; *Notazioni*; *Invocation*; liturgical music.

VAGN HOLMBOE (b. 1909)

Like the man himself, Vagn Holmboe's music offers the most persuasive illustration of complete artistic integrity. Right from the start, this Jutland-born composer dissociated himself from the levity and whimsical humor prevalent in Danish music of the 1920s just as he steered clear of national romanticism and literary orientation. Instead, Holmboe aimed for the high ideals of Carl Nielsen but in his own way. He broadened his vision by close study of foreign folk cultures with particular concern for the Balkans, an interest going back to the 1930s. Naturally, Bartók came into his field of vision, leading to awareness of certain parallels in the music of Bartók and Nielsen — their method of solving melodic, rhythmic and polyphonic problems. For much the same reasons he has mulled over Sibelius, Stravinsky and the atonal revolution. But Holmboe is essentially a composer who has developed from within, a deep thinker as much as an intuitive musician, who is less concerned with "style" than self-discipline, complete honesty, firm structure and very serious personal expressiveness.

If Holmboe's characteristic works (symphonies, string quartets) do not sound fashionably modern, they do not sound dated either. He left obvious traces of folklorism behind by the 1940s as he gained stature and facility through large-scale composition in the major instrumental forms. Rapidly accelerating events and realignments of the 1950s forced him to face the issues of the post Schoenberg generation. His own thoughts about serialism, twelve-tone composition and so forth found summation in his 1961 book *Mellemspil* (Intermezzo).

As a creative musician, however, Holmboe's answer falls on the conservative side of the line by today's wavering standards. His position has been fortified by the unifying principle of metamorphosis. Again and again Holmboe has turned to the rigorous discipline of the symphony and string quartet as proving grounds for his solutions. His tonal relationships generally follow a modal or modified modal-serial linear course; his themes tend to be angular, even austere, but pregnant with growth potential. Later compositions have admitted an ethereal element. A definite but ill-defined Nordic undercurrent persists in Holmboe's music, however, perhaps reflecting the composer's fondness for the mists of the Danish countryside.

Orchestral Music

SYMPHONY NO. 6 (1947)   (33')

Impulses from Nielsen and Sibelius have perhaps reached Holmboe more directly than Rosenberg and Egge, his two closest contemporary peers among Scandinavian symphonists. The Sixth Symphony eloquently displays this inherited Nordic quality and remains one of Holmboe's most outstanding works for orchestra. The composer builds with carefully balanced tension and decisive sonority according to a closely-knit, two-movement plan. His statements are short and direct; his rhythmic and dynamic controls are held tightly. Nothing goes astray in this vital, solid music.

SYMPHONY NO. 8: SINFONIA BOREALE (1952)   (36')

The Eighth was the first Holmboe symphony to reach commercial record catalogues; fortunately the choice well exemplifies the composer's stature and ability. Unlike the highly integrated linkage of the Sixth and Seventh Symphonies, the Eighth introduces fresh material in each of the four separate movements. Ample space exists for complex thematic transformation, metamorphosis all the way but with a topping of incisive rhythmic flourishes giving the work a highly dramatic character. The sardonic second movement (Tempo giusto) generates most excitement at first hearing with its march-like determination, but meaty listening may be found in the other three movements as well.

EPILOG (1962)   (24')

For some reason, probably anti-romantic in origin, modern composers dodge the word "symphony" even when still writing them. Holmboe is partly guilty of this ploy. In the interim between his Eighth and Ninth Symphonies he produced three closely-knit studies in symphonic metamorphosis bearing runish titles *Epitaph* (1956), *Monolith* (1960) and *Epilogue* — symphonies in all but name. *Epilogue* runs the Holmboe gamut of stress and calm with abundant percussive punctuation. A very dark and serious note pervades the whole piece, most evident in a slow central section where *fimbul* (the long night) closes in.

CONCERTO NO. 11 (1948)   (16')

Holmboe's tendency to finish works in batches attained some sort of a record during the 1940s when he added a dozen or so Brandenburg Concerto-type works to his catalogue. Commissions from Copenhagen's Collegium Musicum stimulated several of them. Concerto No. 11 finds three brassmen (trumpet and two horns) interfaced with string orchestra. Holmboe's intense symphonic style eases up in his concertos, but spiky lines and pungent dissonances abound — hardly music for the "little old lady" regulars at Tivoli concerts. While generally playful, this is decidedly not a piece in the "fun" music class.

Chamber Music

STRING QUARTET NO. 1 (1949)

Holmboe had completed a string quartet well before 1949, but that year he heard a performance of the Bartók quartets in Copenhagen, an experience which triggered a flurry of creative activity, the jumping-off point for his serious penetration of the string quartet medium. The results led to some of the strongest and most distinguished contributions yet made to Danish chamber music.

The first quartet of Holmboe's series shares features in common with Bartók: eerie wisps of sound, slinky timbres, motoric rhythms. Yet Holmboe displays a softer lyricism and reduces the harsh impact found in the Hungarian master's quartets.

123

STRING QUARTET NO. 3 (1949)

This quartet received first prize at the ISCM gathering in Oslo in 1953. Events require five movements, but thematic growth remains monocellular; all non-essentials have been stripped from this concentrated music. Each movement is sharply defined by strong, vivid contrasts.

STRING QUARTET NO. 4 (1954)

Bartók's guiding hand has vanished; Holmboe, now a master himself, strikes out alone. A strange melancholy hovers over this quartet, in fact the first movement seems almost desperately grim. An upsurge of cheerfulness finally breaks into the last (fifth) movement, but before this can completely clear the gloomy atmosphere the composer breaks off.

STRING QUARTET NO. 6 (1961)

The finely-honed Sixth Quartet initiated a new phase in the Holmboe quartet series. A more intense dedication to metamorphic principles began to be felt. All construction (in four concise movements) grows from a terse theme given out at the very beginning. Transformation culminates in the swirl of the concluding Allegro spiritoso. Chamber music lovers of the "pipe and slippers" breed will probably receive scant relaxation from this fermentive music, but listeners enjoying a well-played tone game should find Holmboe most rewarding.

STRING QUARTET NO. 7 (1964)

If the Sixth Quartet appears astringent, then by contrast the Seventh seems Schubertian in its warmth. Lyric cantilenas share equal time with unlimbered dissonant counterpoint; Holmboe dances on light pizzicato feet in the second movement (Allegro commodo). Deep emotion runs through the comparatively long Adagio, then a high-spirited finale nips the thread with a friendly smile.

STRING QUARTET NO. 8 (1964)

After the rich glow of the Seventh Quartet, Holmboe returned to a taut five-movement plan in his Eighth Quartet but with fresh examples of his virtuosity uncorked along the way. The part writing now sounds lean, but not hard; textures become spacious and uncluttered, letting in plenty of light. Curious at this late date, the ghost of Carl Nielsen flits in and out of Holmboe's pages. Yet the composer rests assured of his own mastery, his technique dazzling, his synthesis brilliant.

PRIMAVERA (1951)

A three-movement quartet for flute, violin, cello and piano, *Primavera* belongs among Holmboe's more amiable enterprises, a pleasing essay in springtime daydreaming. Sometimes, as in the first movement (Allegretto leggiero e amabile) he evokes pentatonic tinklings recalling Javanese gamelangs.

QUARTETTO MEDICO (1956)

Written expressly for a group of physician-musicians, the five crisp movements of *Quartetto Medico* follow suit with title elaborations like "Andante medicamento" and "Allgro quasi febrilo." Good music as much as good fun, the ensemble consists of flute, oboe, clarinet and piano. Each doctor gets a chance to shine with the lucky pianist getting one movement all to himself.

QUINTET FOR BRASS INSTRUMENTS (1958)

Contemporary music for small brass ensembles often presents taxing problems for players and listeners alike. Too many such pieces sound discoordinated, ragged and ill-suited for the medium. But Holmboe balances his instruments well in this piece written for the New York Brass Quintet. The opening movement (Poco lento) in particular displays rich sonority and almost heroic declaration. Effective use is also made of antiphonal effects.

SONATA FOR SOLO FLUTE (1957)

Holmboe's entry in the Nordic solo flute sweepstakes shows less complexity than comparable offerings from such colleagues as Finn Mortensen and Hilding Rosenberg. All three movements test the skill of the performer (notably a middle movement fugue) but the overall impression is straightforward music with more than an occasional touch of the melancholy Dane.

Keyboard Music

SUONO DA BARDO (1949)

Holmboe's first major "metamorphic" work, the piano suite *Suono da bardo* is certainly one against which the listener must place a star. Immediate ancestry includes Carl Nielsen's *Suite* and perhaps Ravel's *Gaspard de la Nuit,* most evident in the detached coolness of the opening Toccata. But Holmboe intended music of true symphonic character with unfolding and development of germinal ideas from movement to movement. Definitive material surfaces in two middle sections (Fantasia and Metamorphosis) with firm, decisive culmination in the Finale and Postlude. Holmboe has favored the keyboard on only a few occasions, but *Suono da bardo* signs his name in large letters to the history of Scandinavian piano music.

Vocal Music

HEMLÄNGTAN (Longing for Home) (c. 1940)

A setting of Pär Lagerqvist's poem for baritone and male choir, *Longing for Home* finds Holmboe settling for a conventional choral approach. The piece has become a staple in the Scandinavian student repertory.

VANITAS VANITATUM (1953)

This chaste eight-part motet has become the best-known of some twenty Latin liturgical pieces for a cappella choir composed by Holmboe for his important *Liber Canticorum.*

INUIT (Three Igloo Songs) (1956)

Understandably annoyed when people refer to a "Hungarian" or "Slavonic" element in his music (when they probably mean "Rumanian"), Holmboe can reply that as a serious folklorist he has probed other cultures as well. *Inuit,* for instance, finds him focusing on material from Greenland Eskimos. Scored for baritone, male chorus and timpani, *Inuit* provides both exciting and absorbing listening.

For Further Exploration

Symphony No. 3 ("Sinfonia rustica"); Symphony No. 4 ("Sinfonia sacra"); Symphony No. 5; Symphony No. 7; Symphony No. 9; *Epitaph*; *Monolith*; chamber symphonies; chamber concertos; Sonatas; *Tropos*; *Requiem for Nietzsche*; *The Centenary Star*; *The Knife*; Faroese Choral Songs (*6 Yrkingar*); *Zeit*.

FINN HØFFDING (b. 1899)

Høffding belongs to the leaders in Danish music during the quarter-century after Carl Nielsen, a career weighted heavily toward the field of music education as well as composing. Høffding was also among the first to promote musical folk high schools in his country during the 1930s, consequently some of his output has been geared to amateur performers. Generally speaking, however, Høffding has cultivated a variably "modern" idiom retaining a link with tradition and showing several phases of development. Early in the game he followed Carl Nielsen in a couple of symphonies, but a weaning process became evident at the time of his Third Symphony in 1928 when he showed signs of neo-classicism. During the next decade Høffding sought tighter structural organization which led into single-movement consolidation and monothematic elaboration, so-called metamorphosis technique. As for serialism, the first evidence of interest as far as Høffding's creative work was concerned only appeared as late as 1965.

A versatile composer, Høffding's work takes in all forms. If orchestral and chamber music have been his forte, some of his smaller instrumental works show much originality, while his choral writing has gained popularity. His best opera, *Kilderejsen* (Journey to the Spring, 1931), points to a music dramatist of keen perception.

Orchestral Music

EVOLUTION (1939)   (16')

Subtitled "Symphonic fantasy for orchestra," *Evolution* marked Høffding's first application of metamorphosis on a large scale; the main title, of course, refers to the musical universe of the piece itself, not to any specific Darwinian reference. All constructive development flows from an abrupt motive with intervalic third first broached by the kettle drums; variants of this thematic germ take shape gradually to move with gathering intensity toward a final climactic statement. Høffding's tonal fabric shows some stresses and strains, but his clear logic generally masters the challenge. However the grim, almost tragic mood of this piece is not especially typical of this composer.

"DET ER GANSKE VIST —" ("It's Perfectly True —") (1943)   (9')

Høffding really hit the mark with this happy marriage between disciplined metamorphic technique and the world of H.C. Andersen which has achieved status as a Danish classic. In Andersen's amusing little satire of the same name, a perfectly respectable hen loses one of her feathers, an otherwise trifling event but which in this instance trips off a fantastic barnyard scandal pointing to gross immorality in the henhouse. Although faithfully accurate to the course of the story, Høffding's score is no sugar-coated Tivoli tidbit but a full-blooded tone poem lying somewhere between

127

Sorcerer's Apprentice and *Till Eulenspiegel*. Germinal material gets a brisk workout and reaches two thunderous climaxes.

Chamber Music

DIALOGUES (1927)

They say that given some controversial topic, national reactions run like this: Swedes will brood about it, Norwegians will start a fight, while Danes will strike up animated conversation. Høffding musically reproduces the latter situation in *Dialogues* where two countrymen (oboe and clarinet) gabble on in their lively, reedy way. Moderator Høffding keeps the discussants on the topic as he guides the dialogue through "simple," "serious," "sublime," and "happy" channels with a mid-way pause for "altercazione." All that seems lacking are the two bottles of Carlsberg.

CHAMBER MUSIC (1927)

Scored for soprano, oboe and piano, this curious piece comes from the composer's neo-classical period and derives basic format from the baroque trio sonata. Høffding's polyphonic writing in the two end movements drives along with Bach-like pace; the excruciatingly difficult vocal line, however, is something else. The singer is supplied no text, only a special phonetic language invented by the composer for the occasion. Despite firm tonality, much of this piece looks ahead, especially in the darkly expressive second movement where oboe switches to English horn and the piano pounds out complex chords close to tone clusters. Apparently more was taking place in Danish music of the 1920s than most of us realize.

WIND QUINTET (1940)

Almost every Danish composer of the immediate post-Nielsen generation has emulated their great master by coming up with a wind quintet. Høffding's act of musical homage requires four short movements assembled, in a general way, according to the form of the old baroque church sonata. The first three movements, in turn, meditate, chat and sing mournfully. After a terse slow introduction the Finale breaks into a note perfect, but dryly academic, fugue. Høffding's five winds show little adventurous spirit and could use a dash of Stravinsky's rhythmic bite.

Vocal Music

EN PURPURPRIK (Little Purple Dot) (1940)

Wherever Scandinavian glee clubs travel Høffding's *Little Purple Dot* will more than likely go with them. The composer took his text from a wryly humorous poem by Tom Kristensen; this seemingly slight choral "quickie" invariably draws a roar of applause from Danish audiences.

PINSE (Whitsunday) (1959)

This is a gently sentimental song for male choir with lines by Otto Gelsted.

For Further Exploration

Symphonies (4); *The Arsenal at Springfield*; *Overture* for small orchestra; *Variations on "Sørens Far har Penge"*; String Quartets (2); Sonata for Oboe and Piano; *Kilderejsen* (Journey to the Spring); *Pasteur*; piano pieces, choral pieces, songs.

EGIL HOVLAND (b. 1924)

Hovland has steadily maintained his position as one of the most forward-looking and imaginative composers in Norway since the end of World War II. An organist with much liturgical music to his credit, Hovland has also exhibited keen interest in radical new music largely brought to bear in his secular instrumental pieces. His training has been broad and shows catholic exposure under such teachers as Brustad, Holmboe, Copland and Dallapiccolo. Hovland's most representative music exhibits technical finesse along with a cosmopolitan viewpoint; finding anything "Norwegian" in his work proves fruitless. His growth has been increasingly away from classical schematic polyphony towards transparent serial structures and open form which sometimes admit elements of chance.

Orchestral Music

MUSIC FOR TEN INSTRUMENTS (1957)   (11')

This early opus (a Koussevitsky prizewinner at Tanglewood) straddles the line between chamber music and concert music. The first two movements are in the form of quintets — a cheerful opener for woodwinds alone, then strings take over in the second movement for a more serious passacaglia. Both groups join together for the agreeable, decisive finale.

LAMENTI PER ORCHESTRA (1963)   (13')

A concise, attractive three-movement piece, *Lamenti* (Laments) conveys less sadness than joy at finding a composer with a wide range of orchestral devices (including soprano vocalization) at his fingertips. Building on a clearly articulated twelve-note series, Hovland maneuvers his tone-clusters, string glissandi, percussion effects and floating sonorities with an expert hand.

Chamber Music

WIND QUINTET (1965)

Hovland's game for five does not add up to a particularly memorable quarter hour of listening; serial "point music" clichés abound and sometimes the piece merely sounds like a small orchestra tuning up. This may be the result of certain aleatoric allowances in the score. However, the seven abrupt movements of the *Wind Quintet* are by no means entirely devoid of imagination or coloristic interest.

Keyboard Music

VARIANTI PER DUE PIANOFORTI (1964)

In this two-piano piece Hovland plots his course by means of twenty "blocks of music" written down on separate sheets of paper, a sheaf of "variants" derived from a twelve-note row. Certain matters of dynamics, tempo, and rhythm have been left to the players' discretion. Performance

129

may be straight through or the "variants" taken in shuffled order, but the composer has specified that the ending must be with "Omega" (the twentieth "variant"). Hovland's concept proceeds with spellbinding skill, a field of shifting tone segments joined by strong feeling for plan and pattern despite the introduction of chance. Fascinating touches occur when the players reach into the sounding board for exotic plucked effects (shades of the Cowell-Cage school). Personal opinion places this Hovland opus with the best new music from Norway.

ELEMENTA PRO ORGANO (1966)

Some unusual features of this piece (two assistant performers with labial pipes, matchsticks between keys to hold chords down) suggest more radicalism than actually exists. In reality Hovland has written an entirely comprehensible organ fantasia in five short movements based on a twelve-note row. "Completorium," the final movement, even works in a Gregorian hymn.

Vocal Music

LØFT TROENS SKJOLD (Raise the Shield of Faith) (1956)

In general, Hovland's choral-religious music leans in a more conservative direction than his instrumental output. The present example can stand in evidence, a motet for the 21st Sunday after Trinity. However, nothing stodgy or dry mars the superior devotional quality of this music.

HOW LONG O LORD (1967)

Hovland's setting (in English) of Psalm 13 for unaccompanied eight-part choir exhibits austere, sometimes intense, realization of the text.

For Further Exploration

Festival Overture; Concertino for 3 trumpets and strings; Second Symphony; *Concert Overture*; *Symphonia Sacra*; Suite for Orchestra; Trio for Violin, Cello, and Piano; *A Norwegian Te Deum*; *Magnificat*; *Rorate* for organ, orchestra, voices, and tape.

DAVID MONRAD JOHANSEN (1888-1974)

No composer since Grieg has been more consistently identified with Norwegian national romanticism than David Monrad Johansen, although other currents (impressionism, Bachian polyphony) have washed across his pages. In earlier works Johansen displayed an unadorned homophonic style laced with folklorisms which clung to the Grieg tradition. After studies in France and Germany, his horizons widened during the late 1920s, by a return to Norwegian themes but with greater intensity. The same spirit sustained labors on a detailed, romantically oriented life of Grieg which appeared in 1934; despite subsequent controversy, this remains the closest yet to a definitive biography.

By the middle 1930s, desire for greater universality prompted Johansen's return to Germany where he sought more abstract paths leading through counterpoint. Significantly, the mature composer's sojourn in the Third Reich seemed to shield him from the more radical ideas and styles of the period. The war and its aftermath brought some reverses, but with advancing years Johansen has continued composition with emphasis on vocal and chamber music.

Orchestral Music

SYMPHONIC FANTASY (1936)   (20')

This impressive toccata and fugue in some ways typifies much Norwegian composition between the two World Wars — correct, contrapuntal and Germanic. When in Germany, the composer had studied under Herman Grabner, in turn a pupil of Max Reger's, further solidifying a tradition in Norway sustained by Sinding. But *Symphonic Fantasy* is by no means an example of academic dullness; clarity of line and orchestral resourcefulness lend distinction to the piece. Elaborate thematic development precedes a more subdued gathering of forces before the final sweep into an invigorating three-part fugue. Resolution appears on a note of triumphant sonority.

PAN (1939)   (15')

Johansen's symphonic poem *Pan* came out of a radio commission for a work to honor Knut Hamsun, the Nobel laureate novelist, on his eightieth birthday. While programmatic inferences may be read into Johansen's eloquent and dramatic work, listeners unfamiliar with Lieutenant Glahn, Eva, Edvarda and other characters in Hamsun's novel *Pan* need no knowledge of their complex relationship to enjoy the music. The composer molds his ideas by means of freely treated sonata form fleshed out with ample Nordic lyricism. Touches of a Sibelian nature help arouse visions of the forests and skerries of North Norway where the novel is set; curiously, Johansen has been reported to deny such specificity in this music. Be that as it may, *Pan* beautifully enshrines the Nordic sound.

131

Chamber Music

QUINTET FOR FLUTE, TWO VIOLINS, VIOLA AND CELLO (1967)

Serene and mellow music from Johansen's seventy-ninth year, the quintet seems to represent a refined type of national romanticism. Following an ambiant introduction (Grave), the players settle down to moments of fleeting Griegishness where *slåtter* references peep in. Second half of the work consists of a set of twelve mostly somber variations in the form of a passacaglia.

Keyboard Music

PIANO SUITE NO. 2: FROM THE GUDBRANDSDAL VALLEY (1922)

Few parts of Norway are more steeped in lore and traditions than Gudbrandsdal, the valley of the river Laagen which sweeps across East Norway as part of the old royal highroad from Oslo to Trondheim. This is the country of the original Peer Gynt, trolls and Sigrid Undset's epic novel *Kristin Lavransdatter*. In his delightful ethnic piano suite, Johansen unashamedly continues the line of Grieg's folk-song settings with loving elaboration. Each of these eleven old tunes has its own little story to tell; for instance the unexpectedly violent rumblings from No. 9 ("The Flying Wind") refer to a legend about a country fiddler who was lying drunk after a wedding and listened to the wind howling through the house. Authentic and colorful, the "Gudbrandsdal" Suite would seem basic to any representative collection of Norwegian music.

Vocal Music

VOLUSPAA (1926)

Voluspaa (often translated as *The Sibyl's Prophecy*) initiates the *Poetic Edda,* that landmark of Old Norse-Icelandic literature relating the full panorama of ancient Nordic cosmology: the creation of the Universe, a titanic war between gods and giants, destruction of the earth followed by an idyllic vision of the new world to come. In giving musical treatment to these epic lines, Johansen faced precedent. J.P.E. Hartmann, for one, had worked the mine of eddic material many years before. Johansen, however, did not succumb to melodramatic temptation. He chose a direct path through the poem allowing the march of events to stimulate his fertile melodic imagination.

The cantata falls into three logical sections symbolizing past, present and future. Each employs a different soloist — bass, alto, soprano. The result is a well-balanced, integrated score with a generous spread of melody. Memorable moments abound: the virile choral invocation, the troll shepherdess with her harp, the understated (non-Wagnerian) war preparations of the Valkyries, the terrible warfare of the gods — "Axe-time, sword-time, shields are sundered, wind-time, wolf-time 'ere falls the world . . . ." The concluding moments, a hymn to the New Age, retain the honest, non-contrived excellence of the entire work. The odd corners of Scandinavian music conceal many treasures; Johansen's *Voluspaa* unquestionably lies among them.

132

MOR SYNG (Mother Sings) (1915)

The full title of Johansen's Opus 1 reads: *"Mother Sings* and other poems by Idar Handagard." But of these three settings only the title song has reached the status of a minor Norwegian song classic. This tender, affecting lullaby ventures no further than the limits of Griegian songcraft.

NORDLANDS TROMPET (The Trumpet of Nordland) (1925)

Johansen was born in the far northern district of Nordland and has written several pieces rendering homage to his birthplace. In these songs he joins forces with Peder Dass, the redoubtable seventeenth-century pastor at Alstahaug, whose homespun verse lovingly immortalized the daily joys and hardships of his fisherfolk parishioners. Nordland is not the world of Edvard Grieg, so Johansen's songs depart from drawing room intimacy to favor an outspoken, hearty outdoor style recalling the spirit of Sinding or Jack London. These seven splendid songs with epilogue deserve three-star rating on any representative list of Scandinavian music.

FEM BIBELTEKSTER (Five Biblical Texts) (1946)

Like Oscar Wilde's *De Profundis,* this craggy, tortured music amounts to an almost frightening confession from a soul in torment. Considering some of the difficulties faced by the composer after the Occupation, their composition perhaps became a necessity.

PA GRAVBAKKEN VART DETTE SONGI (This Was Sung by the Graveside) (1965)

Johansen's brief funeral lament for six-part mixed choir (lines by Arne Garbog) provides a moving expression of grief largely through telling use of chromatic cadences.

For Further Exploration

Symphonic Variations; Piano Concerto; Violin and Piano Sonata; Piano Quintet; Suite for Cello and Piano; *Draumkvaedet* (choral ballad); *Ignis Ardens* (cantata); piano suites; songs and choral pieces.

HALFDAN KJERULF (1815–1868)

With the passing of romanticism, interest in Kjerulf outside Norway has fallen almost to zero, a situation which should be recognized with regret. Norway's outstanding composer in the generation preceding Grieg and Svendsen was essentially a poet of sweet memories. Kjerulf spoke with a soft, quiet voice at times lost in the nationalistic turmoil about him. But if Kjerulf's political sympathies favored conservatism and kept him aloof, as he put it, from "all this Norwegian business," his delicate sense of melody could penetrate to the very heart of national romanticism. Strong, emphatic Norwegian feeling counted as a matter of principle to Ole Bull, served as a research project for Ludvig Lindeman, but formed a carefully weighed coloristic device for Kjerulf; for him ethnic flavor entered through a side door. Few Scandinavian composers have surpassed Kjerulf in terms of sheer beautiful melody or the ability to grasp the essence of calm, reflective poetry; on these points Kjerulf as a songwriter met his peer only in the best of Grieg.

Vocal Music

SONGS

Kjerulf was a well-trained professional (including a spell at the Leipzig Conservatory), but he restricted himself to the small forms, "small tone children" as he called his two-hundred-odd solo songs, quartets for male voices and some fifty piano pieces. As a songwriter Kjerulf seldom strayed beyond strophic form. His continual alertness to shifting textual meaning often led to subtle, discreet tempo changes in his accompaniments which can stand as models of economy and refinement. When treating a Norwegian subject, Kjerulf's harmonic imagination and resourcefulness clearly anticipated Grieg. The seeming simplicity of Kjerulf's songs, however, can prove deceptive; to perform them well is not easy.

One of Kjerulf's earliest compositions struck the native note, *Nökken* (The Water Troll) for tenor and male quartet, written about 1829. Ethnic perception continued in *Brudefaerdin i Hardanger* (Bridal Procession on Hardanger Fjord, 1849), which still ranks as one of Kjerulf's best-known compositions, a piece musically matching the famous Tidemand and Gude painting of the bridal barge gliding over the mirrored stillness of the fjord's surface. The piece exists in numerous arrangements for soloist and/or chorus.

A higher level of inspiration, however, occurs in Kjerulf's solo song settings, particularly those taking the poetry of Johan Sebastian Welhaven. Superb examples include the melting *Ved Sundet* (At the Cove), the contemplative *Hvile i Skoven* (Rest in the Woods) and the arresting *Lokkende*

134

toner (Enticing Sounds), a distantly heard troll bride's lament realized much in the Griegian manner although Grieg was only three years old when this song was written.

At a fairly early date Kjerulf established identification with Bjørnson's poetry leading to numerous gem-like songs: *Ingrids Vise* (Ingrid's Ballad), *Synnöves Sang* (Synnove's Songs), *Sovnen* (Sleep) and *Ved sjøen den mørke* (At the Dark Lake). There is more musicality in these songs than "quaintly fascinating ditties," a curious comment from Grove's Dictionary. Theodore Kjerulf, the composer's brother, supplied the verse for several charming songs, as in *Syng, Nattegal du!* (Sing, You Nightingale!) Elsewhere, Kjerulf ran the gamut from mere salon sweetness as in *Hun er Sød, Hun er Blød* (She Is Sweet, She Is Soft) to more Norwegian nature moods like *Paa Fjellet* (On the Mountain). Kjerulf's range of song sometimes went beyond Norwegian literary sources; English, Spanish and French verse also received his attention.

For Further Exploration

Songs; choral pieces; Humoresques and Intermezzi for piano.

PETER ERASMUS LANGE-MÜLLER (1850–1926)

If ever called upon to name a typical Danish composer, this listener would sidestep more renowned figures like Niels Gade and Carl Nielsen in preference for the more reserved Peter Lange-Müller. Born into a well-to-do family, Lange-Müller enjoyed the means and leisure to paint, read poetry, dream and play the piano under excellent teachers. But severe migraine headaches, later connected to chronic eye disease, plagued him from youth and made sustained study or protracted work a nightmare. Therefore what Lange-Müller could compose quickly usually shows him in best light although his two symphonies and smattering of other instrumental pieces, such as the suite *In the Alhambra,* are far from deplorable. Despite obvious difficulties with his health, Lange-Müller completed some seventy-seven opus numbers and, for a few years, conducted Copenhagen's Concert Society.

After 1900 not much issued from Lange-Müller; yet he lived for another quarter century enjoying his grandchildren and secluded villa "Sophienberg" just north of the Danish capital. This quiet life encountered no serious interruption until one winter's day the elderly gentleman-composer suffered a fatal street accident. He died as one of Denmark's most beloved artists; today Lange-Müller's portrait hangs with his country's immortals in the galleries of the National Museum, Frederiksborg.

Vocal Music

SULAMITH OG SALOMON (The Sulamite and Solomon) (1877)

Lange-Müller's characteristic understated nostalgia and subtle harmonic coloration lay in the future when he composed this youthful, impassioned Opus 1 song cycle, poems taken from B.S. Ingemann. At times this music recalls the ecstatic outbursts from Schumann's "year of song," notably *Frauenliebe und Leben.* The seven songs in Lange-Müller's cycle form a unified narrative telling of the love for King Solomon by one of his wives: the eager awakening of the Sulamite's young love, rapturous culmination in the apical number *Sang på Brudekarmen* (Song in the Bridal Coach), then a shift in mood to sorrowful resignation upon the death of her beloved King. Few Danish songs from the romantic period contain the boldly stated emotion and eroticism which Lange-Müller brought to his work.

DER VAR ENGANG (Once Upon a Time) (1886)

Two more dissimilar types than the introspective Lange-Müller and the bluff, bohemian poet Holger Drachmann would be difficult to imagine, but their pooled talents created one of the most successful shows ever presented on the Danish stage. *Der var engang* is singspiel, a type of operetta elevated to the status of national classic. Foreign listeners might

136

well consider the cozy Danishness of the whole thing a preposterous blob of treacle. But take it or leave it, here is a thoroughly authentic Danish stage piece in which Lange-Müller came up with some of his most infectious tunes and knew exactly how to parcel them out.

Passing over the plot, (a loose adaptation of *Taming of the Shrew*), the heart of this consummate Danish fantasy beats in two key numbers: the heavily romantic, haunting *Serenade* and the soaring patriotic sentiment of *Midsommarvise* (Midsummer Song), both for tenor, chorus and orchestra. The remaining dozen or so set pieces ably enhance the nostalgic fairyland atmosphere: the Table Music, Gypsy scenes, hunt music, and wedding numbers all exhibit strong native flavor and undaunted zest.

SOLO SONGS

As the composer of some two hundred songs, Lange-Müller can be seen in retrospect as the last great champion of the Danish *romanse* tradition, the legitimate heir of Peter Heise. Though hardly an innovator like Carl Nielsen, Lange-Müller did as much for Danish song despite his narrower sphere and aura of decadence. His telling use of quasi-impressionistic tone color in piano accompaniments does much to convey strange half-lights tinged with late-romantic melancholy.

It would be wrong to consider Lange-Müller's songs as products of stuffy nineteenth-century drawing rooms; on the contrary, many of them followed local tradition by being written for the popular theater. Lange-Müller's songs often had to face the acid test of glaring footlights; playwrights sought him out because he could set words melodically and work fast. Yet the composer never felt the need to "write down" or cheapen his music. His songs seldom probe deeply, but they invariably do justice to their texts and often carry more subtlety than first meets the ear.

Russian verse (in Danish translation) often appealed to Lange-Müller largely due to the influence of Thor Lange, a minor figure in Danish literary history but one of the composer's old school chums. Some of Thor Lange's material was set in the collection *Eight Folksongs* (1888), which includes such Lange-Müller evergreens as *I Wurtzburg ringe de klokker* (The Bells Ring for Joy in Wurtzburg), the strongly poetic *Hyrden drager sin kappe på* (The Shepherd Dons His Cloak) and the wistful *Silde den Aften* (Late That Evening). The previously composed *En rand af diset hede* (A Ring of Misty Heat) sets Tolstoy's lines in an unusual way. Subdued emotion appears in *Himlen ulmer svagt i flammerødt* (The Sky Glows Flaming Red), another Russian song but a Lange-Müller offering of the highest order.

Turning to Danish verse, the listener encounters pure gold in Lange-Müller's *Five Danish Songs* (1882). Here is *Ved solgang* (Towards Sunset) which favorably compares to the finest *romanser,* a song of softly flowing melody recalling Kjerulf. The same set includes *Frisk vejr* (Chilly Weather) where voice and piano enter into swift dialogue. The Vilhelm Kaalund song *Alverden er syg* (The Whole World Is Sick) receives passionately agitated treatment from the composer.

Of some odds and ends: the wonderfully bright and airy song *Firenze* comes from the drama *Letizia* (1893) as does a sad song of farewell, *Yderst i slaebet det lette* (At the Edge of the Light Train). *Solen springer ud som en rose* (The Sun Rises Like a Rose), from the play *Comus,* on the other hand, sounds merely routine. *Gjenboens forste Vise* (The Neighbor's First Song) employs folk-like simplicity, unusual for Lange-Müller but dramatically apt. One of the composer's most enduring songs unfortunately owes its long popularity to oversweet lyricism, but the sincere feeling in *En Engel har rørt din Pande* (An Angel's Touch) cannot be denied.

For Further Exploration

First and Second Symphonies; Violin Concerto; *In the Alhambra*; incidental music for *Renaissance*; *Spansk Studenter* (The Spanish Student), *Fru Jeanna* (Lady Jane), *Tove*; cantatas; songs; piano pieces.

Bronze Age Lur (Courtesy *Det Danske Selskab*)
Compenius Organ, Frederiksborg Castle (Courtesy *Det Danske Selskab*)

Drottningholm Court Theater

Bellman's cittern and original edition of *Fredman's Songs*.
City Museum, Stockholm.

Niels W. Gade   Franz Berwald

Ole Bull and Fossegrimen, statue in Bergen

Edvard Grieg

Carl Nielsen

Wilhelm Stenhammar

Fartein Valen

Hilding Rosenberg

The Mima scene from Blomdahl's *Aniara*

Per Nørgård

Arne Nordheim und Zubin Mehta

The Nordheim/Haukeland "sound sculpture" at Storedal, Norway

LARS-ERIK LARSSON (b. 1908)

A so-called middle way exists in Swedish music as well as in economics, and Larsson exemplifies this position better than any composer in his country. Trying to fix a specific Larsson idiom is difficult because he has gotten into the habit of shifting gears from time to time: romanticism, Nordic lyricism, neo-classicism, dissonant polyphony and hesitant serialism mark the principal changes. Folkloric stereotypes, however, have been avoided as has monumental striving, points of separation from composers like Alfvén on the one hand and Rosenberg on the other. Generally speaking, Larsson has traveled light. His attempts to capture attention as a formal symphonist have backfired — his Third Symphony (1945, but since withdrawn) has been described as a "great fiasco." His most endearing music, on the other hand, speaks with unrivaled directness and shows a smooth, very Swedish, melodic flow capable of astonishing beauty. But there is considerably more to Lars-Erik Larsson. Since 1946, when he entered higher academic circles, he has cultivated a more complex, "modern" idiom indicating no desire to hide from the challenges of his time. If nothing else his larger orchestral works reach the listener along uncluttered lines, and while these more demanding pieces perhaps have added little to Larsson's enormous popularity in Sweden based on his earlier style, they point to his sense of artistic responsibility and alert musical intelligence.

Orchestral Music

LITEN SERENAD (Little Serenade) (1934) (10′)

Reaction does not necessarily mean regression. During the 1930s Larsson and Dag Wirén independently sidestepped controversy by taking up short, simplified forms. Such light, diverting music came as welcome aspirin to Scandinavian listeners of this period pained by the first serious inroads of modern music. Scored for strings only, *Little Serenade* is a neat, four-movement charmer with no serious pretentions.

SERENAD OCH LITEN MARSCH (Serenade and Little March) (1936) (6′)

The original version of these small-scale, diverting pieces called for chamber ensemble; the string orchestra version came later. Educational in purpose, but by means of entertaining neo-classicism, *Serenade* employs waltz tempo; *Little March* struts with tongue in cheek.

PASTORAL SUITE (1938) (13′)

Larsson's *Pastoral Suite* rivals Alfvén's *Midsummer Vigil* as the most often-played orchestral piece written in Sweden. Almost unbelievably, this ecstatic, spontaneous-sounding music is derived from odds and ends left over from the composer's days at the Swedish radio. Scored for modest orchestra, *Pastoral Suite* opens with an ethereal vision, then promptly hustles off as a breezy Overture. An eloquent Romance provides slow

139

movement contrast, music which touches the heart of Larsson's exquisite gift for melody. An agitated, transparent Scherzo concludes the piece. Record collectors have long been familiar with Larsson's *Pastoral Suite,* but why this marvelous classic has failed to win its spurs outside the North remains a mystery.

EN VINTERSAGA: EPILOG (Epilogue from A Winter's Tale) (1938)   (3')

Larsson has prepared a whole suite from his *Winter's Tale* incidental music, but only the Epilogue movement seems to have caught on with Scandinavian music lovers. Here is Nordic sound in capsule form: elegiac nostalgia as a simply stated, gripping melody.

FARLIGA VÄGAR: "MELODI" ("Melody" from *Dangerous Roads*) (1942)
(3')

The composer's gift for striking, peculiarly Swedish melodic inflection has been put to use in a number of film scores; "Melody" from *Dangerous Roads* is one of them, a melancholic tidbit carrying Larsson's unmistakable autograph.

MUSIC FOR ORCHESTRA (1949)   (23')

During the 1940s Larsson felt the need for critical self-examination, a broadening of powers apart from the limitations of neo-Mozartianism and his own brand of open-faced lyricism. The call to new directions led him to the comparative austerity of chamber music and linear counterpoint. Both Bartók and Hindemith stand as obvious godparents for *Music for Orchestra,* a three-part study in motivic growth indicating radical renewal of Larsson's goals. By no means did he entirely forsake lyricism or expressive elegance, but now he worked with more austere, harsher themes, fragments of themes and taut rhythmic organization. *Music for Orchestra* stands as one of Larsson's clearest, most convincing statements, a work rich in content and character.

CONCERTO FOR VIOLIN AND ORCHESTRA (1952)   (25')

Friends of the "old" Larsson with his outgoing Nordic feeling might react adversely to the comparative astringency of the Violin Concerto, yet a few hearings prove his best qualities as a composer are retained if delivered in a more rigorous modern language. Lyrical motivation is abundantly present, but carefully controlled. Equal attention is paid to striking a balance between a natural tendency to let the solo violin rhapsodize and the demands of the concerto principle itself. Larsson somewhat liberalizes classic sonata plan strictness by allowing thematic material to overlap between movements: a trenchant opener designated Moderato, an expectedly poetic (and very fine) Andante pastorale and summation in terms of a lean, forceful Allegro molto. Dedicated to the Belgian violinist André Gertler, the Larsson Violin Concerto is one of the composer's most important works.

ORCHESTRAL VARIATIONS (1962)   (17')

Larsson had "privately" toyed with atonality as far back as 1932 (he had been, for a short period, a pupil of Alban Berg's), but nothing came of these limited experiments until atonality and dodecaphony began dominating European musical thought in the late 1950s. Although Larsson had already tested a modified serial technique (*Three Pieces for Orchestra,* 1960), his second large-scale atonal undertaking, the *Orchestral Variations,* has overtones of "Foundation music" or "keeping up with the Joneses." The work seems more respectable than progressive; its symmetry pleases, the right level of intellectual objectivity is reached and niceties of instrumentation admirably observed. But events within the whole seem to occur because the textbook says so. "Correctness," less than inspiration born from inner necessity, wins the day.

LYRISK FANTASI (Lyric Fantasy) (1966)   (8')

Lyric Fantasy lends credibility to the suspicion that the "real" Larsson is a romantic at heart. Here he fulfilled a publisher's request to supply a new work for small orchestra. The outcome? Music of breathtaking beauty, a cool, wistful return to the world of the *Pastoral Suite.* But now, a quarter-century later, Larsson looks back upon the memory of things past with almost Mahleresque resignation to evoke a pellucid mood of limpid, sustained melancholy.

CONCERTINI FOR SOLO INSTRUMENT WITH STRING ORCHESTRA (1955–1957)

Larsson's twelve junior concertos, Opus 45, hold a special position among his works; a display of sterling musicianship which might bear comparison to Hindemith's celebrated *Kammermusik* series from the twenties. Amounting to a roll call of the standard symphony orchestra, Larsson wrote his concertini primarily to strengthen the repertoire of the community orchestra. The solo parts are of professional caliber, but the accompanying orchestral material is calculated to lie within the capabilities of well-directed amateurs.

Whatever the composer's stimulus, the concertini all bear his characteristic urbane imprint with substantial musical values placed well ahead of dry pedagogy. At no point does Larsson convey an impression of "writing down" either to the performers or audience.

Concertino No. 3 for clarinet has climbed higher in general favor than its companions. This is a superb, laconic little work from mellow start through perky finish. Subtitled, "Hommage à Mozart," it proves most worthy of the work's celebrated ancestor.

Double bass players should rejoice in what Larsson has given to them in Concertino No. 11 — an amusing, gruff-throated satire on his own, well-oiled "divertimento" style.

Concertino No. 5 for French horn proves predictably elegant and fully enjoyable.

The full concertino series, in numbered order, runs as follows: Concertino No. 1: flute; 2: oboe; 3: clarinet; 4: bassoon; 5: horn; 6: trumpet; 7: trombone; 8: violin; 9: viola; 10: cello; 11: double bass; 12: piano.

DUE AUGURI (1971)   (14')

A brace of felicitations from Lars-Erik Larsson which were written for the bicentennial of the Royal Academy of Music, *Due Auguri* exhibit a degree of whimsical waywardness seldom encountered in this fastidious and usually serious composer. But the humor displayed is genuine and, needless to say, sophisticated, as may be judged from the two "auguries'" designations: "Omaggio Conservatorio" and "Ricamo all'Academia" ("academic embroidery.") While full effect of these slight pieces doubtless depends on being privy to "in" jokes around musical Stockholm, the average listener is invited to smile along with the unbuttoned Lars-Erik.

Chamber Music

QUATTRO TEMPI (1968)

Although he has delivered himself of three string quartets, Larsson has left the more lofty aspects of chamber music to others, but he can give a deft account of himself when the occasion arises. In *Quattro tempi,* designated a divertimento for wind quintet, Larsson presents a neat set of mood pictures, vivid sketches of the four seasons with more than a tip of the hat to the instrumental vocabulary of Carl Nielsen. Summer, Autumn, Winter and Spring have been depicted several times before in musical terms, but seldom with such fluency or grace.

Keyboard Music

SONATINA NO. 1 (1936)

Larsson has never shown himself to be a keyboard giant, but his occasional drifts in this direction are accompanied by liveliness, formal grace and a clear sense of sticking to the point. His First Sonatina lies stylistically near the crossroads of Mozart and Prokofiev, a piece in four snappy movements that makes judicious use of acidic harmony.

SONATINA NO. 2 (1947)

This is a substantial little opus a shade more intense and assertive than the pre-war Sonatina No. 1.

CROQUISER FOR PIANO (1947)

The French term *croquis* means a rough draft or preliminary sketch and conveys the intent of Larsson's six short piano essays under that designation: Capriccioso, Grazioso, Semplice, Scherzando, Espressivo and Ritmico. In these *croquis* the more controlled and tightened-up neo-classicism of the sonatinas gives way to easier breathing and a more relaxed type of piano writing.

Vocal Music

PILARNA (Willows) (1932)

Although sounding much like a folk song, this a cappella favorite for male choir is not. The realization is pure Larsson, the most popular from a set of six choral settings of poems about trees by Sigfrid Siwertz.

FÖRKLÄDD GUD (The Disguised God) (1940)

Some of Larsson's most memorable creative work stems from his experience in broadcasting during the thirties and forties when he served as a conductor with the Swedish radio service. Among other projects he revived the "lyric suite," a type of melodrama where spoken poetry alternates with musical expansion of the text. None of Larsson's other lyric suites have proven equal to *The Disguised God,* a work of sensational

142

popularity which has gone on to hundreds of performances in Sweden and helped make Larsson's name known all over Scandinavia.

Literary underpinning comes from *Love in the 20th Century* by Hjalmar Gullberg, notably those poems of Hellenic purity linking the humble tiller of the soil to an eternal divine presence on earth, a subject taken from Greek mythology which tells of Apollo living among mortal men for a year disguised as a shepherd. Each of four recitations leads to ravishing musical response within a simple but perfectly balanced schedule: prelude — chorus — solos with chorus — chorus — solo with chorus — final chorus — epilogue.

In this pantheistic composition, Larsson raises Swedish lyricism to one of its supreme heights, music as clear and fresh as a mountain spring. There are also ancient Greek echoes thanks to the composer's frequent use of the mixolydian mode. His direct, homophonic vocal writing and modest demands on the orchestra place *The Disguised God* well within reach of most non-professional performing groups, and the existence of an English translation means the work can travel. *The Disguised God* offers a stunning example of what a motivated twentieth-century composer can accomplish using only the fundamentals of his art.

MISSA BREVIS (1954)

Larsson's austere "mini-mass" has been considered one of the more important examples of recent Swedish choral music, and no doubt music of this type sounds more impressive when heard in a church. In recordings, however, the effect seems bland. Assembled with fastidious craftsmanship, the piece uses the traditional Latin text set in a three-part vocal line with balance between homophony and polyphony. The work also lives up to its title: the Kyrie scarcely has ended before it seems time for Communion.

For Further Exploration

Sinfonietta for Strings; Concert Overture No. 2; *Ostinato*; Saxophone Concerto; Cello Concerto; *Gustavian Suite*; *Intimate Miniatures*; String Quartets; *The Princess of Cyprus*.

INGVAR LIDHOLM (b. 1921)

A forceful, dynamic personality, Ingvar Lidholm carries the highest credentials to support his leading position within the ranks of Sweden's "middle generation" composers. His background has included studies under Hilding Rosenberg, participation in the historically important "Monday Group," a turn at Darmstadt, and a finishing period in Britain with the influential modernist Mátyas Seiber. Seasoning has also included the performing side of music: viola playing in the Royal Opera Orchestra and the conductorship of a regional orchestra. Appointments to the Royal College of Music and the staff of the Swedish Broadcasting Corporation round off the picture.

As a composer, Lidholm has directed his main effort toward the orchestra with a strong minor in choral music. Vestiges of Carl Nielsen and Hindemith had been shaken off by the mid-fifties when Lidholm developed his characteristic brand of hard-line serialism. Somewhat later the aggressive block sonorities and shimmering "sound curtain" textures of the new Polish school became incorporated into his style, but Lidholm has not built his reputation by rote imitation. Intuitive purpose, strong feeling for form and carefully detailed craftsmanship go into all his music ranging from the most explosive piece for orchestra to choral music of Apollonian purity.

Orchestral Music

TOCCATA E CANTO (1944)   (14')

Deep seriousness with parallel lucidity bestows more than passing interest on Lidholm's first major work. No groping or fumbling occurs. In *Toccata* the young composer exhibits firm command of a polyphonic and keenly expressive tonal language; his phrases, well-separated and sharply defined, proceed with logic. *Canto* is more personal and pays respects to Carl Nielsen.

CONCERTO FOR STRING ORCHESTRA (1945)   (13')

On the surface a work similar to *Toccata e Canto,* but Lidholm sustains a less austere mood and moves with greater freedom. The first of two movements, titled Largo espressivo, has apt designation, music of elevated thought yet warm and compassionate. Balance and contrast are provided by a second movement, Allegro molto. Here in a sinewy and active context Lidholm displays joyous, affirmative and ardently Nordic feelings.

MUSIC FOR STRINGS (1952)   (15')

The liberating effect of postwar modernism evidently set the course for this coherent, if derivative, three-movement study for strings. Broken, abrupt rhythms and harsh, motoric accents suggest the ghost of Bartók lurking behind the woodwork. As with most of Lidholm's music, however,

144

dull moments seldom intrude. The composer has made two versions of *Music for Strings* available: a concert version for string orchestra with an alternate for string quartet.

RITORNELL (1955)   (18')

Bäck's *Chamber Concerto,* Blomdahl's Third Symphony and *Ritornell* from Lidholm proved particularly decisive in bringing Swedish music abreast of the times during the fifties — the first major victories won by the "Monday Group." The title for *Ritornell* was governed by events within the piece itself, a sort of symphony with each of four segments joined without interruption by recurrence of tone series material. Complex rhythmic interplay and subtle manipulation of timbre further enliven organic growth. The urgency so often found in Lidholm's orchestral music works at full force in *Ritornell's* final pages.

RITER (Rites) (1959)   (23')

Dance stimuli in one form or another pointed out a major direction for the "Monday Group" composers, most of all for Blomdahl, but *Riter* put Lidholm firmly in his company. As a ballet suite the piece consists of five well-designated sections: Ritual Dance, Procession, Sacrificial Dances, Epilogue. The ballet's basic message, taken from Erik Lindegren, states that raw power eventually defeats all human striving from birth through death. Lidholm's taut, hard-boiled, even brutal score, with its strident rhythms and mechanistic passage work, more than amply elaborates that cheerless proposition.

POESIS (1963)   (15')

Poesis is a striking tour de force composed for the 50th anniversary of the Stockholm Philharmonic. Large forces are marshaled for what the composer has called "a kind of instrumental drama in which the *tutti orchestra* is placed in a dramatical relationship to a few individual solo instruments." *Poesis* epitomizes the potency latent in orchestral language since Webern. Conventional serialism gives way here to block sonorities and quickly juxtaposed sound fragments; rhythms appear in various guises and, since traditional "themes" are absent, serve a vital purpose. Events unfold from function, music creating itself as it passes through a highly fluid universe, so the listener must seek other than traditional signposts. Lidholm has suggested three: tautness of structure, the "psychodynamic curve of events" and exchange between solo groups and the whole orchestra. Listeners past the initiation phase of music since Webern should find *Poesis* a fascinating experience, a veritable blockbuster of a piece.

Chamber Music

FOUR PIECES FOR CELLO AND PIANO (1955)

Lidholm was among the first Scandinavian composers to adopt serial procedures, although in 1955 traces of assertive polyphony of the Bartók/Hindemith stamp still clung to his music. But some of the salient features of serialism are present too, such as the apparent random fall of the melodic line and the textural value assigned to single notes. These are good, solid pieces written with minimum of waste motion. The final movement (con

145

espressione) quotes homage to Dallapiccola whom Lidholm then regarded as a musical "brother."

Keyboard Music

KLAVERSTYCKE (Piano Piece) (1949)

Lidholm's Piano Sonata from 1947 reputedly marked his first entry into dodecaphony. But his 1949 *Piano Piece* seems more tonally oriented. Here is a forceful, well-constructed étude quite in keeping with the composer's dynamic personality.

STAMP MUSIC II (1971)

Here is an odd one — music specifically created for a postage stamp. To commemorate the bicentenary of the Royal Academy of Music, the Swedish Post Office issued a special stamp showing three concentric circles with clef signs and some scattered notes. Realization evidently requires as much from the performer as from the composer of this sparse "score." *Stamp Music II* is intended for organ, *Stamp Music I* for solo voice. Neither version makes easy listening.

Vocal Music

LAUDI (1947)

Laudi carries the mark of a master composer with a natural feel for choral writing. Lidholm selected three Biblical texts in Latin and renders them in a plastic, linear manner entirely modern in concept despite touches of archaism. *Homo natus* is vigorous but troubled; *Haec dicit Dominus* repentent; *Laudate Dominum* jubilant.

FYRA KÖRER (Four Choruses) (1953)

Lidholm's treatment of four poems from Åke Nilsson succeeds admirably because of judiciously applied tone color and expressive, unusual harmony. The four selections are: *Tidens pelare* (Pillar of Time), *Havet* (The Sea), *Uppbrott* (Decampment) and *Efteråt* (Afterwards). All provide worthwhile listening with special praise for the final number where solo soprano wafting over choral ground swells proves particularly memorable.

PIECES FROM THE A CAPPELLA BOOK

Beginning about 1950, Lidholm embarked on a choral project originally conceived for teaching purposes and consisting of works of graded difficulty. Some of the finest classical and Swedish poetry found its way into the *A Cappella Book*. While not familiar with the entire contents, this listener can vouch for the singular beauty of *Three Strindberg Poems* and the austere *Two Greek Epigrams*.

Canto LXXXI, however, marks the summit of the *A Cappella Book*, possibly Lidholm's finest piece of choral writing. The knotty lines come from Ezra Pound with emphasis on the recurring injunction "Pull down thy vanity." No slick tricks or sensational effects distract from the composer's intense preoccupation with his difficult text.

SIX SONGS (1940–1945)

In these gem-like songs from his early days as a composer, Lidholm comes close to the deeply poetic mood and Nordic soulfulness of Ture

Rangström. The Swedish poets Hjalmar Gullberg and Eric Härninge served as sources for five of the texts, but the most ravishing song appears with *Madonnans vaggvisa* (Madonna's Cradle Song), words by Lope de Vega.

NAUSIKAA ENSAM (Nausicaa Alone) (1963)

The remote magic of classical antiquity has engaged Lidholm on previous occasions but never so completely as in this extended dramatic monologue, almost an operatic scene, for soprano, orchestra and sparingly applied chorus. The island princess Nausicaa makes a brief appearance in the Odyssey of Homer, but Swedish novelist Eyvind Johnson explored her erotic psyche more thoroughly in this poem which Lidholm set to music. By almost impressionistic means the composer evokes the atmosphere of wind and sea even down to little details like cowbells tinkling by the shore. Heart of the score, however, beats in the taxing, broadly lyrical song of Nausicaa herself as she contemplates the sleeping guest Ulysses. The text contains a provocative line in reference to "this island which the storm reaches but not the wars."

For Further Exploration

Mutanza; Motus-Colores; Sonata for solo flute; *Skaldens natt* (Night of the Skald); Piano Sonata.

FINN MORTENSEN (b. 1922)

One of Norway's more prominent modernists, Mortensen took some training from Klaus Egge but much has been acquired on his own. In an initial spate of compositional activity, resulting in a symphony and some chamber music, Mortensen worked in a clearly tonal and contrapuntal idiom. But contact with Niels Viggo Bentzon helped point his direction toward the twelve-tone parade giving him the distinction of being Norway's first thoroughly committed atonalist since Fartein Valen. The 1960s have found Mortensen perfecting his serial technique with "eruptivity" sometimes used as a cementing principle. In 1972 Mortensen succeeded Klaus Egge as Chairman of the Norwegian Composers Society, an indication of the full acceptance of new music by the Establishment.

Orchestral Music

FANTASY FOR PIANO AND ORCHESTRA (1966) (14′)

For all practical purposes a concertino, this Mortensen opus retains such traditional features as a "slow movement" and cadenza but the piece speaks entirely in contemporary serialist language. Although cerebral, nothing truly formidable appears, thanks to the composer's lucid sense of form and precise balancing of instruments. In addition, Mortensen has taken cues less from the Schoenberg-Webern school than from the more free-style "mother chord" ideas long used by such old modernist warriors as Ernst Krenek. This gives his works advantages of unity through thematic binding. Mortensen's *Fantasy* is a solid achievement worthy of many hearings.

Chamber Music

QUINTET FOR WIND INSTRUMENTS (1951)

Although an early piece, Mortensen's Quintet brought him to general attention and has remained near the top of his works list in performance frequency. All three movements abound in counterpoint and subtle thematic relationships, yet technique lies subordinate to crisp and cogent dialogue. Carl Nielsen's Wind Quintet may still reign as king in Nordic quarters, but the sprightly neo-baroque vitality coming from Mortensen affords worthy contrast.

SONATA FOR SOLO FLUTE (1953)

The short-lived Alf Andersen attracted several solo flute pieces from Swedish and Norwegian composers with Mortensen's tribute among the more outstanding. Solo flute music of any length runs the risk of limited appeal because of inherent dryness of timbre. But for aficionados Mortensen has supplied ample rapid runs, long-held notes, shakes and octave leaps, a true three-movement sonata from his pre-serial days which fully exploits the silvery brilliance and mellow contrasts of the featured instruments.

148

Keyboard Music

FANTASY AND FUGUE FOR PIANO (1958)

Even to wide-open, tolerant ears much atonal composition seems to lack clear purpose apart from determination to sound unromantic and impersonally objective. Mortensen's *Fantasy and Fugue,* however, still possesses some traditional overtones. Germinal material, lean and pointillistic, evolves from the *Fantasy*; an embroidered bridge passage connects to *Fugue* where the basic material further digests in a context of retrograde motion and inversion. All determinants of the piece seem to respect classical balance and precision.

SONATA FOR TWO PIANOS (1964)

Excruciating difficulties face any brave pair of pianists sitting down to this example of new Norwegian music. The composer has retained the original meaning of "sonata," that is, a piece to sound. He allows his performers a certain degree of freedom as the work progresses; for example, when the score signals "Improvisation" each player "dials" in one of several "chord boxes" by means of small wheels (dials) affixed to the score. Each chord aggregate carries specific directions concerning dynamics, tempo and touch. If the listener keeps his ear close to developments, Sonata for Two Pianos can captivate. From a quiet, even hesitant beginning, the music moves on to probe and search; gradually speed accelerates and volume grows. By half-time both players have become locked into frenzied dialogue; torrents of notes rain down like hail. Mortensen's fascinating orgy of pianistic sound never resolves its problems. It reaches a limit of tolerance, then simply stops.

For Further Exploration

Symphony (Op. 5); *Pezzo Orchestrale*; *Evolution*; *Tone Colors for Orchestra*; Piano Concerto; String Trio; Piano Quartet; Piano Sonata.

CARL AUGUST NIELSEN (1865–1931)

The fortunes of Carl Nielsen's symphonies and other works have shown fluctuation between acceptance and continued obscurity since his death. Peaks appeared during the late 1950s when Danish orchestras reintroduced Nielsen to the British public; another came into view about 1965, the Centennial Year, when Leonard Bernstein stepped forward as a champion for the cause. Other conductors and soloists have favored Nielsen on their programs, yet none of Nielsen's works have really joined the international repertoire, the Wind Quintet possibly excepted. Status as a classic figure still eludes Nielsen; he remains outside the Pantheon although in good contemporary company, for instance Roussel, Suk, Pijper and Szymanowski. How long this situation will continue becomes anyone's guess; perhaps Nielsen will always remain an underrated, skipped-over composer at least in concert halls. Nielsen on records, however, is an entirely different matter. Almost all his important work has been available at one time or another, often in multiple recordings. On this basis, Nielsen can no longer qualify as a "neglected" composer.

Carl Nielsen displayed a dual creative personality: the assertive, two-fisted symphonist on one hand, the gentle, grass roots people's songwriter on the other. His basic concepts of the art were spelled out in a series of forceful essays published as *Levende Musik* (Living Music, 1925). The softer side of Carl Nielsen, his close identification with native soil, radiates from the pages of his other book, the autobiographical *Min fynsk Barndom* (My Childhood on Funen, 1927); both give close insight into Nielsen's art and character.

History has shown Carl Nielsen to be the pivotal figure in Danish music, yet care must be taken in trying to hold him up as a typical Danish composer. His importance lies in the very fact that he was not typical. He took comfortable old Danish music by the scruff of its neck and shook hard; his was a big fist breaking windows to let in fresh air. The startling tonal freedom and evolutionary development of Nielsen's style still baffles some listeners, even in Denmark where for many years contrary voices could be heard in the sincere belief that Nielsen had sacrificed his God-given gifts on the altar of modernism. Others have expressed grave concern over the raw-nerved, perverse streak running through the composer's late works written when he sometimes admitted discouragement and bitterness at the failure of his music to take hold of a broad audience. Closer examination and familiarity, however, shows that almost all of Carl Nielsen's music carries the will to win and the glow of good health. It can speak harshly and with resolute power, but the serene and gentle countryside from which Nielsen came is never entirely forgotten.

150

Orchestral Music

LITTLE SUITE FOR STRINGS (1888)   (15')

Nielsen's Opus 1 met immediate acclaim at its Tivoli premiere and has continued as a Danish favorite ever since. Title understates the substance of this lucid three-movement piece which sports moments of distinct individuality beyond others leaning toward Grieg and Svendsen. The center movement (Intermezzo) displays particular interest, an appealing waltz developed with contrapuntal expertise.

SYMPHONY NO. 1 IN G MINOR (1892)   (34')

Nielsen never felt the necessity to make apologies for his First Symphony, a work he always felt a fit companion for his others. Most listeners will agree. Although a robust Nordic-romantic quality overlays the piece, this warm, strong music reveals clear fingerprints of the master symphonist to come. This seems particularly true of the well-wrought and clear-headed end movements which show the young composer in full command of his material. Incidentally, the First Symphony seems to have been the vehicle for America's initial encounter with Nielsen's orchestral music: the Theodore Thomas Concerts, Chicago, October 19–20, 1908.

SYMPHONY NO. 2: THE FOUR TEMPERAMENTS (1902)   (30')

The lithe, forceful Second Symphony brings some of Nielsen's stylistic hallmarks into sharp relief: pithy themes, rhythmic snap, irrepressible energy and dramatic coherence. The easy melodic flow of the two inner movements (Allegro comodo e flemmatico and Andante malincolico) contrasts sharply with the bounce and dance-like vigor of the outer two (Allegro collerico and Allegro sanguineo). In fact, choreographers have pressed music from "The Four Temperaments" into service as a ballet.

The idea to translate the four classic humors of man (choleric, phlegmatic, melancholic and sanguine) into a symphony reportedly occurred to Nielsen after he spotted comic depictions of them on the wall of a Zealand taproom. Although the composer issued a sort of "program" for this work many years after its composition, the Second Symphony left his writing desk a fully developed abstract work for orchestra, a true symphony in every meaning of the word.

SYMPHONY NO. 3: SINFONIA ESPANSIVA (1911)   (35')

The "espansiva" finds Nielsen a seasoned symphonist bursting with the full-blooded joy of living and determined to sing a broad hymn to the marvels of tonality. The composer displays almost unbelievable invention in the Third Symphony with new suppleness and power brought to commonplace devices like waltz and fugue: his instrumentation scintillates. In movement II (Andante pastorale) wordless soprano and tenor add melismatic lines over a langorous orchestra, an evocation of boyhood summers on Funen. The noble tune starting up the last movement (Finale: Allegro) might well have been the envy of Sir Edward Elgar. The wonderful Third Symphony provides an ideal banner to raise for Nielsen in quarters where his work is less than fully appreciated.

151

SYMPHONY NO. 4: THE INEXTINGUISHABLE (1916) (37')

The Danish subtitle, *Det Uudslukkelige,* presents most listeners with a linguistic impossibility, but this hard-hitting symphony speaks plainly enough. The Fourth shows toughening of Nielsen's idiom, an urgent need to vent his strong humanistic feelings and to express "the basic will to life" which took on added meaning for him after August, 1914. He admitted to a friend that the climactic ferocity of the kettledrum duel in the finale (Allegro: Tempo giusto) meant "something about the war." Decidedly, this is not the type of music usually expected from the tranquil Kingdom of Denmark. All four movements lock together as a masterful symphonic arch; resolute hope eventually arises out of turmoil, a symphonic paraphrase of the composer's words: "Music is life, and, like life, inextinguishable . . . ."

SYMPHONY NO. 5 (1922) (39')

Some opinions hold the Fourth Symphony comes closest to Nielsen's ideal; others cite the monolithic Fifth as his consummate masterpiece. True, the epic struggle erupting in the "Inextinguishable" continues here, but now events are thrown out across a much broader canvas. The opening moments are extraordinary, an almost maddening state of suspended animation while what amounts to primordial germ plasm congeals as from a great void (Tempo giusto); without pause the music passes into a determined ostinato leading into a great hymnal section (Adagio) where the cacophany and frenzied rat-a-tat of the snare drum almost tears the symphony to pieces. But the hymn overcomes chaos and then all subsides. Part II (Allegro — Presto — Andante, poco tranquillo — Allegro) is considerably more complex and conventional, a symphony within a symphony, four contrasting sections held together by a contrapuntal web which surges toward unity and a final cry of victory.

SYMPHONY NO. 6: SINFONIA SEMPLICE (1925) (32')

Following exhausting labor on his Fifth Symphony, two changes cut across the path of Nielsen's career: his health began to fail (angina pectoris) and his work began probing entirely new, unconventional directions, areas difficult for his friends to follow and properly appraise compared to the logical line of his development from the First through Fifth Symphonies. Commentators have since used terms like "nervous breakdown" or "creative degeneration" to express their apparent bafflement at the music written by Nielsen during his final years. Equally valid, however, is the contention that chronically ill or not, experimentation became the aim of the composer; he had awakened in himself the desire to explore new forms, tone relationships and, above all, capabilities of instrumental timbre. Many of his ideas have borne fruit a generation later.

Wailing has arisen among those taking a dim view of late Nielsen that his Sixth Symphony represents a work unworthy of its author, the last pathetic gasp of a sick and worn-out symphonist. But against this highly subjective view stand some obvious facts. The "Sinfonia semplice" came from a veteran composer fully in touch with reality, well aware of what he felt compelled to say and perfectly entitled to issue a personal statement no matter how wry, harsh or sardonic. If not necessarily the greatest, the Sixth might qualify as one of the most unique symphonies to issue from Scandinavian sources.

Both neo-classical and radical signals from the 1920s find reflection in the Nielsen Sixth; structure becomes lightened and simplified; emphasis is placed on meticulous instrumental control. The magnificent opening movement (Tempo giusto) develops some gem-like ideas. The controversial Second Movement (Humoresque) is a puzzler: do these chopped-up, perverted sounds represent satire or the ravings of a musical degenerate? Proposita seria, the slow movement, does suggest weakened invention; material pregnant with arresting possibilities is presented, but somehow these fail to develop. The cynical finale (Tema con variozioni) convulses with violent contrasts to end in self-mockery. Nielsen's "tragic" symphony may show some disturbing flaws, but the work holds a cold fascination all its own.

VIOLIN CONCERTO (1911)   (34')

Nielsen was handed his first violin when a mere tot and much of his life was spent as an orchestral violinist; with this intimate knowledge, a violin concerto from his hand might have broken into the masterwork class. Unfortunately, his single attempt in this form, introduced at the same time as the Third Symphony, generally works with unadventurous, late-romantic conventions even though the composer tinkers with standard concerto form. But beautiful moments do appear. Most lyrical interest arises during the extended first movement (Praeludium — Allegro cavalleresco); the second half consists of an elaborate rondo.

FLUTE CONCERTO (1926)   (18')

Compared to the large orchestra for the Violin Concerto, line-up for the Flute Concerto appears spartan. But listeners should note inclusion of a solo trombone, a protagonist fully as important as the solo flute. Flutist Gilbert Jespersen, a devotee of French music, was in mind when Nielsen conceived this concerto, therefore a solo part of elegant refinement. Frisky humor, however, takes over as Nielsen "roasts" his friends with an increasingly bold set of trombone comments; the intruder even manages the final word — a jolting raspberry — to bring the work to a close on a note of irreverence after a long chase for stable key relationships.

CLARINET CONCERTO (1928)   (27')

The last of Nielsen's orchestral scores well demonstrates his keen interest in exploring the subtle timbre and inner nature of a given instrument. Prickly and astringent, the Clarinet Concerto bristles with problems for performers and listeners alike as the music treads its thorny path through four uninterrupted movements; tempo and lyric fancies shift without warning within a typically late-Nielsen framework of conflicting key relationships. As in the Fifth Symphony, the composer employs the snare drum as a hostile counterforce. The Clarinet Concerto, for these reasons, may repel the casual listener. Growing familiarity, however, will eventually disclose an intriguing mixture of wry humor and abrasiveness. Unfortunately, nothing short of an absolutely immaculate performance can bring most listeners to this level of awareness.

HELIOS OVERTURE (1903) (12′)

Generally speaking, Nielsen took a dim view of program music; music was an art for listening without the need for "flowers, posturing, nor philosophizing," he said. The concert overture *Helios* does have strong programmatic connotations, however, although at a simple level. The piece depicts the rise, noonday glory and retreat of the golden Aegean sun. One of Nielsen's more overtly romantic works, *Helios* provides stimulating moments in the full-blooded resonant vein of the Second and Third Symphonies.

SAGA-DRØM (Saga Dream) (1908) (9′)

Also known as "The Dream of Gunnar," this enjoyable short symphonic poem paints a general picture of saga times instead of a blow-by-blow account of Gunnar's grimly prophetic dream of death as rendered in the old Icelandic *Njal's Saga*. More thoughtful than dramatic, *Saga Dream* contains passages calling up the ghost of J.P.E. Hartmann, particularly in the concluding pages where brass mingle darkly with strings.

AT THE BIER OF A YOUNG ARTIST (1910) (5′)

Given the subtitle *Andante lamentoso,* this elegy for the young, deceased painter Oluf Hartmann originally took shape as a string quintet; the string orchestra version, however, is more commonly performed. An entirely conventional example of north European *Trauermusik,* the piece conveys feelings of grief with appropriate dignity and restraint.

PAN AND SYRINX (1918) (8′)

One of Nielsen's most interesting orchestral pieces, the tone-poem *Pan and Syrinx* forms a Nordic approximation to Debussy's *Afternoon of a Faun.* The composer designated it as a "Nature Scene for Orchestra," a work embellishing the classic tale explaining how Pan came by his pipes. Pan chased the nymph Syrinx, but just at the moment of capture the pitying gods transformed her into a reed. The music artfully conveys Pan's lustful dancing and bleating along with beguiling use of coloristic effects. Expert scoring for woodwinds points ahead to works like the Clarinet Concerto and Sixth Symphony. An odd number in the Nielsen catalogue, the composer's skill and imagination brings off this bucolic escapade quite well.

RHAPSODY OVERTURE: AN IMAGINARY TRIP TO THE FAEROES (1927) (10′)

Nielsen's correct estimate of his orchestral travelogue was "just a piece of jobbery." But even so he produced an enjoyable imaginary boat trip through North Atlantic fog banks to the lonely outlying islands. The horizon gradually brightens and at landfall the mists have cleared. All embark to the joyous strains of a Faeroese folk hymn.

ALADDIN SUITE (1919) (25′)

Besides two operas, Nielsen fashioned incidental music for over a dozen stage productions. A few snippets survive, but by and large Nielsen's work as a theater composer lies submerged. The score for Ohlenschläger's perennial *Aladdin,* however, has passed the test of time. Nielsen's *Aladdin* music finds mere cleverness edging into front position with more than a hint of slickness, notably the brash Oriental Festival March and whirling Negro Dance. But not all of Nielsen's exoticism came second hand. A veteran traveler, his visit to the Middle East might account for the perceptive "Charles Ives" approach taken for The Market Place at Ispahan, where four orchestras play simultaneously in different tempos to conjure up the sunbaked color of it all.

SAUL AND DAVID: PRELUDE TO ACT TWO (1901)   (4')

Still in the repertoire of Copenhagen's Royal Theater, Nielsen's Old Testament opera is reputedly a work of nobility worthy of its subject. This richly sonorous fragment, building a picture of David, confirms that view.

Chamber Music

STRING QUARTET IN G MINOR (1888, rev. 1900)

Nielsen produced four string quartets (discounting juvenalia and student efforts) but none after 1906, a fact deplored by many because of his enormous capacity for instrumental writing. The G minor, his first quartet, makes up in hearty good spirits what may be lacking in terms of formal perfection. Unison playing dominates at the expense of balanced part writing, but the breath of life is everywhere in evidence. The slow movement (Andante amorsoso) and scherzo (Allegro molto) deserve special praise.

STRING QUARTET IN F MINOR (1890)

The F minor Quartet proved Nielsen's first composition to get abroad with early performances documented not only in Europe, but also in the United States. The bounce and genial air of this music do not preclude tension-filled moments notably in the splendid first movement (Allegro non troppo ma energico). The Finale (Allegro appassionato — allegro molto — presto) gallops with equal determination if a shade less flair.

STRING QUARTET IN E-FLAT (1898)

Sometimes considered Nielsen's most perfectly developed string quartet, the Third bursts with self-confidence and forceful counterpoint sometimes verging on excessive assertion and intensity. If not his most immediately enjoyable, the work certainly stands as Nielsen's boldest creation in quartet form.

STRING QUARTET IN F (1906, rev. 1923)

The F major Quartet originally bore the subtitle "Piacevolezza" indicating that peace and tranquility had come to replace the stress and striving of its E-flat predecessor. Warmth and gentle humor flow abundantly from the Fourth Quartet; part writing is restrained, almost chastely classical.

QUINTET FOR STRINGS IN G (1888)

'Eighty-eight was a fruitful year for young Carl Nielsen with completion of his Little Suite for Strings, the G minor Quartet, and the present Quintet. However, this work waited until 1937 for publication as a posthumous opus. Comparative obscurity should not blind listeners to the congeniality and craft displayed in this sunny music, clearly one of Nielsen's legitimate children. The warm melodicism of the fourth movement (Finale: Allegro molto) brings particular delight.

SONATA NO. 1 IN A FOR VIOLIN AND PIANO (1895)

Nielsen's two violin/piano sonatas measure up to his more important and rewarding compositions, although each shows vast difference in concept. The First Sonata comes as a meaty slice of late-romanticism built on rich chords and cascades of parallel octaves much in the Brahms tradition, but a Danish note also appears, evidently derived from Gade. Structure is broad and content full. Despite influences, Nielsen shows sufficient strength to be his own man. The last movement, bearing a typical Nielsen designation Allegro piacevole e giovanile, swings out with one of his most lovable tunes.

SONATA NO. 2 FOR VIOLIN AND PIANO (1912)

Excess enthusiasm might be curbed simply by stating that here is probably the finest duo sonata from Scandinavia since Grieg. Nielsen has jettisoned excess baggage and tightened any loose bolts in this incredibly efficient sonata strategically placed between the Third and Fourth Symphonies, a time when Nielsen's idiom began to harden and he leapt forward into new ideas about progressive tonality. Now his themes have become terse and angular, his melodic thoughts restless and searching; not a note is wasted even when he hammers home his argument at the end with insistent note repetition. Listeners who know Nielsen only from his symphonies are urged to seek out this work promptly.

SERENATA IN VANO (1914)

The Italian means what it looks like — a serenade in vain. Here the composer has assembled the gnomish combination of three winds, cello and double bass, the idea being to caricature a rag-tag band of rustic musicians. They warm up, render a serenade, then march off unconcerned about lack of appreciation. Less obvious than Mozart's tired *Musical Joke,* the eccentric *Serenata in Vano* sometimes recalls the mood of Grieg's *Peer Gynt* music or the deliberately grotesque folkishness of Mahler.

WIND QUINTET (1922)

Few nineteenth-century composers bothered with the wind group tradition left them by Mozart, Reicha and Danzi; but Nielsen, as much as Hindemith or Stravinsky, can take his share of credit for twentieth-century revival. Nielsen wrote his Wind Quintet when at the peak of his powers. Although flashes of humor peep out, his purpose went far beyond a work of impudent or breezy character. Serious reflection and concern for instrumental timbre form its main attributes. Structure is rather complex: Allegro ben moderato — Minuet — Praeludium form one unit; Tema con variazioni (based on Nielsen's own hymn tune "My Jesus, make my heart to love Thee") comprises the second, and most affecting, portion of the work.

FANTASY PIECES FOR OBOE AND PIANO (1889)

These tart little pieces make easy listening. Total time of six minutes divides equally between a wistful Romance and a perky Humoresque.

CANTO SERIOSO (1928)

Canto serioso might give some clue to what Nielsen may have had in mind for a horn concerto. More than a trifle, but less than a finished work, this piece for horn and piano provides a good warming-up exercise for horn players but adds nothing to the composer's stature.

PRELUDE WITH THEME AND VARIATIONS (1923)

Apparently, Nielsen felt that one Violin Concerto from his hand was sufficient, but in later years he again pondered his chosen instrument leading to two substantial, highly characteristic concert works for unaccompanied violin. First of these, *Prelude with Theme and Variations,* responded to a request from violinist Emil Telmányi (the composer's son-in-law) for something new to play during their joint visit to London in 1923. Frank borrowings from native rootstocks rarely entered Nielsen's instrumental work; in this instance he uses an original theme, but one with decided Danish folk flavor. The Prelude is florid and wrapped in demanding virtuosity; the eight variations are succinct and compelling.

PRELUDIO E PRESTO (1928)

Nielsen's second monument to the solo violin astounds with sheer technical demands, challenging music which all but drains the violin's virtuoso possibilities. Display music as such lies outside Nielsen's usual range of interests, but here he indulges in violinistic fireworks without loss of integrity. Few of Nielsen's pieces sound so "modern" as this one, partly because of unusual effects and tone-clusters.

Keyboard Music

FEM KLAVERSTYKKER (Five Piano Pieces) (1890)

Carl Nielsen a keyboard composer? Not only that, but some of his most rewarding music falls into this area. Though a professional violinist and no piano virtuoso like his Swedish friend Wilhem Stenhammar, Nielsen made enormous progress as a piano composer at various intervals throughout his career. Sidestepping juvenalia, Nielsen's first piano pieces amount to pleasantly derivative tidbits echoing Grieg and Hartmann, but a start had to be made somewhere. Titles of these little lyric sketches are: Folktone, Humoresque, Arabesque, Mignon, and Elf Dance.

HUMOROUS BAGATELLES (1897)

The six short character pieces comprising *Humorous Bagatelles* may have been intended for kiddie ears, but to play them even passably would tax the musical understanding and digital capacity of any but the precocious child. Solid technique is demanded by the angular leaps of *Spraellmanden* (Jumping Jack), the toccata velocity of *Snurretoppen* (Spinning Top), and the Mozartian precision of *Spillevaerket* (Music Box). Recognizable Nielsen traits also appear in the three remaining, though slightly less interesting, bagatelles: *God dag, god dag* (Hello, Hello), *En lille langsom vals* (A Little Slow Waltz), and *Dukkemarch* (Doll's March).

SYMPHONIC SUITE FOR PIANO (1894)

Most informed critics, Busoni included, seem agreed that here Nielsen simply overloaded the pianoforte; such massive, rock-ribbed music would doubtless have been better served spread out in the orchestra. Analogies for *Symphonic Suite* have been sought in the equally heavy F minor Piano Sonata by Brahms, but this comparison is really unfair. Even in his comparatively early sonata (Op. 5) Brahms showed the bearing of a keyboard titan; Nielsen commands more enthusiasm than authority. But if a pianist can dampen the work's more bombastic passages, hold rhythm firm through all four movements, and lighten texture in the lower octaves, *Symphonic Suite* can reveal much of interest.

CHACONNE FOR PIANOFORTE (1916)

With several of his greatest orchestral works behind him, Nielsen returned to the keyboard to score a direct hit. *Chaconne* shows a metamorphic structural plan. Starting with a venerable dance form and an unpromising sequence of bass notes, the composer advances through twenty compact, continual variations including an arresting midpoint climax before subsiding to a state of tranquility. Strict musical rules, in other words, become transformed into some of his most carefully shaded poetry. *Chaconne*'s serious introspection and certain technical details like dabbed right hand figuration suggest relationship to the Grieg *Ballade*.

THEME WITH VARIATIONS FOR PIANO (1916)

Much of Nielsen's piano writing speaks in short five-note phrases, closely bunched note-groups obviating the need for passing fingering. These pianistic idiosyncrasies somehow fit effortlessly into the traditional formalism of *Theme with Variations*. This is generally engaging music, highly imaginative arabesques and fantasies woven around a serious chorale-like theme.

SUITE (1920)

Several paths cross here: harmonic experimentation, the icy brilliance of Ravel, the restless tonality and five-note modules characteristic of Nielsen himself. The happy result impresses this listener as Nielsen's ultimate statement for piano. The composer freely interprets the usual meaning of "suite." His plan centers on six contrasting sections differentiated by tempo changes rather than arrangement as separate, self-contained movements. Originally the composer wanted to entitle the piece "Den Luciferiske"; meaning of this appears obscure because nothing particularly satanic or diabolical emerges from these pages unless the piece be considered "devilishly" difficult to play.

TRE KLAVERSTYKKEN (Three Piano Pieces) (1928)

Like his symphonies, Nielsen's piano music shows constant progressiveness; solutions to yesterday's particular problem raise fresh challenges today. The present opus, really a type of sonata, belongs with the composer's more "far-out" pieces which received scant understanding when first heard in Denmark. Here Nielsen dips into atonality with bunched note-groups verging on use of tone-clusters. Syntax sounds terse and sinewy. People who consider Nielsen a "romantic" should adjust their thinking to the realities of his music with *Three Piano Pieces* a good starting point.

158

KLAVERMUSIK FOR SMÅ OG STORE (Piano Music for Young and Old)
(1930)

The composer indicated these as "Twenty-four five-tone little pieces in all keys" and wrote them with didactic intent. They display moments of humor and originality. Some of the more angular numbers bring to mind Bartók's *Mikrokosmos*.

FESTIVAL PRELUDE (1900)

Like any other composer Nielsen is entitled to lay an occasional egg. The present opus had origins in a few solemn bars published in a newspaper as Carl Nielsen's official greeting to the twentieth century at New Year. Both organ and piano versions have been published.

TWENTY-NINE SMALL PRELUDES FOR ORGAN (1929)

These short organ preludes plus two published posthumously served the composer as preliminary studies in organ sonority for his great work *Commotio*. By subserving the creation of *Commotio* these little pieces could be dismissed as otherwise insignificant minions, but hearing them reveals more than utilitarian worth. The prevailing mood is sober and dispassionate.

COMMOTIO FOR ORGAN (1931)

The impulse driving Carl Nielsen to the organ loft at sixty-six to compose a mammoth, ascetic organ fantasia (512 bars, 25 minutes playing time) remains vague. Emelius Bangert, organist at Roskilde, may have initiated interest; an organ builder's reform movement coming out of Germany during the 1920s perhaps also stimulated his imagination. The Latin "commotio" here refers to "movement," not "commotion." In a letter to Bangert the composer plainly stated his purpose in sticking to strict form and firm counterpoint with repression of "all personal feelings." Cerebral nature established, what about form? Much of *Commotio* suggests a mosaic, but actually the ground plan follows the baroque toccata fairly closely: a Fantasia and Fugue followed by an equally elaborate Andante sostenuto and Fugue. Fugue I climaxes on an arresting, starkly resonant open fifth, a midpoint signal. Fugue II demonstrates more "swing" and builds to majestic resolution.

Nielsen left no registration for *Commotio,* but any thought that he was indulging in transplanted orchestral music has no foundation in fact. His last major statement was unquestionably music for organ; *Commotio* says something essential about the genesis of music as such, a message Nielsen delivered as objectively as possible through the ageless medium of pipes and air.

Vocal Music

MASKARADE (Masquerade) (1906)

Both of Nielsen's operas, the serious *Saul and David* and the comic *Maskarade,* appeared before his fortieth year, thus making them part of his earlier, more conservative period The basic plot for *Maskarade* comes from Holberg's comedy, but librettist Vilhelm Andersen performed radical surgery to adapt the work to the operatic stage. Prime attention centers

159

on situation comedy, not character delineation. The involved story boils down to a stock boy-meets-girl situation complicated by betrothal by contract and mistaken identity. Yet both Holberg and Andersen/Nielsen managed to turn such thin gruel into a delectable dish.

The opera leads off with a crisp, no-nonsense overture, an established Danish concert favorite in its own right. Act I introduces the hung-over hero (Leander) and his valet (Henrik) who mull over the day's problem: Leander has fallen in love with an unknown girl at the previous night's ball. The hero pours out his feelings in the first-class aria, "Se, hvor bag min Vinderslem" (See, How Through My Window). After much banter the hero's mother (Mrs. Magdelone) enters to disprove her years in an infectiously melodic dancing scene. Finally, the irascible father (Jeronimus) and the prospective father-in-law (Mr. Leonard) come aboard to further complicate matters.

Act II carries overtones of *Die Meistersinger*: a poetic Prelude, the Night Watchman with lamp in hand, gabled rooftops. Leander and Henrik dupe the bumpkin assigned to guard them, pop into costume and head for the masked ball (and the lady in question) across the street.

Events culminate in Act III, the masked ball, where Nielsen hits full stride; he almost bursts with fun-loving music as in the Cotillion Scene with its robust *Hanedans* (Rooster Dance). Eventual unmasking finds the comedy played out. The "old folks" have made fools of themselves while Leander and his mystery girl find true love and share some golden moments in their superb duet starting with "Min Herre! Je døbt Eleonora" (Sir! My Name Is Leonora). All ends on a mixed note of happiness and befuddlement.

Maskarade has waited too long for international recognition. Nielsen's expert touch shows at nearly every turn. Although male voice predominance puts Act I slightly off balance and most conductors trim down the length of Act III, the opera's action steps smartly, thanks to Nielsen's ready supply of appropriate melody and firm command of his busy, expressive orchestra.

Maskarade has been carelessly dubbed Denmark's National Opera. Although long popular with Danish audiences, outspoken patriotic sentiment in the work hovers around zero. The Danes do have patriotic operas, but *Maskarade* is not among them. In fact, most of the citizens of old Hafnia portrayed come away either as clowns or victims of satirical Danish humor — hardly glorification of "The People."

MODEREN (The Mother) (1920)

The chronic Slesvig-Holstein problem — something to do with Danish-speaking Germans and German-speaking Danes on the borders of the Reich — took a swing in Danish favor as a byproduct of the Treaty of Versailles; several thousand North Slesvigians returned to "mother" Denmark after fifty-six years of German rule. Nielsen's music for Helge Rode's play celebrating this deeply patriotic event seldom reaches performance except as bits and pieces. Some fifteen separate vocal and instrumental

160

numbers are involved ranging from frank chamber music like the soulful *Tågen letter* (The Fog Is Lifting) and *Børnene spillar* (Children Playing), both for flute and harp, through songs to numbers for orchestra. The songs are the real finds in this score; two of them have become extremely popular in Denmark, *Min pige er så lys som Rav* (My Girl Is as Fair as Amber) with its melting balladic character and the affecting *Så bittert var min Hjerte* (So Bitter Was My Heart). Other numbers like the orchestral Prelude to the Seventh Tableau, a March and *Som en rejselysten flåde* (Like a Fleet Eager to Sail) for chorus find Nielsen in his strongest national mood.

JACOBSEN SONGS (1891)

Of Carl Nielsen's many works for solo voice, only a few can really qualify as "art" songs. Instead, as time went on, he created his own popular style with decreasing interest in the *romanse* tradition. But two early collections devoted to the poems of Jens Peter Jacobsen still retain links with the songs of Grieg and Lange-Müller. Here is found *Irmelin Rose,* a Danish classic, and *Genrebillede* (Genre Picture); both songs recall the chivalric past.

HOLSTEIN SONGS (1894)

Excellent items appear among these six songs in the Opus 10 collection devoted to the poetry of Ludvig Holstein. *Sommersang* (Summer Song), *I Aften* (Tonight) and the extremely beautiful *Aebleblomst* (Apple Blossoms) all lie within the sphere of the Nordic *romanse*. In *Sang bag ploven* (Song Behind the Plow), however, Nielsen broadens his vision; without resort to actual folk song he probes a hidden pocket of native feeling not entirely unlike the lingering sorrow of *A Shropshire Lad*.

Although not part of the Opus 10 set, three of Nielsen's best songs again turn to Holstein for inspiration and make up part of the music for his play *Tove* (1908). These are: *Vi sletternes sønner* (We Sons of the Plains), *Jaegersang* (Hunter's Song) and *Glenten styrter fra fjeldets kam* (The Kite Soars Down).

DU DANSKE MAND (Thou Danish Man) (1906)

JENS VEJMAND (Ben the Stone-Breaker) (1907)

Like Edvard Grieg, Nielsen could write what some mistook for genuine folk songs. These two classics firmly link Carl Nielsen's name to the Danish common man. Both were greeted with outspoken enthusiasm when first heard and continue as national favorites. *Du Dankse Mand* assumes no pretension beyond direct, almost primitive love for country. *Jens Vejmand* is completely disarming, a simple strophic setting telling of the poor old road-mender eking out his daily bread making little ones from big ones; but when he dies, ironically, nobody bothers to find a stone for his grave.

MISCELLANEOUS SONGS

In partnership with Thomas Laub, Nielsen helped change the course of Danish song by diverting it from romantic into popular channels. For a model, the partners turned back to the "folk tone" of J.A.P. Schulz.

Further stimulus came from the Folk High School Movement long established in Denmark thanks to the vision of N.F.S. Grundtvig. Group singing is basic to the Folk High School idea and both Nielsen and Laub made many contributions to official song books. In this way their new, populist type of song quickly reached the very roots of Danish society.

While Nielsen's later songs were not entirely devoted to Folk High School *gebrauchsmusik,* collections like *En snes danske viser* (A Score of Danish Songs, 1915–1917), *Sangbogen Danmark* (The Denmark Songbook, 1924) and *Ti danske småsange* (Ten Danish Songlets, 1924) closely reflect the Folk High School spirit. Few of these songs are likely to appeal to concert singers; they were not composed for this purpose in the first place. But listeners desiring fresh insight into the well-rounded genius of Carl Nielsen might well enjoy them. Here are some good examples:

Saenk kun dit hoved, du blomst (Lower Your Head, Pretty Flower)
Underlige aftenlufte (Twilight Fragrance)
Jeg baerer med smil min byrde (I Carry My Burden with Joy)
Tit er jeg glad (Often I'm Happy)
Grøn er vårens haek (Green Hedges in Spring)
O, hvor er jeg glad i dag (Oh, How Happy I Am Today)
Den danske sang er un blond pige (Danish Song Is Like a Fair Young Girl).
Havet omkring Danmark (The Sea Around Denmark)
Jeg laegger mig så trygt til ro (I Go to Rest in Peace)

FYNSK FORAR (Springtime on Funen) (1921)

Nielsen's "lyric humoresque" for soloists, chorus, and orchestra can count similar fantasy cantatas from Weyse and Gade among its ancestors. In some ways Nielsen's hodgepodge of bucolic moods proves disappointing; nearly all he had to say occurs in the first half. In proper frame of mind, Nielsen might have done wonders with this text, regional depiction by Aage Bernsten, but when he finally got around to serious work on the piece he was deeply involved with the Fifth Symphony. However, a few magic moments do appear: the soprano solo *A se, nu kommer våren* (Now Spring Is Coming), and the almost painfully Danish tenor song *Den mild dag er lys og lang* (The Mild Day Is Bright and Long).

AFTENSTEMMING (Evening Mood) (1908)

Compared to his deep and lasting interest in solo song, Nielsen showed sparing attention toward the unaccompanied chorus. *Aftenstemming,* however, has held fast in Scandinavian collegiate circles. The text (by the romantic poet Carsten Hauch) is translated musically into a dreamy mood with a few unconventional harmonic progressions thrown in.

DANMARK, I TUSIND AR (Denmark, for a Thousand Years) (1917)

Nielsen's hopeful but turgid patriotic hymn holds less than major importance for non-Danes.

THREE MOTETS (1929)

Among the last of Nielsen's principal works, *Three Motets* take up the Psalms of David in the austerity of Latin. *Afflictus Sum,* the lead-off motet, restricts itself to the narrow spectrum of contralto through bass voices, dark choral hues dramatizing the lurking fear of death. Full vocal range appears with *Dominus regit,* a comparatively relaxed setting of the familiar "The Lord is my Shepherd." Pure serenity flows from the final *Benedictus Dominus.* Chaste, neutral light shines from these polyphonic pieces paying homage to the ghost of Palestrina; in them Nielsen again demonstrated the broad range of his creative genius.

For Further Exploration

Saul and David; Hymnis Amoris; Søven (Sleep); theater music; cantatas; songs.

BO NILSSON (b. 1937)

Bo Nilsson has revealed himself a rewarding composer with a mysterious and delicate talent. His activities first came to general attention in Germany, not his native Sweden. Before he was twenty, Nilsson had made contact with radical circles at Darmstadt and Cologne where he arrived preformed and knowing. Pioneer use of serialized open form, chance techniques and electronic sound may be attributed to him, but more important was his ability to assimilate quickly a style of his own within the highly abstract, conformist patterns of the main serialist camp. This shows obvious points in common with Boulez and Stockhausen, but instead of their tendency toward expansive constructivism, Nilsson specialized in brief, explicit statements using small-sized ensembles often with vocal component and with strong affinity for contemporary poetry.

Sharp lines between orchestral, chamber and vocal music become difficult to draw in the case of a composer like Bo Nilsson; his typical opus seldom plays beyond a few minutes. Rich luminosity, crystalline timbres and aphoristic form serve as main guideposts to this interesting composer's complex, yet direct, music. His refined and calculated technique bends to the service of his cocksure manner of personal expression.

Ensemble Music without Voices

FREQUENZEN (1956)   (4')

A fastidious study in cool and bouncy *Punktmusik, Frequency* for jazz combo and percussion understandably earned Nilsson his early reputation as a Wonder Boy. Today, the radical chic has paled, but the work's clear diction and sense of proportion remain.

SZENE II (1961)   (6')

Bo Nilsson favors German titles. His second *Scene* for chamber orchestra belongs to a set of three with present scoring divided among trumpets, violins and percussion (piano, vibraphone, harp, celeste.) So armed, the composer sets up another of his clangorous, finely chiseled soundscapes of brief duration but shimmering intensity.

SZENE III (1961)   (5')

Listeners outspoken in their hostility towards "modern" music are gleefully referred to this Nilsson opus, a piece guaranteed to enrage. Nilsson gives no quarter in this hard-edged, metallic music with its savage thrusts and controlled rustlings of anger which, unable to be held back, finally erupt into one of the juiciest instrumental tantrums in contemporary music. A must for the avant-garde buff.

REVUE (1967)   (7')

A curious hybrid, *Revue* starts off with Nilsson's customary cascade of brittle and crystalline timbres (including sounds from empty bottles)

164

but midway he changes course entirely. Without warning, a deeply moving, tonal elegy for strings takes over, presumably a nostalgic "review" of things past. Nilsson manages this unexpected dovetailing of abstract serialism and overt romanticism with enviable finesse.

Chamber Music

DÉJÀ-VU (1967)

Essentially a single movement for wind quintet, *Déjà-vu* makes incisive and even contemplative comment on the poetry of Gunnar Ekelöf. Ekelöf carries the reputation of a surrealist, but Nilsson's musical involvement is linear, down-to-earth and quite substantial.

Keyboard Music

QUANTITÄTEN FOR PIANO (1958)

Listeners who relish the dessicated sonatas by Boulez or the *Klavierstucke* from Stockhausen will find this Swedish tidbit familiar ground. Silences balance against the point-sound of isolated notes and terse tone clusters.

STENOGRAM FOR ORGAN (1969)

A sampling from the more radical fringes of the new Swedish organ school, *Stenogram* extends Nilsson's ideas about dynamic development as against the Webernesque affinities of his earlier works. Chord masses emerge as thick, turgid wads of tremendously amplified sound. The performer, virtually assaulting the manuals, is called upon to produce massive percussive effects. This music is less unpleasant than it is disturbing.

Vocal Music

STUNDE EINES BLOCKS (A Block of Time) (1958)

Toward the end of the 1950s, Bo Nilsson became primarily engaged in the phonetic aspects of vocal music. Inspired by the "concrete expressionist" poetry of Öyvind Fahlström, this cycle of six terse songs is deeply involved with both subtle and obvious allusions to the absurd. An accordion plays a prominent role in the proceedings while the singer shifts from vocalizing to *Sprechstimme* (speech song) as occasion demands. A pleasing feature of *Stunde eines Blocks* (title taken from the name of the first song) is the composer's sovereign command of instrumental color.

BRIEF AN GÖSTA OSWALD (Letter to Gösta Oswald) (1959)

In shaping this cantata-like tribute to the late poet Gösta Oswald, the composer divided his attention equally between the phonetic aspects of his texts and the timbral qualities of his musical resources: alto and soprano voices, women's choir, loudspeakers and large orchestra. The result strikes this listener as a Nordic counterpart to *Le Marteau sans Maître* (The Hammer Without a Master, composed by Pierre Boulez only a few years previously). Both are wickedly difficult examples of unrelenting serial formulation with sufficient incandescent beauty to qualify as masterpieces.

Nilsson opens his work with an eruptive prelude designated *Séance*. Two fairly short Boulez-like songs follow: *Ein irrender Sohn* (The Wandering Son) and *Mädchentotenlieder* (Girl's Death Songs). The critical

165

message, however, is reserved for last, a setting of the Oswald poem *Und die Zeiger seiner Augen wurden langsam zurückgedreht* (And the Clockhands of His Eyes Turned Slowly Backwards), where Nilsson dispenses with clipped, aphoristic form to lay out a movement of some fifteen minutes' duration. Textures remain brittle, harsh and fragmentary up through a frenetic climactic finish, telling reflections of today's art which can both create and destroy itself.

For Further Exploration

Versuchungen; *Entré*; *Caprice*; *Reaktionen*; *Zeiten in Umlauf*; *Zwanzig Gruppen*; *Attraktionen* (string quartet); *Design* for violin, clarinet, piano; film music.

ARNE NORDHEIM (b. 1931)

Because of his international outlook and man-on-the-go personality, Arne Nordheim has become the most widely known representative of post-serial Norwegian music. A given week might find him operating in Warsaw, Tokyo or Long Beach. Basically, the seedbed of Nordheim's fertile creative imagination has always been a strong feeling for poetry and keen sensitivity to sound as such. Much of his music derives from some literary or visionary starting point, but the resultant soundscape is what matters most.

In earlier days, the irreverence of John Cage helped Nordheim achieve a sense of independence which he has never lost, often manifest by a breezy attitude toward formal schools or doctrinaire systems. But, at the same time, Nordheim sees nothing contradictory in his free use of "open control" in his musical structures and his insistence that he should not be cast as an experimental or even vanguard composer.

"I am really a traditional composer," Nordheim claims. Supporting evidence consists not only of his carefully written scores using, for the most part, conventional notation, but also the immediacy and lack of cerebral pretense in his work as a whole. Intellectual, mathematically complex music in fragmented techniques is not his aim. Instead he plans carefully for the "lyrical" episodes in his works — not as literal major/minor melodies, of course, but the lyric-poetic feeling emerges clearly enough from Nordheim's intuitive manipulation of chord complexes and carefully weighed sheets of sonority and timbre.

The sixties found Nordheim deeply involved in electronic means of expression, but more recent works from the early seventies indicate a return to possibilities inherent in the modern symphony orchestra.

Orchestral Music

CANZONA PER ORCHESTRA (1961)   (13')

The temptation arises to label Nordheim's first large-scale concert piece "impressionistic." But trying to pin down any specific "impression" would be misleading despite an atmosphere laden with subtle color and vivid sonic imagery. Actually, *Canzona* is a concerto for orchestra, poetry in sound but the poem not specified. Form relates to thematic cells brought forward by individual instruments then tightly woven into an orchestral fabric. By turns the piece shimmers at instrumental extremes, bursts with climactic intensity and fades away like the chimerical passage of a mirage.

EPITAFFIO PER ORCHESTRA E NASTRO MAGNETICO (1963)   (11')

Perhaps Nordheim's masterpiece to date, *Epitaffio* builds an elaborate, highly expressive statement by means of standard orchestra wedded to electronically taped choral effects. The piece took shape in Nordheim's mind under the spell of the epigrammatic Salvatore Quasimodo poem, "And suddenly it's evening":

> Everyone is alone on the heart of the earth
> pierced by a ray of sun:
> and suddenly it's evening.

The musical result with its limpid blocks of tone which weave and wander hints at the spacious surrealism of painters like Dali and Tanguy — silent planes littered by grotesque shapes and cold shadows formed by an unseen sun. An austere, almost Arctic beauty hovers over *Epitaffio,* an allusion which the composer does not deny.

GREENING FOR ORCHESTRA (1973)   (16')

Despite an opening siren screech, gentle gongings, timpani thumpings and a section entailing 48-part contrapuntal cacophony, *Greening* is neither chaotic nor an example of avant-garde posturing. What Nordheim actually offers stands on tradition, a symphonic essay for large orchestra built on straightforward ABA form and the long established principle of metamorphosis. Events germinate from a simple three-note cellule and grow in an atmosphere of vegetative luxuriance which the composer aptly likens to organisms proliferating on culture media. As in many of his compositions, Nordheim takes spatial arrangements into careful account. "The percussion is rich in bell sounds," he explains, "and has been split into five groups surrounding the orchestra like a hedge to protect my seedlings during their growth."

SIGNALS (1967)

Three instruments may not properly constitute "orchestral" music, but in Nordheim's hands accordion, electric guitar and percussion add up to resources of formidable potential. Intent of the piece seems to be dialogue set into motion by cues (signals) passed around by the players. Effects of timbre are carefully calculated. Technically, *Signals* puts forth some dazzling moments, but there are other times when Nordheim veers close to slickness for its own sake.

LISTEN FOR PIANO (1971)

On the strength of persuasive live performances from Delores Stevens and a superb recording of Elisabeth Klein (the dedicatee), this listener feels safe in declaring *Listen* one of the most interesting piano pieces to come out of Scandinavia (or even Europe) in some time. Although such pioneers as John Cage and Henry Cowell used bizarre methods to get at the timbral possibilities in the piano, Nordheim needs only the keyboard and pedals to extend the range of the instrument in a manner seldom heard before.

In *Listen,* Nordheim again falls back on his tried-and-true responsorial gambit but non-electronically. Note sequences are held for the full effect of the overtones which then enter into full partnership with the player. The keyboard, in effect, carries on a dialogue with its own ghost. Echoes and dying vibrations collide, contrasts arise and fade. "What I want to explore," says Nordheim, "is the situation of people listening, and in the process of listening having also the possibility of choice." After some ten minutes, when the pianist ceases to stir the tonal blend, disintegration continues within the sounding board which Nordheim considers the supreme moment of *Listen*.

Electronic Music

RESPONSE I (1966)

Response I consists of a give-and-take game between two sets of heavily equipped percussion and sounds previously taped, the control panel operator acting somewhat as a referee. Musically, *Response I* carries conviction. Some of the events are planned, others fall into the aleatoric category. The piece might be considered a species of futuristic jazz.

SOLITAIRE (1968)

Nordheim can once again step to the head of the class for delivering *Solitaire,* truly a first-rate demonstration of musical inventiveness and coherence. Almost literal suggestiveness occurs, as in the vivid "rainstorm" episode, but main value of the piece lies in the logic and clarity of its design. Too much electronic music seems to ramble endlessly, but *Solitaire* presents a refreshing beginning, middle and end, a statement of symmetrical shape with a single seminal tone as reference point.

Originally conceived as a "cantata" (fabric of the piece contains a camouflaged voice reciting Baudelaire), *Solitaire* included coordinate lighting and dance effects when first presented at the opening of the Sonja Henie-Niels Onstead Art Center outside Oslo. But neither seems essential for effective realization.

WARSZAWA (Warsaw) (1968)

Nordheim's "Warsaw Concerto" for electronic tape can prove a terrifying, gut-wrenching experience. Neither polemic nor propaganda, *Warszawa* strikes this listener as a blunt canvas of horror, a veritable *Guernica* in sound. Events start off with what must be an air raid — crashing bombs, splintering glass, even the drone of disappearing aircraft, vintage 1939. Huge wails of pain lead to more simple textures such as dripping "water" sounds and a child's voice distantly intoning snatches of a grimly distorted folk song. Nordheim probably had no intention of musically recreating a World War II newsreel, but for those who remember, this association is inevitable.

COLORAZIONE (1968)

Arne Nordheim considers *Colorazione* (Colorings) among his pet progeny, an extended semi-electronic rhapsody calling for Hammond organ X-66 and percussion instruments played "live" in conjunction with material from electronic filters and ring modulators — devices capable of wide distortions and manipulations of tone. This particular programmed situation depends on "tape delay," the percussionist and organ player responding to material just played. Nordheim's controlled feedback may not touch the depths of musical profundity, but the intended vivid coloring of his tone surfaces meanders purposefully through episodes of what he calls "play on time, color and space." A worthy sound tapestry, *Colorazione* merits consideration for anyone's "five-foot shelf" of electronic music.

169

PACE (1970)

Produced on a return visit by the composer to Warsaw, *Pace* (Peace) stands in direct antithesis to the shuddering agony of *Warszawa* concocted two years previously. *Pace* employs the transformed sound of three voices (man, woman and child) reading a declaration of human rights plus bell sounds. The general atmosphere is one of unruffled pleasantness, the utopian peaceable kingdom where the lion lies down with the lamb. An apt subtitle might read: "Music for Shangri-la."

Vocal Music

AFTONLAND (Evening Country, 1957)

Nordheim's early song cycle takes up four world-weary songs by Pär Lagerqvist with projection realized by means of solo soprano and chamber ensemble. In turn, these dream visions reflect longing, an invocation to nature, alienation and the poet as a desert wanderer at night. The composer supports his vocal line with fragile, often exquisitely subtle timbres from strings and muted percussion, a generous demonstration of Nordheim's innate feeling for mood as transmitted through nuances of tone color.

ECO (1968)

A major Nordheim opus, *Eco* again finds the composer reacting to the poetry of Salvatore Quasimodo but expanding his forces as compared to *Epitaffio*. Here he has created a type of cantata using large chorus, soprano solo and orchestra (minus violins). Concentrated and tightly knit, *Eco* brings shattering tonal imagery to bear which underscores the voices with their cries of "active pain." This dire mood strikes home from the very start of the piece, a cascade of brittle microtones falling into a wail of voices like a million glass splinters descending on Dante's Inferno. Elsewhere, Nordheim calls up the expressive potential of modern choral articulation to carry his text (the poems "I morti" and "Alle fronde dei salici"). *Eco* scarcely makes a relaxing listening experience, but the terrible clarity of Nordheim's vision, accurately delineated, lies beyond any dispute.

Note on Nordheim's "Sound Sculpture"

Nordheim is more than a composer; he is also a musical engineer, perhaps among the first of a new species. One of his most publicized projects is a "sound sculpture" created in conjunction with Arnold Haukeland on the grounds of a home for the blind at Storedal, a few hours' drive south of Oslo. This large, non-representational object was designed "to sing," to use tone as an aid for the blind so they might "see" the statuary in all its dimensions. Some dozen photoelectric cells are scattered about the statuary; these become activated by light setting off, in turn, tones from a built-in "musical engine." Sound patterns emerge all day long, varying with the time and the season.

A somewhat similar challenge was undertaken at Expo 70 in Osaka, Japan, where Nordheim rigged a special electronic system in the Norwegian pavillion to provide six months of continuous music.

For Further Exploration

Floating for orchestra; String Quartet (1956); Partita for viola, harpsichord and percussion; Partita II for electric guitar; *Lux et Tenebrae* (electronic music); *Osaka-Music* (concert version); *Dinosauros* for accordion and electronic sounds; *Katharsis*; *Favola*; music for *One Day in the Life of Ivan Denisovich* and other film scores; *Zimbel*.

PER NØRGÅRD (b. 1932)

With Per Nørgård the musical explorer runs up against one of the North's more enigmatic figures. Trying to fix his stylistic position or artistic aims amounts to finger-chasing a drop of mercury across a glass table. Does Nørgård really represent Nordic music since Webern, or is he merely one symptom of its ills? The question holds importance because along with Arne Nordheim and a few others, Nørgård has been held out as the younger generation's white hope.

Nørgård's works list indicates no idleness; he has composed profusely and wide variety occurs. Orchestral pieces, chamber music, songs, film scores, theater and ballet music, a "shocking" opera for adults and Christmas music for school children all have swept across his desk to reach an understandably confused public. At one time, Nørgård seemed to polarize with a down-to-earth quasi-popular style on the one hand counterbalanced by a more "serious" and "exclusive" serial commitment. But systems as such seem to alienate Nørgård; he prefers the visionary modernism of Messiaen to the constructivism of Stockhausen. By falling in with Danish music's trend towards the "New Simplicity," unmistakable signs of anti-music have come from Nørgård, deliberately colorless pieces with or without electronic admixture in which time sense becomes ablated. Possible seepage from the psychedelic and rock subcultures adds further complexity to this composer who seems to run in several directions at once. "I am not so concerned with the process of statement," this puzzling introvert has declared, "as of the process of being."

Consciously or not, Per Nørgård (once a student in Paris) may be living out the singular esthetic of Erik Satie, possibly the first musician to exploit the possibilities of sheer boredom. The listener, baffled by Nørgård's erratic course and mystifying statements, might profitably refer back to the "white music" of Satie's *Socrate* as an illuminating ancestor of Nørgård's *Iris* not to mention the more obvious relationship between works like *Parade* and *Le Jeune Homme à Marier*.

For Satie, the lessons of experience meant restriction while satisfaction heralded death. He deliberately invoked boredom to subdue the listener, to provoke him beyond all provocation as a means of upholding his own freedom. But few subsequent composers have been prepared to accept calculated boredom as a valid premise for their art. There seems little doubt that a type of free-floating timbral music has replaced much of the ubiquitous serialism of the 1960s; no law states music must "express" anything. In this Nørgård stands on firm ground. Such composers as Morton Feldman and Terry Riley are his soulmates. But how much further

172

Nørgård can go with so-called "state-of-the-mind" music in his quest for "pure being" remains an unresolved question.

Orchestral Music

KONSTELLATIONER (Constellations) (1958) (22')

In this early, respectable piece Nørgård delivered himself of a richly ornamented study for strings in the concerto grosso tradition. A solo group of twelve mixed strings contrasts against full string choirs. Some concessions are made to serialism (as in rhythmic organization), but dissonant polyphony supplies the real glue between the "solo" group and the rest of the band. Movement one, called "Constellations," speaks as a spirited allegro; a plaintive movement designated "Contrasts" holds the center; the concluding "Alternations" recalls the Magyar abandon of Bartók. While *Constellations* may run long for its message, the piece proves readily accessible and surefooted.

LE JEUNE HOMME À MARIER (The Young Man Gets Married) (1964) (49')

Ballet music for a scenario by Eugène Ionesco, *Le Jeune Homme à Marier* documents the zany side of Nørgård's make-up. The ballet takes a hard slap at "bourgeois" marriage rites; the music follows suit as a collage of parodic clichés mixing scraps of familiar wedding music with extra-musical noise effects somewhat in the spirit of Erik Satie. How much derives from theatrical necessity as against perverse eccentricity for its own sake is difficult to decide from recorded performance alone. Presumably, the score faithfully mirrors stage business — a hapless young chap thrown to his three-headed bride like a terrified rabbit to a boa constrictor.

IRIS (1967) (13')

A pair of large works, *Iris* and the companion *Luna* represent Nørgård's presumably mature thinking in terms of the orchestra. No work can be fairly evaluated from a single hearing, but exposure to *Iris* in concert performance left this listener with the distinct feeling of having encountered true "beat" music. The surface of the piece scarcely moves, with little of interest breaking a sea of subdued orchestral sonority. Rhythm, direction, action, contrast have no place here. Nørgård is not without defenders or apologists; one of them has explained that in *Iris* the composer aimed to transfer electronic sounds to the orchestral palette. This may be. But he may also have concocted something definable as musical marijuana.

Chamber Music

QUARTETTO BRIOSO (1958)

Chamber music of all sorts has always interested Nørgård, with this work his first formal play with string quartet. A fairly conservative piece from the composer's formative years, *Quartetto Brioso* makes use of metamorphosis principles with a core theme uniting the three movements in a process of continuous development. The first movement can be described as churning and hard-driven, the second a contemplative Adagio and then forceful resolution in a movement actually entitled "Metamorphosis."

173

LE BAL SONAMBULE (The Somnambulist's Ball, 1966)

A trifle for accordion with support from mouth organ and electric bass, this little piece arose as music for a radio play calling for "lingering melancholy." Nørgård complied admirably with a very simple dream fantasy evolving from the merest wisp of a waltz melody.

BØLGER (Waves) (1969)

Speaking of *Waves,* a piece for solo percussion, the composer openly declares that it "deals with ambiguity." Facing a semicircle of drums, woodblocks and the whatnot available to the percussionist, the player methodically tinkles and bonks his way from one end of the assemblage to the other. The underlying musical motivation depends less on rhythm than on permutations of a basic rhythmic pattern ending with a too-cute touch of "instrumental theater" (the player bounces a rubber ball off the tympani). Actually, nothing particularly ambiguous emerges from *Waves.* Virtuoso technique is required as the piece progresses from mild interest to tedium.

RONDO (1964)

Rondo, like *Waves,* bears dedication to the Danish percussionist Bent Lylloff but requires six players arranged in a circle for proper execution. In addition to other percussion instruments in his sphere of responsibility, each player is furnished with a drum pitched differently from the others, giving the work a certain cohesion by means of a "chain of pitches," to use Nørgård's own phrase. The net effect recalls Varèse's pioneer *Ionisation* written more than thirty years previously.

Keyboard Music

SONATA IN ONE MOVEMENT (1953)

The piano has meant a great deal to Nørgård, one of the main avenues for his complex creative development. The single-movement form of the early "one-movement" Sonata is a product of what the composer has called his "construction phase." The piece makes a pleasant and worthwhile discovery, music of clarity and imagination. Antecedents seem less related to the Nordic colorists than the bright-sounding pianism of the inter-war French school.

SONATA NO. 2 (1957)

Burdened by a reputation of awesome difficulty, the Second Sonata had to wait until 1969 for its first full performance. The work is, I think, essential for an understanding of the enormous talent Per Nørgård can command for composition when he chooses to work within one of the traditional forms of music. Sonata No. 2 seems a direct descendent of the great Lizst B minor Sonata with something of Carl Nielsen's ideas about movement structure thrown in. The piece falls into two halves, a grand fantasia designated Andante, molto espansivo, followed by a more compressed Presto and Allegro maestoso played as a unit. Passionate intensity abounds, but Nørgård's youthful energies must not be confused with abandon; his sonata is a sonata in all respects, music of purpose, direction and more than a hint of genius.

NINE STUDIES (1959)

Studies makes an apt title for these terse essays in arid pointillism. In one of them pedal thumpings add a novel note.

FOUR SKETCHES (1959)

Further pages from the composer's sketchbook with brevity paramount (sketching is completed for all four pieces in a matter of three minutes). A suggestion of lyric intimacy does arise, however.

FOUR FRAGMENTS (1960)

Nørgård's pointillistic dabblings may show logic but the effect on the listener is less than rousing.

GROOVING (1968)

Grooving holds the distinction of being one of Nørgård's most widely performed as well as exasperating compositions. Listeners either love it or hate it. Nørgård explains: *"Grooving* is grooving, digging into the inner calm of the mind; the tones stretched out as strings in distant invisible worlds . . . ." The quarter hour needed to take this trip seem interminable as an undulating line of single notes spins on and on, moving glacially into a concluding episode where crescendo and diminuendo are treated almost in serial fashion. "Written for Mrs. Elizabeth Klein and dedicated to myself," Nørgård's tedious message both bores and irritates; status as a minor classic in new music seems conferred, however.

INTRODUCTION AND TOCCATA FOR ACCORDION (1953)

"Classical" music for accordion comes along rarely, but Nørgård demonstrated his dexterity while providing a piece for his friend Lars Bjarne. Agreeable and unpretentious, *Introduction and Toccata* is a smooth blend of Bach and modern dance rhythms.

For Further Exploration

Sinfonia austera; Symphony No. 2 (in one movement); *Fragment IV*; *Luna: Recall*; *Ceremonial Music 1968*; *Voyage into the Golden Screen*; *Lila*; *Calendar Music*; Second String Quartet ("In Three Spheres"); Third String Quartet ("Inscape") Trio for clarinet, cello and piano; *Tune-in*; Wind Quintet ("Whirl's World"); *The Labrynth*; *Gilgamesh*; *Babel*; *It Happened in Those Days*; *Tango Chikane*; songs; organ music.

175

KNUT NYSTEDT (b. 1915)

Besides composing, Nystedt has built up a reputation as an organist and founder-conductor of *Det Norske Soloistkor* (The Norwegian Soloist Choir), one of Scandinavia's outstanding performing organizations. Close association with America also belongs to his career profile starting with studies under Aaron Copland just after World War II. Several of Nystedt's works have received first performances in the United States, and while American concert audiences may not be too familiar with his larger pieces, some of his choral songs have become well known in church and collegiate circles.

Nystedt cannot be said to have arrived at an idiom irreducibly his own. Not surprisingly, his music has drawn both from the Bible and Norwegian folk sources with swings between post-romanticism and modern cosmopolitanism. Perhaps Nystedt has filed a more contemporary edge on his vocal and chamber music than in his large pieces for orchestra.

Orchestral Music

DE SYV SEGL (The Seven Seals) (1960)   (27′)

The cataclysmic prophecies of St. John have received full-blown chorus-orchestra treatment from such composers as Franz Schmidt and Hilding Rosenberg. Why Nystedt with his mastery of choral writing chose the orchestra alone to portray these dire Biblical visions when others have found voices indispensable is hard to understand. *The Seven Seals* consequently comes out as soupy program music struggling to depict the Four Horsemen, the ominous breaking of the Seventh Seal, glorification of the Almighty. St. John's portentious text deserves more awesome clout than Nystedt has provided.

Chamber Music

STRING QUARTET NO. 3 (1956)

Nystedt's aptitude for the string quartet apparently came from childhood memories of his father's amateur group progressing through the quartet classics at home. In his Third Quartet, Nystedt deals with neo-classical material in definable sonata form. The work shows clear-headed internal logic as well as a personal imprint. There are four traditional movements, all concise and immediately accessible.

STRING QUARTET NO. 4 (1966)

A striking work, one flowing like a precipitous Norwegian mountain stream. The idiom is modern enough (a fair share of tone clusters and extended tonality) but neither cerebral nor formularized. The composer works with a single-movement plan and spins off events in generally fast-moving sequence. Resolution takes place with decisiveness and flair.

176

Listeners on the lookout for new adventures within the venerable string quartet tradition are urged to become acquainted with this exciting music.

Keyboard Music

PIÈTA (1961)

The moderately short *Pièta* possesses a non-distracting, meditative character, a piece suitable as a prelude to church services or quiet music during Communion. Written in a free atonal manner, *Pièta* takes inspiration from a stained glass window depiction of Mary holding the body of Jesus.

Vocal Music

PAL SINE HØNUR (Paul's Chickens)

This smooth arrangement of a Norwegian folk tune provides all the requirements as a warm-up piece for choral singers and audience alike.

DE PROFUNDIS (1964)

Nystedt's choral prayer *De Profundis* represents one of his more advanced choral compositions in which sweet harmony has given way to choral dissonance, speech-singing and snatches of interwoven Gregorian melody. The eloquence and sincerity of the piece bring out textual meaning with etched clarity. *De Profundis* has been widely praised wherever performed; one commentator has gone on record to call it "the finest Norwegian church music work of our time." This listener cannot argue with that evaluation.

THE MOMENT (1962)

A fluid and expressive song setting in which Nystedt embroiders the Kathleen Raine poem *The Moment* with ghostly gong sounds and silvery punctuation from the celesta. The vocal line is taken by a soprano with considerable reliance on declamation. Subtle motivic repetition underlies musical commentary on the unfolding poem which falls into three closely connected sections. The text is in English.

THE BURNT SACRIFICE (1954)

Partly revised in 1967, *The Burnt Sacrifice* employs conventional means to recount events in the Book of Kings (Chapter 18) but with deep understanding and telling effect. This work, subtitled "Biblical Scene" for narrator, chorus and orchestra, takes the listener back to the tense dramatic moment on Mount Carmel when Elijah called upon the Lord to send fire, consume the offered sacrifice and rebuke the false prophets of Baal. Like Honegger, Nystedt demonstrates a flair for putting across Old Testament messages in straightforward, readily grasped form. The final pages, a hymn of praise for the Lord God, soar on wings of sheer inspiration.

For Further Exploration

The Land of Suspense; Concertino for English horn, clarinet and strings; *Festival Overture*; Divertimento for 3 trumpets and strings; Symphony for strings; *Collocations for Orchestra*; *Via Gratiae*; *Ungdom* (Youth); String Quartet No. 2; choral works; organ music.

177

GÖSTA NYSTROEM (1890–1966)

Rosenberg, Pergament, Nystroem: the three names looming largest on the small, struggling front fighting to modernize Swedish music during the 1920s and 1930s. Much of this period, however, found Nystroem in Paris trying to decide whether music or painting would claim the lion's share of his creative drive. Music won and he returned to the North in 1932. A certain amount of French eclecticism, by way of D'Indy's circle, came home with him, perhaps most evident in Nystroem's precise sense of orchestration and leanings toward a declamatory rather than overtly lyrical song style. A few tricks from the impressionists also colored his work, a sharpened feeling for color and atmosphere. But the totality of Nystroem's rich tone painting received fertilization time and time again from one specific source — the sea.

Nystroem went through life hypnotized by the sea. Restless ground swells, deep-hued blues and purples, the hard glitter of sun on water and the shimmering haze of distant horizons never ceased to fascinate this painter-composer, and in fact threatened to consume him. But he sometimes broke free of haunting seascapes and marine visions. In the arresting Second Symphony, for example, Nystroem stepped ashore. Later years also saw him adopt a newer and more current style along with greater objectivity. Yet as late as 1959 Nystroem could state with utter sincerity: "I cultivate absolute, pure music, but I am oddly enough at the same time an unrepentent romantic."

Orchestral Music

SYMPHONY NO. 2: SINFONIA ESPRESSIVA (1935)   (30')

The masterful but sadly neglected Second Symphony finds Nystroem putting his visions aside to issue a strongly disciplined and determined non-romantic statement. His purpose was "an intensive musical event," and these words from the composer admirably state his case. The symphony is an organizational marvel with the four movements interlocked like the cantilevers of a steel bridge. The basic building materials are raw and austere but they grow by accretion to mighty proportions. Events begin with only a solo violin, but as the music gathers intensity each choir of the orchestra enters on calculated cue to build sonority through numerical strength. Step follows step until the full orchestra has been assembled to deliver the final thrust. Although a "Nordic" atmosphere hangs over "Sinfonia espressiva," its artistic conviction aims at universality.

SYMPHONY NO. 3: SINFONIA DEL MARE (1948)   (38')

Composed at Capri, Nystroem's inevitable sea symphony releases the pent-up feelings of many years. Realization takes place in the course of a single vast movement sweeping like an azmuth drawn from horizon line to horizon line of a dove-gray sea. A stunning highlight appears at midpoint, respite from storm-tossed waters in the form of a song for soprano setting Ebba Lindqvist's *Det enda* (The Only Thing). "Like one who flees from his true love," these lines run, ". . . so I have fled from the sea." But yearning never ceases, even for "one breath of wind from the sea." This passage along with its rich and fluent orchestral commentary belongs to Nystroem's most inspired moments.

THEATER SUITE NO. 4: THE MERCHANT OF VENICE (1936)   (16′)

Not much about the character of Shylock and friends, but Nystroem's music dispenses ample Venetian atmosphere thanks to quaint and colorful pluckings on mandolin, guitar and harpsichord merged into a pit-sized orchestra. Much of this music recalls the dance flavor of the Renaissance masque. Special praise goes to a nocturne movement entitled "Frescobaldiana," a langorous evocation of sultry Adriatic nights.

SINFONIA CONCERTANTE FOR CELLO AND ORCHESTRA (1944)   (36′)

Sharper contrasts than provided would be welcome in a work of this scope. Nystroem brings a beautifully shaped melody into the final movement (Lento), but otherwise dwells too long on a somber, wistful message, soon wearying to the listener. Strong material for backbone seems lacking, unfortunate because in this mid-period work the composer strives sincerely for warmth and lyric intimacy. His intentions, in this instance, earn more respect than the music.

CONCERTO RICERTANTE FOR PIANO AND ORCHESTRA (1959)   (24′)

Ricercante points to a characteristic of Nystroem's style, a tendency to recapitulate melodic germ cells. In the present concerto he churns along somewhat in the neo-classical manner of Prokofiev or Martinu, music of motoric impulse and fleeting melody built on firm but amiable lines. A curious footnote appears at the end of the score: "God help me, the sea is so vast and my boat is so small." Nystroem's hint of despair seems at odds with an otherwise confident, outgoing piece. The Swedish artistic soul, however, can prove baffling.

Vocal Music

SÅNGER VID HAVET (Songs by the Sea) (1942)

Nystroem's set of sea pictures lacks the literary unity of a true song cycle; the five songs take texts from assorted native poets with common ground only manifest in their subject matter. Perhaps the most lyrically arresting moments accompany the third number, Gullberg's *Havets visa* (Sea Song). More dramatic treatment is reserved for the fine setting of Ragnar Jändel's *Jag har ett hem vid havet* (I Have My Home Near the Sea). *Ute i skären* (Out on the Skerries), *Nocturne* and *Jag väntar månen* (I Await the Moon), the remaining songs, sustain a marine mood although less memorably.

SJÄL OCH LANDSKAP (Soul and Soil) (1950)

In the poetess Ebba Lindqvist, Nystroem encountered a brine-loving soul-mate whom he enshrined in his *Sinfonia del Mare* and other works.

179

But in the song collection *Soul and Soil,* the sea gets left behind for the bittersweet memories of life in general. Each of these songs conveys deep, somber Swedish temperament expressed as verse-melody starkly contrasted against austere keyboard accompaniment. Non-Swedes may justifiably find these songs difficult listening compared to the more open *Songs by the Sea.* Titles are: *Vitt land* (Wide Country), *Onskan* (Wishing) and *Bara hos den* ... (Only with This ...).

HAVET (The Sea)

A brief, meditative choral work dwelling on the composer's favorite topic, *Havet*'s idiom remains generally conventional despite a tinge of dissonant harmony. Text comes from the rarified Swedish poet Vilhelm Eklund.

For Further Exploration

Sinfonia breve; Sinfonia Shakespeareana; Sinfonia seria; Sinfonia tramontana; Ishavet (The Sea of Ice); Concertos for strings (2); Violin Concerto; *The Tempest* (incidental music); Viola Concerto ("Hommage a France"); *Overture Symphonique;* String Quartet (1956); *Herr Arnes Penningar* (Sir Arne's Money); *Ungersvennen och de 6 prinsessorna* (The Swain and Six Princesses); *På reveln* (On the Reef); piano pieces; songs.

WILHELM PETERSON-BERGER (1867–1942)

One of Sweden's more popular composers, Peterson-Berger entered whole-heartedly into the spirit of the so-called 1890s movement, a surge of new romantic feeling in art and litrature inspired by the pulse beat of Swedish folk life and the idyllic beauty of the provincial countryside. Fascinated by the lore and landscape of the northerly Jämtland district, Peterson-Berger built a villa here, on Frösö Island, named *Sommarhagen*; at first the place served as the composer's summer retreat, but eventually this became his permanent residence.

Yet Peterson-Berger led anything but the life of a recluse. For many years he was in the central swirl of Swedish musical and literary life; from his vantage point on the staff of the Stockholm newspaper *Dagens Nyheter* he kept close watch on developments in European music which led to his reputation as a staunch Wagnerian and pugnacious critic, a fearless voice wielding an expert — and sometimes cutting — pen. Peterson-Berger's copious writings cover much territory and display perceptive concern for *Svensk musikkultur* along with reverence for certain Nietzschean theories about "Appollonian" and "Dionysian" polarity in art.

Fortunately for his posthumous reputation, little of this heady stuff penetrates the bulk of Peterson-Berger's music which takes direction from Nordic romanticism exemplified by composers like Grieg and Emil Sjögren. His work seeks to capture the hills, forests, flowers, lakes and very air of northwest Sweden but in a generally manly and beguilingly melodic way; his lack of pretension and discreet use of folk tone coloration, even when he worked with larger forms, are decidedly refreshing. Peterson-Berger ruled as a king of smaller forms, however; in these he sometimes skirted banality, yet his sharpened sense of literary values and remarkable melodic fertility grant his many songs and character pieces for piano moments of rare distinction.

Orchestral Music

SYMPHONY NO. 3 IN F MINOR: SAME ÄTNAM (Lapland) (1915)   (45′)

Scandinavian music lovers are apt to regard Peterson-Berger as the composer of a few familiar evergreens, but there were times when he could surpass mere competence in the management of extended musical structures. His Third Symphony marks one of those occasions, a work most authorities place ahead of the composer's four other symphonies (the First Symphony came in 1903, the Fifth as late as 1933). This engaging tribute to Lapland neither debates great issues nor wrings out the composer's heart, but its balanced four-movement plan proves congenial to the use of authentic Lapp thematic material. Scoring is both delicate and imaginative

181

with special compliments deserved by the impressionistic third movement (Tranquillo), a vivid depiction of the Arctic summer night.

ROMANCE FOR VIOLIN AND ORCHESTRA (1915)   (10')
Originally written for violin and piano (orchestration later by other hands), this songful, richly poetic music was dedicated to Karl Tirén, a railway employee whose collection of Lapp folk songs inspired the Third Symphony. Second half of the piece relies on one of the composer's warmest, most memorable melodies.

CONCERTO IN F-SHARP MINOR FOR VIOLIN AND ORCHESTRA (1928)   (32')
Why continual exposure to Sibelian murk when Scandinavia offers alternate violin concertos like this light-filled example from Peterson-Berger? "This concerto," the composer admitted, "is the pet child among my instrumental works — the only girl among the five boys, my symphonies." And, this listener would add, a real Swedish beauty at that. Designation for movement one (Allegro moderato, ma appassionata) adequately summarizes the whole concerto's declarative content, music of unashamed romantic eloquence. After an extended first movement complete with cadenza, the composer relaxes with a rhapsodic Andante tranquillo e cantabile, then directly on to a generally frisky Finale elaborating a curious "Chinese" theme. Being a music critic for many years naturally led to Peterson-Berger making enemies eager to castigate his creative work, but in this stellar Violin Concerto written comparatively late in his career, the often-labeled miniaturist took his detractors completely by surprise.

DANSLEK FROM "RAN" (Playful Dance from "Ran") (1900)
A trite but tuneful tidbit from one of Peterson-Berger's early music dramas, *Danslek* has seen long service as salon music.

Keyboard Music
FRÖSÖBLOMSTER (Flowers from Frösö) (1896–1914)
In the three books of *Frösöblomster,* little pianoforte bouquets much indebted to Grieg's *Lyric Pieces,* Peterson-Berger worked within a fairly narrow range of thoughts and moods, but as might be expected he scattered many a melodic pearl along the way. Typical pleasantry appears in *Rentrée, Lawn Tennis, Gratulation* and the puckish *I skymingen* (At Twilight), all pieces from Book I. These lie side by side with more serious, meditative moments such as *Frösö kyrka* (Near Frösö Church) and *Sommarsång* (Summer Song) where the melancholic side of Swedish folk tone gets affectionate phrasing. Similar comments apply to *Långt bort i skogarna* (Far Off in the Forest) and other numbers in Book II where joy and sadness often mingle closely together. *Intåg i Sommarhagen* (Entry into Sommarhagen), a popular specimen from Book III, takes the form of a merry, extroverted march celebrating the composer's joy at moving into his country house.

Vocal Music
ARNLJOT (1909)
Because of a heroic theme and frequent revivals, *Arnljot* leads all others in the claim for Sweden's "national opera." Acting as his own

librettist, Peterson-Berger (with more than a glance at *Lohengrin*) went to saga history to assemble in *Arnljot* a music drama bursting with patriotic pride and a host of spear-carriers. The convincing plot (drawn from the same sources as Bjørnson's drama *Arnljot Geline*) tells of the viking hero Arnljot who returns to his Jämtland home only to find his beloved Gunhild betrothed to his rival Gudfast. Swords are drawn during a *Thing* (law-making assembly), and for this crime Arnljot is condemned as an outlaw. He flees north, a fugitive among the Lapps feeding on thoughts of revenge when he hears of the White Christ and meets Harald Haraldsson (St. Olav); their destinies merge. Climax of the opera occurs at the Battle of Sticklestad (near modern Trondheim in Norway) where both Arnljot and Harald receive mortal wounds. The wronged viking dies a repentent Christian with love for his Swedish fatherland the last words from his lips.

On the surface, *Arnljot* might appear a bastard child of the Wagnerian household, but the work really adheres to a more traditionally conservative pattern of arias and set pieces with little obvious reliance on leitmotiv elaboration. In *Arnljot* the Wagnerian influence becomes diluted with the composer's strong sense of locale and feeling for distinctive Swedish lyricism. All three acts possess abundant dramatic and musical coherence brightened by fluent poetic touches. Act I contains some choice writing for a chorus of skalds, while Arnljot's fervent "Homeland Greeting" (*Hälsningssång*) marks another high spot. By any operatic standard, *Arnljot* with its deeply penetrating patriotism and quasi-modal melodic contours remains a viable work of art, certainly one of the most characteristic expressions of Swedish national feeling.

SONGS

Although badly underrated by the world at large, Peterson-Berger ranks among the most productive and accomplished practitioners of Nordic songcraft. Earlier years found him drawn to Danish and Norwegian poetry including a group of songs inspired by Bjørnson (*Marits visor,* 1896). But the intensification of Swedish nationalism during the 1890s lured Peterson-Berger increasingly toward his native ethos. Before the end of the century his songs identified closely with Swedish folk spirit as in *När jag för mig själv in mörka* (When I Walk Alone in the Forest), *Ditt namn jag hade skrivit* (Your Name I Have Written), *Bland skogens höga furustammar* (Among the High Fir Trees) and *Som stjärnorna på himmelen* (The Stars Shine above Me). The last is an exceptionally beautiful folk hymn inviting arrangement by several other composers. The composer's beloved Jamtland hills received attention too, as in *Fjällvandring* (Roaming in the Mountains).

Peterson-Berger's folklorism became more sophisticated in his three volumes of *Svensk lyrik* (Swedish Lyrics) especially the second, devoted exclusively to the Dalecarlian bard Erik Axel Karfeldt. Here is the cream of his song production.

Karfeldt, and his *alter ego* Fridolin, was a poet after Peterson-Berger's heart. In the Fridolin poems (about a dozen set by Peterson-Berger) a learned man of peasant extraction returns to the countryside of his forefathers, a sort of poet-peasant richly identifying with life close to the soil. So Swedish are the full-bodied rhythms and sensuous imagery of these poems that they amount to Dalecarlian wall paintings in rhyme.

Of the score of Fridolin songs and other Karfeldt settings, the infectious dance melodies given to *Sång efter skördeanden* (Song after Harvest), *Böljebyvals* (Billowy Waltz) and *Aspåkerspolska* (Aspaker Polka) make quick friends. Love's intensity springs from *Intet är som väntans tider* (Nothing Is Like Times of Waiting) and *Dina ögon äro eldar* (Your Eyes Are Flames of Fire) while love's cooling meets understanding in *Längtan heter min arvedel* (Longing Is the Name of My Inheritance), one of Peterson-Berger's most typical (and popular) songs. Poet and composer enjoy an expansive mood in *Månhymn vid Lambertsmässan* (Hymn to Man at St. Lambert's Feast). The darker, almost macabre side of Dalecarlian folk life, recalling the "Death Dances" of the Middle Ages, appears in *Jorum*. More cheerful moments return in *En madrigal* (A Madrigal) and *Humlevisa* (Hops Song).

Peterson-Berger set Karfeldt's poems almost as soon as they came off the press. This held true even in later life with the three lesser-known songs from *Hösthorn* (The Autumn Horn) written in the late 1920s. Their quality remained high: *Vandring* (Wandering), *Humlor* (Bumblebees) and the prayerful *Gammal ramsa* (Litany). An isolated Karfeldt song, *Dalmarsch* (Dalecarlia March) is so popular that it has become Peterson-Berger's signature tune. Here is a robust song worthy of Bellman.

Without the Karfeldt volume Peterson-Berger's *Svensk lyrik* would be less memorable, but two of the stronger songs in the balance of the collection are von Heidenstam's *Höstsång* (Harvest Song) and Fröding's *En visa om kärlek* (A Song of Love).

For Further Exploration

Symphonies Nos. 1, 2, 4 and 5; Sonatas for violin and piano (3); Piano Suites; *Domedagsprofeterna* (The Doomsday Prophets); *Adils och Elisiv*; Cantata for the Royal Opera; choral music; songs.

184

TURE RANGSTRÖM (1884–1947)

Ture Rangström might well be considered the most Swedish of all composers; under him the secret Swedish "soul" attained some of its most sublime expressive moments. The usual run-of-the-mill national romanticism with folkloric trappings held slight interest for Rangström. Early in life Strindberg had told him to "look for the key in the Swedish lyre," sage advice for a young man of Rangström's temperament which prompted him to soak himself in poetry and a venerable church music tradition instead of more obvious references to race and soil. "Perhaps even my interest in music," Rangström once confessed, "was born out of poetry, for it was the *word,* the burning word that gave me my inexorable desire to write music." In a very true sense, Rangström strove to become a musical poet, not just a romantic singer or mere adjunct to the verse of others. He wanted, as he said, to clothe poetry "in a new garment." This dream of his youth persisted unspoiled virtually all Rangström's life.

Expectedly, Rangström's idealistic visions found greatest fulfillment in terms of song; his larger works display certain undeniable weaknesses which have been attributed to scanty formal training in composition. But otherwise Rangström developed an idiom adequate for his purpose. His own personality was rich in fantasy, energetic and full of contradictions. The distinguishing feature of his music, what made him a classic, was his unparalleled gift for the purest, most exalted lyricism.

Orchestral Music

SYMPHONY NO. 1 IN C SHARP MINOR: AUGUST STRINDBERG IN MEMORIAM
(1914) (33')

Strindberg powerfully affected Rangström's artistic maturation, a catalyst helping to free his creative process. Unfortunately, this symphonic act of homage misfires. Excessive emotional heaving and wild flailing about dominate the outer movements (Ferment and Battle), although quality improves in the quieter middle movements (Legend and Troll Rune) thanks to the composer's flair for Nordic imagery. Perhaps only an orchestral wizard in the Richard Strauss class could capture the perverse, explosive essence of Strindberg on a musical canvas. While Rangström's effort commands moments of admiration, the symphony as a whole totters badly.

DIVERTIMENTO ELEGIACO (1918) (15')

Although the best elements of Rangström's art found basis in the written word and picturesque impulses, abstract composition by no means lay beyond his reach. No better proof exists than in the sterling suite for strings *Divertimento Elegiaco.* The piece compares admirably to more celebrated Scandinavian counterparts, Grieg's *Holberg Suite* and Nielsen's

185

Little Suite. All come from the same family. In his suite, Rangström has subdued what his friends termed *"Sturm und Drang-*ström" in favor of compact organization and warm, direct expression; each of the four movements mirrors a well-defined and executed poetic mood: Preludio visionario, Scherzo leggiero, Canzonetta malincolia and Giga. Once Rangström stated: "How wonderful it would be if Swedish song, our deepest melodic nature, should try to permeate a Swedish instrumental style with its spirit." In *Divertimento elegiaco* that wish came true.

Keyboard Music

MÄLARLEGENDER (Lake Mälaren Legends) (1919)

Stockholm enjoys a beautiful location at the confluence of Lake Mälaren with the Baltic; both placid and turbulent waters course through and around the town affecting Stockholmers like the Seine does Parisians. Rangström's extensive piano suite, which he called "Three Musical Vignettes to Strindberg's 'The City Journey' " joins the poet in praise of the Swedish capital and its outlying small islands, or skerries. Mood rather than specific snapshots dominates the suite; its three movements show adequate, if not always idiomatic piano writing. The work might sound better in the composer's own alternate orchestral version. Still, as musical tributes to cities go, Rangström's spurts of charm and quasi-impressionistic lyricism leave little unsaid.

SPELMANSVÅR (Fiddler's Spring) (1943)

One of Rangström's few pieces in frank folkloric style, *Fiddler's Spring* makes generous use of *polska* material. The "raw" sound and imaginative figurations of traditional country fiddlers are well preserved in this suite; parts of the third movement, not surprisingly, sound almost identical to Grieg's *Slåtter.*

Vocal Music

SONGS

Ture Rangström, like Hugo Wolf, seized the "inner meaning" of his song texts — a thoroughbred man of letters as well as musician placing message in the foreground sometimes at the expense of musical substance. But he avoided complexity in his large number of songs and could lavish heavenly melody on them; stark accompaniments often operate a step away from the vocal line to supply little more than summarized background of chordal and figurative suggestion. The dramatic quality of Rangström's songs was enhanced when he orchestrated about one-third of their accompaniments. Rangström worked within a reasonably broad spectrum of poets — mainly contemporary Swedes plus a smattering of other Scandinavians and German romantics — but he felt special affinity for the verse of Bo Bergman.

Bergman inspired some of Rangström's best-known songs, notably the graphic *Vingar i natten* (Wings of the Night), a soaring love lyric entitled *Melodi,* and the serene *Bön till natten* (Prayer to the Night); full romantic moods develop in *Pan* and the exceptionally attractive *Flickan under nymånen* (Maiden under the New Moon). The *Sturm und Drang*

186

aspect of Bergman's poetry comes to the fore in *Tristans död* (Tristan's Death), not really a distinguished song, in which the composer dramatizes grief to the point of bombast, but in *En gammal dansrytm* (Old Dance Rhythm) he employs waltz acceleration to add a touch of intoxication in a song lying close to the bizarre erotic suggestiveness of Strindberg's *Miss Julie.*

Of songs from other poets, Rangström does an exceptional job with *Den enda stunden* (The Only Moment) where he communicates Runeberg's words with exquisite lyricism and almost frightening intimacy. Assertive feminism gets aired in *Sköldmön* (Valkyrie), a heady but banal song taken from Karin Boye's *Shield and Sword.* Better results appeared when Rangström worked with Strindberg's verse as in *Villemo, Villemo* (Villemo, Why Did You Leave Me?). In a few instances Rangström supplied poems of his own, notably in the song collections *Havets sommar* (Summer Sea) and *Notturno.*

UR KUNG ERIKS VISOR (From King Erik's Songs) (1918)

Although Gustav Fröding published his five *King Erik's Songs* at different times during his comparatively brief productive career, they show remarkable unity of mood, dwelling as they do on the bitter gall of life as tasted both by the poet and his royal subject. Erik XIV, the sixteenth-century Swedish king, led a tragic existence ending ultimately in insanity and imprisonment. A man of vast talent and potential, the wretched monarch managed to poison the very air about him and destroy all he loved. Passionate grief runs through all the King Erik's songs, most dramatically displayed in the opening number. But the remarkably vivid middle song, *En visa till Karin när hon hade dansat* (Song to Karin after Her Dancing), looms high in all Rangström's work, a gripping picture of the half-mad king imagining that the garland crown he sets on the head of his beloved wife contains a poisoned thorn. Anguish finally turns to defiant bitterness in *Kung Eriks sista visa* (King Erik's Last Song) where the royal prisoner mocks his hated brother, John: "Thy neck I made — and thou would'st be free, thou hast thy neck — go, break it!" Soon after, according to legend, Erik's enemies had him served a bowl of poisoned pea soup.

KRONBRUDEN (The Crown Bride) (1915)

At their very first meeting in 1909, Rangström and Strindberg discussed possibilities for an operatic rendering of *The Crown Bride,* a Dalecarlian folk play completed by Strindberg but a few years previously. Although Rangström made the suggestion to trim away the last two scenes, radical revision of the text became unnecessary because the playwright virtually handed the composer a libretto. Musical himself, Strindberg had peppered his play with actual folk song quotations along with meticulous notes on authentic costumes and native customs.

Both plot and setting of *The Crown Bride* bear similarity to Janáček's roughly contemporaneous *Jenufa.* Both operas are intense portrayals of folk life in which passions lead to infanticide and redemption. Both heroines suffer from the machinations of relatives, but Kersti, heroine of

187

The Crown Bride, must also suffer harassment from trolls. But in neither opera do the morbid aspects of plot constitute the prime center of attention; what really matters in both works is the strength and character of the peasantry, the implied soul of the nation.

Following a brief exposure to Rangström's opera (taped performance with score in hand), this listener came away with a strongly positive impression that *The Crown Bride* might be the composer's masterpiece. The work is long, but Rangström's flow of radiant lyricism seldom falters while his choral passages convey the honest heartiness of the idealized folk spirit. Hopefully, this extremely interesting and well-wrought opera will someday reach a broader audience.

For Further Exploration

Symphony No. 2 ("My Country"); Symphony No. 3 ("Song under the Stars"); Symphony No. 4 ("Invocatio"); Festival Prelude; *Intermezzo drammatico*; Partita for Violin and Orchestra; *Ballad* for piano and orchestra; *A Little Stockholm Music*; String Quartet ("Night Piece after E.T.A. Hoffmann"); Romance for cello and piano; *Medeltida* (The Middle Ages); *Gilgamesj*; piano music; choral pieces; songs.

KNUDAGE RIISAGER (b. 1897)

An artist who may be eminent in a small nation may easily go unrecognized throughout the rest of the world. The Danish composer Knudage Riisager is a specific case in point. Following studies in Copenhagen and Paris (including preceptorship under Albert Roussel), Riisager has had a long career of solid achievement, a works list covering a variety of forms and consisting of over two hundred separate pieces. Riisager has built his local reputation on solid craftsmanship and a generally less-than-serious style often spiced with subtle Danish humor. He is a dance composer with few peers anywhere. Yet apart from an inadequate smattering of recordings issued to date and occasional mention in ballet programs, this wonderful composer usually draws a blank outside Denmark.

Neglect of Riisager seems doubly unfortunate because his music is immediately approachable and gives great pleasure on first hearing. After World War I, when Riisager returned to Copenhagen from the ferment of Paris, he struck people as a young radical. But the wit and clarity of his work eventually disarmed his critics, and during the 1940s his distinctive flair for ballet music culminated in a series of scores for Harald Lander, Birgit Cullberg and other choreographers giving him a measure of international recognition, at least within dance circles. But the full range of Riisager's abilities remains to be exported; his is a very special talent, and among Scandinavian composers he stands out as distinctively as a red-coated Danish postman.

Orchestral Music

PRIMAVERA (1934) (5')

The flyleaf of the printed score for this concert overture carries a quotation from Pascal: "The heart has its reasons which reason does not know." A heartfelt, if condensed, salute to the first signs of Spring, the overture opens and closes on a note of jubilation with a reflective pause midway to listen to the chirping of the birds. A feeling that life can be good forms the essential mood of this music.

I ANLEDNING AF — (On the Occasion of —) (1934) (14')

Danish children's songs form the basis for this miniature suite, a sort of musical birthday present which has become a longtime "pops" favorite at Tivoli concerts. Riisager treats his simple, tuneful material in straightforward fashion without resort to cute tricks or gimmickry.

CONCERTINO FOR TRUMPET AND STRING ORCHESTRA (1933) (12')

A typical bright and bracing Riisager opus, the Trumpet Concertino has proven a useful alternative to the overworked Haydn concerto whenever first desk trumpeters get their rare chance to star in a soloist's role. The piece attracted much attention at the 1938 ISCM Festival in London,

189

although first performance had taken place in Denmark four years earlier. Stylishly neo-classical, the well-etched themes, balanced contrasts and lucid, precise orchestration immediately bring to mind such witty composers as Jean Françaix and Francis Poulenc. The spark of invention remains with Riisager through all three movements (Allegro; Andantino semplice; Rondo: Vivace) aided by deft interplay between trumpet and strings as well as sustained good humor.

QARRTSILUNI (1938)   (12′)

Qarrtsiluni originally took shape as pure concert music, but the piece has become inextricably associated with Harald Lander's celebrated Eskimo ballet of the same name launched in 1942. Starting point for the composer related to the journals of the Arctic explorer Knud Rassmussen, a particular passage where an old Eskimo woman gave explanation for the sudden quiet among her people: "This silence," she said, "is what we call 'qarrtsiluni,' which means that you are waiting for something to burst." The "burst" referred to means the sudden return of the sun to Greenland after long months of winter's darkness. This mood of Arctic awe appears immediately in Riisager's score, a shimmering opening chord for full orchestra. The rest of the piece is essentially a choric fantasy building up over a long ostinato corresponding (in the ballet) to the beat of the shaman's drum. Qarrtsiluni has been compared to Stravinsky's Rites of Spring. A few superficial resemblances do appear, but Riisager's work is far less fierce and explosive.

TOLV MED POSTEN (Twelve by Mailcoach) (1939)   (12′)

According to Hans Christian Andersen, New Year's Eve brings a big mailcoach clattering up to the town gate with twelve passengers stuffed inside. Each alights in turn presenting his passport to the sentry on duty; each represents a month in the calendar year. The work has been presented as a one-act ballet (choreography by Børge Ralov), but Riisager's adaptation for concert purposes usually includes only six characterizations: January, April, "Miss May" (whom Andersen has wearing a summer dress with galoshes), July, August and October. In terms of sheer vivacity and instrumental color Riisager surpasses himself in these little seasonal sketches expressed as well-knit, infectious tunes of folk character. An utterly irresistible score, Twelve by Mailcoach amounts to one of the choice "finds" in Danish music.

ETUDE (1947)   (11′)

The crowning achievement of the Lander-Riisager partnership, Etude constitutes a balletomane's dream — a production uncluttered by plot. The basic choreographic idea simply consists of showing the development of the ballerina's act from fledgling state through various upward phases to artistic perfection. Musically, Riisager does for Karl Czerny and his notorious pedagogical Études for aspirant pianists what Respighi did for the lesser Rossini, and Tommasini for Domenico Scarlatti, the bringing of half-forgotten music back to vibrant life by means of the modern orchestra. He treats these generally considered dust-dry tunes with pliant freedom and meticulous workmanship. In all, the full ballet score requires music for sixteen scenes; much less is presented in the dazzling concert suite.

Chamber Music

SERENADE FOR FLUTE, VIOLIN AND CELLO (1936)

Although Riisager has written formal string quartets, the bulk of these belong to his early days; more typical of the mature composer is chamber music for diverse instrumental combinations. In these pieces Riisager shows fondness for neo-classic blends of string and woodwind tone. The present Serenade provides a good example of the composer's approach, the intimate Riisager making highly civilized and diverting music in the cool, reserved French manner.

Vocal Music

SONGS

Riisager cannot be accused of neglecting singers; over a hundred songs and short pieces for male chorus appear in his works catalogue. Yet this largely points to a byway; Riisager's main effort has gone in different directions. Most of his industrious vocal output seems never to have been intended for more than local consumption. Two of his best-known songs supplied wartime morale building: *Mor Danmark* (Mother Denmark) gained understandable popularity while the Germans held the country and Riisager was ready with another patriotic hit, *Danmarks Frihedssang* (Denmark's Freedomsong) when they marched out.

For Further Exploration

Symphony No. 4 ("Sinfonia gaia"); *Slaraffenland* (The Land of Cockaigne); *Les Victoires de l'Amour;* Partita for Orchestra; *Shrovetide Overture; Erasmus Montanus Overture*; Little Overture for Strings; *Bellman Variations; Summer Rhapsody; Niels Ebbesen* (incidental music); Violin Concerto; *Sinfonietta*; Wind Quartet; Sonata for two solo violins; Sonata for violin, cello and piano; Concertino for five violins and piano; *Danish Psalm; Canto dell'infinito* (Song of Infinity); *A Merry Trumpet* (collection of piano pieces); solo and choral songs.

JOHAN HELMICH ROMAN (1694–1758)

A steadfast admirer of Handel, Roman returned to his native Stockholm after travels on the Continent and two periods of study in London to take charge of the court orchestra, promote public concerts and lay the groundwork for modern Swedish music — efforts justly earning Roman the designation "musical father of his country." But Roman's posthumous reputation dwindled sharply. His mass of largely unpublished music joined piles of poorly catalogued material at the Academy of Music, on estates and in university libraries. Not until the opening years of the twentieth century did curiosity spark revival which later grew to full-scale scientific inquiry at the hands of Swedish musicologists, notably Ingmar Bengtsson. Sifting the genuine from the spurious has been the main task for Roman scholars, but thanks to their labors a formerly vague picture is now greatly clarified and a deserving eighteenth-century master restored to active circulation. The gathered evidence now supports the stature and quality of Roman as a composer, the northernmost representative of the late baroque instrumental tradition.

Orchestral Music

SINFONIAS (c. 1735–1745)

Roman's twenty-odd compositions entitled "sinfonia" are a milestone in Swedish instrumental music. They straddle the line between the baroque suite and the less weighty products of the pre-classical *style galant*; generally speaking, they amount to lively sprouts from the Neopolitan school and the French overture. Their purposeful harmonic progressions, energetic thematic profiling and imaginative rhythmic organization mark Roman a kapellmeister well above his contemporary average and one not adverse to original solutions for compositional problems.

Of the smattering of Roman sinfonias so far committed to microgroove, the Sinfonia in D major (BeRI 23) and one in E minor (BeRI 22) consist of generally vivacious music and have immediate appeal.* The less striking Sinfonias in G major (BeRI 9) and in B major (BeRI 11), apparently written some years earlier, are typical examples of the pre-classical pocket symphony.

DROTTNINGHOLM MUSIC (1744)   (24′)

Among Roman's more celebrated works stands a twenty-four movement suite for orchestra composed as wedding music for Crown Prince Adolph Fredrik and his bride, Lovisa Ulrika of Prussia (sister of

---

*Of various systems for numbering the Roman sinfonias, the author has adopted the Ingmar Bengtsson listing ("BeRI number") on advice of Swedish authorities.

192

Frederick the Great). The festivities took place at the lakeside Drottning-holm Palace, a setting which might have put Roman in mind of Handel's *Water Music* which runs in a similar vein. Handel's broad majesty may be lacking in Roman's festive suite, but he did write idiomatically for his band of winds and strings and laced his sturdy tunes together with plenty of rhythmic flexibility. Most modern performances of the *Drottningholm Music* use a trimmed-down version, but even in truncated form this suite should give baroque buffs cause to rejoice.

VIOLIN CONCERTO IN D MINOR (c. 1730) (13')

An experienced violinist and oboist himself, Roman contributed several concertos for both his favored instruments. Of his four known concertos for violin, the D minor (edited by Hilding Rosenberg) stands out as one of Roman's most attractive pieces in any category. Fluent and delightful throughout, the concerto is organized in customary fast-slow-fast pattern. In the opening, buoyant Allegro, Roman gives his themes a more thorough working-out than usual. A gracious cavatina then bridges over to an equally brief but decisive finale.

OBOE CONCERTO IN B-FLAT MAJOR (c. 1730) (15')

About 1730, along with his disciple and successor Per Brant, Roman organized an unprecedented series of public concerts using Stockholm's impressive House of the Nobility as the regular gathering place. Most of Roman's concertos presumably came about in response to this stimulus, with the composer himself a likely soloist. The amiable B-flat major Oboe Concerto proceeds with smooth assurance recalling the grace and fluency of Telemann.

OBOE (OBOE D'AMORE) CONCERTO IN D MAJOR (c. 1730) (15')

Another fine example of Roman's instrumental art, the D major Concerto remembers Handel but sounds vaguely more "modern." A favorite of Bach and other German composers of the baroque era, the oboe d'amore was pitched a minor third below the standard instrument and sends out a less pungent tone.

Chamber Music

ASSAGGI (c. 1735)

Music for solo violin occupies a prominent place in Roman's instrumental production. Of these pieces, considerable importance attaches to a series of experimental multi-movement sonata-like "essays" or "studies" which the composer generically called *assaggi*. Geminiani stands as the chief spirit behind these highly interesting works which are often musically rich as well as prime sources for the art of late baroque violin technique. In the case of Assaggio No. 6 in B minor (BeRI 324), Roman conveys dignity along with virtuosity, connoisseur music happily free of pedantry or mannerism.

FLUTE SONATAS (1727)

Only a tiny fraction of Roman's music saw publication during his life time with the notable exception of a set of twelve sonatas for transverse flute and thorough bass. These are typical examples of the trio sonata familiar to friends of K.P.E. Bach and Telemann. Sonata No. 6 in this collection has moments of stodginess but generally manages a tone of elegant, well-crafted diversion. Sonata No. 8 in A major (BeRI 208) conveys more sparkle and signs off with what sounds like a merry folk tune.

Both in Roman's time as well as today, instruments in the performing trio might vary with violin replacing the flute. Some of Roman's "violin sonatas" are therefore only transcriptions of his trio sonatas for flute.

Keyboard Music

SUITES FOR HARPSICHORD

Roman rarely enters the mind as a keyboard composer, but like most of his contemporaries various facets of music were all parts of the day's work. Some dozen keyboard suites attributed to his hand survive with some particularly frisky writing found in the third movement of a Suite in C.

Vocal Music

JUBILATE

The musicological problems of sorting, classifying and editing Roman's copious vocal output has proceeded much more slowly than with his instrumental compositions. Not that they are less important; far from it. Roman's historical significance in Scandinavian music rests on his promotion of Swedish song with accompaniment and his conscious effort to marry the Swedish language to church music. Although Roman actively produced and conducted opera he, strange to say, never wrote one.

Dramatic flair, however, comes out in *Jubilate,* a setting of Psalm 100 for chorus and orchestra, a piece most probably by Roman, but certainly the work of a loyal Handelian.

GUD ÄR VÅR TILLFLYKT (God Is Our Refuge)

Accepted as genuine Roman, this rendering of Psalm 46 provides a choice example of Swedish religious music from the first half of the eighteenth century. As with *Jubilate,* content and expression strike an admirable balance.

For Further Exploration

Sinfonias; sonatas; keyboard music; motets; Swedish Mass; songs.

HILDING ROSENBERG (b. 1892)

Hilding Rosenberg, a gardener's son from Scania, may be said to have done more than any other individual in channeling the course of modern music in Sweden. Once a ridiculed and heckled radical, this determined "lunatic" reached his seventies able to look back on his long career from a mountain top, a musician hailed as Nestor for an entire generation of younger composers. Rosenberg, above all, lifted the onus of provincialism from Swedish music.

Rosenberg made a great teacher because of his ability to inspire as a man. When interviewed, this tall, unstooped septuagenarian admitted the old man's span of years, yet he showed the responsiveness and alerted interests of a far younger person. Rosenberg has never disengaged from the life around him. He spoke sincerely of the need for a man's daily work and of art's ultimate derivation from nature; whenever possible he sinks his own hands into garden soil to reaffirm that mystical relationship. An instinctive musician, Rosenberg only reached his goal as a completely integrated artist after years of self-discipline and upward struggle. The perspective of his life has been both spacious and deep.

Rosenberg's command of the materials of music can only be described as encyclopedic. His work covers all forms and variants of all forms to the point of a mountain of manuscripts. Of course, in terms of communicative value and listening interest, all these pieces are not equal, but this composer's craft and concern never come into question. The radical element in Rosenberg's music belongs to ancient history, the twenties, when he took cues from such unlike models as Sibelius and Schoenberg. His more characteristic works began flowing in earnest from the middle 1930s after much striving for individual synthesis. In Rosenberg's mature utterances the listener becomes conscious of an expressive linear foundation, austere melodies with a whiff of Gregorian ancestry flowing into patterns of polyphonic growth laced with animating rhythm. A lighter side to Rosenberg's art also exists, but his almost religious belief in the power of music to purify stands foremost, with peak fulfillment found in his vast choral-symphonic statements. An almost Biblical seriousness, a certain aloofness and refusal to play to the gallery warn listeners not to expect colorful excitement or sensual gratification. As with some Swedish people themselves, Rosenberg's music generally maintains a certain cool reserve and formality; both time and patience are required to appreciate it fully. Infatuation with folk life has been left to others.

When the winds of change began to blow past him, the leaves of this sturdy old oak began rustling with twelve-tone music, but whether or not the impact of the postwar serialists really touched Rosenberg's deepest convictions is an enigmatic question. Certainly the breakup of all tonality and the rage for experimentation typical of the 1960s did not always meet with his approval, but on the whole his adjustment to rapid change at an advanced age has proven remarkably smooth. Virtually all of Rosenberg's music exists against a background glow of humanism; depersonalized abstraction is foreign to his nature. "Technique is important," Rosenberg has stated, "but Man is also important."

Orchestral Music

SYMPHONY NO. 2: SINFONIA GRAVE (1935)   (35')

Although preceded by two versions of a First Symphony as well as a set of so-called Church Symphonies, the "Sinfonia grave" really marks the start of Rosenberg's mainline symphonic offering. Subtitle appears apt — a weighty Nordic opus of serious purpose and determined eloquence recalling Hindemith in its dignified solidity. In "Sinfonia grave" the composer made a summarized declaration of his experiences as a man and musician up to this point in his life, the fruit of at least seven years gestation and revision. The symphony contains a few echoes from Sibelius and Stenhammar, but on the whole it is a product of Rosenberg's own mind. The strongly rhythmic opening movement (Allegro energico) and concluding pages of the third movement (Allegro risoluto) convey a special kind of splendor and strike this listener as some of Rosenberg's finest music. The middle movement, however, runs into some difficulty as the composer tries to juggle the requirements of an adagio and scherzo at the same time.

SYMPHONY NO. 3 (1939)   (36')

Originally conceived as a symphonic drama for radio, Rosenberg's Third Symphony carried "The Four Ages of Man" as a title with readings from Rolland's *Jean Christophe* preceding each movement. Literary trappings, however, were discarded in subsequent revision. While not a through-and-through atonal work, the tightly constructed first movement (Moderato: Allegro) does build from an unpromising twelve-note motive darkly stated at the outset by cellos and basses. Main thrust of the symphony, however, holds off until movement three, a turbulent, aggressive Allegro con fuoco inspired by the trials and turmoil of adult life. The fourth and final movement (Andante semplice), little more than a senescent epilogue, avoids all heroics to close the fourth age of man on a note of simple dignity.

SYMPHONY NO. 4: JOHANNES UPPENBARELSE (Revelation of St. John) (1940)   (75')

Rosenberg had long pondered The Book of Revelation before starting on his Fourth Symphony; to him, this portion of the Bible meant "a vision of mankind's distress and suffering . . . a struggle of unconquerable belief in the final victory." In all likelihood the outbreak of war in 1939 spurred his need to organize his thoughts musically. Despite full soloist-chorus-orchestra apparatus, the Fourth Symphony is a very personal work, a type of symphonic cantata closer to, say, Brahms' *German Requiem* than the

196

straining, diffuse epics of Gustav Mahler. Forward pace of the Apocalyptic text breaks off at intervals to admit a series of unaccompanied chorales written in pure homophonic style, but taking texts from the contemporary "mobilization poetry" of Hjalmar Gullberg. These moments of sublime intimacy give this long but noble work a poignant extra dimension.

SYMPHONY NO. 6: SINFONIA SEMPLICE (1951)   (25')

For his Fifth Symphony Rosenberg erected an oratorio-like monolith even vaster than his "Revelation of St. John," to be followed by the immense opera-oratorio tetralogy *Joseph and His Brothers*. Evidently, by 1950, Rosenberg had worked monumental gigantism out of his system making a return to the comparative simplicity of his Sixth Symphony a natural event. "Sinfonia semplice" is possibly the smoothest of all Rosenberg's symphonies, music displaying the composer's expected elevated purpose, but here stated in a more restrained atmosphere almost neo-classic in its four balanced movements. Non-essentials have been weeded out, leaving a somewhat austere framework which the composer fills with terse drama, dry elegiac melody and rhythmic intensity.

CONCERTO FOR VIOLIN AND ORCHESTRA NO. 2 (1951)   (32')

The Second Violin Concerto, dedicated to the American-Scandinavian violinist Camilla Wicks, finds Rosenberg in top form. The laconic phrases and vehement rhythms of his symphonies step aside here for warm lyricism and a relaxed ramble through the three full movements of the standard concerto. The solo violin sometimes indulges in wayward banter, but Rosenberg's well-controlled orchestra prevents undue loquacity. Few if any clouds mar the horizon; it is sunshine all the way.

CONCERTO NO. 3 FOR ORCHESTRA: LOUISVILLE CONCERTO (1954)   (20')

Rosenberg's one turn "at bat" with the Louisville team's contemporary music recording project happily resulted in one of his most congenial scores. This salute to the New World could win many friends for Rosenberg if more widely known. Sturdy in construction and prompt in impact, the "Louisville Concerto" presents a model of musical efficiency. Not the least of its attractions appears in the final movement where Rosenberg incorporates a brisk theme reputedly of Lapp origin.

RESA TILL AMERIKA: SUITE (Journey to America) (1932)   (20')

Rosenberg's first opera, *Journey to America,* took up the pathos and humor of nineteenth-century emigrations from Scandinavia to the new world. In the end, however, the hero returns to stay beside his sorrowing sweetheart. While Kurt Weil and the jazzy *Zeitopern* ("now opera") style of postwar Berlin supposedly influenced Rosenberg, little hint of this crops up in the three-movement concert suite extracted from the full score. In the Harbor, the first movement, has impressionistic overtones and the second movement, Intermezzo, is as a soulful Nordic dirge. The suite rounds off with Railway Fugue which catches the rhythmic clicking of train wheels to end the piece in a surge of orchestral power.

ORFEUS I STAN: SUITE (Orpheus in Town) (1938)   (12')

No recognized musical form has escaped Rosenberg's determined pen.

Orpheus in Town, written for the Stockholm choreographers Vera Sager and Julian Algo, represents his major venture into ballet. The brilliantly orchestrated dance suite taken from the original score mingles thirties ballroom practice with driving "machine age" rhythms and other exotica including snatches from Gluck. The gist of the ballet has the Carl Milles sculpture group of Orpheus and friends erected in front of the Stockholm concert hall spring to life. Orpheus feverishly seeks his Eurydice in the market squares and nightclubs of the modern metropolis. Rosenberg selected six vivid choric episodes for his suite and hung them together in imaginative fashion: Rhythm of the Times, Bartender's Dance, Girl's Dance, Dance of the Negress, Trio Dance and Tango constitute the chosen numbers. Although not a particularly characteristic piece, *Orpheus in Town* abounds in vitality and shows Rosenberg at his most immediately communicative.

Chamber Music

STRING QUARTET NO. 5 (1949)

The crux and culmination of Rosenberg's intense involvement with chamber music begins and ends with the string quartet. His love affair with the abstractionist versus humanistic possibilities of this medium first appeared in the early twenties; full flowering has required a quarter of a century. The Fifth is vigorous and pithy, an astringent quartet in polyphonic linear style with motoric animation as a prime asset. Certain passages suggest Stenhammar, possibly an act of thinly disguised homage from Rosenberg to his onetime mentor.

STRING QUARTET NO. 6 (1953)

Rosenberg's string quartets generally make difficult listening. The Sixth is no exception. The piece may show coherence and balance on paper, but at the performance level the impersonal nature of its ideas and constantly shifting tonal centers cause the mind to wander. In at least three of the four movements inner compulsion seems lacking although everything is stated concisely. Firmer ground appears in movement three (Presto) where incisive rhythms help clarify goals.

STRING QUARTET NO. 7 (1956)

With his Seventh String Quartet Rosenberg entered an atonal phase, a time when he came to serious grips with serial methodology. Although he had known Schoenberg's work first hand in his youthful days, Rosenberg never has been one to truckle to "slide rule" formulas in his compositions. Consequently, his brand of dodecaphony generally continues what he had developed stylistically before. "It is the melodic and polyphonic in this technique which has inspired me," Rosenberg has explained, "not so much the sonorous aspect." Serialism, then, has not meant a radical departure for the composer, but merely a path to new polyphonic freedom. The comparatively tame Seventh Quartet is an essentially lyrical and friendly work.

STRING QUARTET NO. 8 (1957)

Historically, Rosenberg has thrown out a salvo of like pieces with each challenge encountered. But for the listener, each must be taken as it stands. In the Eighth Quartet, conservative use of twelve-tone technique subserves intense, declarative motives worked out in three generally austere movements. But Rosenberg's efforts to solve musical equations sound studied when compared to other players in the contemporary string quartet game like Elliott Carter or Witold Lutoslawski.

SONATA NO. 1 FOR SOLO VIOLIN (1921)

The deeply serious musician's inevitable reverence for J.S. Bach lies well forward among the motivating factors leading to Rosenberg's demonstrable interest in extended music for solo violin. His 1921 Sonata (apparently touched up in certain details at a much later date) falls into two broad movements, the second being a stimulating set of variations spiced by a hint of folk fiddling. By its very nature the solo violin sonata tends toward forbidding complexity, but in this work Rosenberg holds to his elevated plateau without sacrifice of clarity or warmth.

SONATA NO. 2 FOR SOLO VIOLIN (1953)

If the First Violin Sonata seems expansive, the Second shows the results of severe pruning and contraction. Rosenberg's typical dry lyricism, technical facility and constructivist thinking show tightening up all down the line. Something of a companion piece for the Sixth String Quartet composed the same year, the sonata seems more concerned with transition rather than summation, and the composer requires only two brief movements to make his point.

SONATA NO. 3 FOR SOLO VIOLIN (1963)

From the very first bars (Poco largamente) of his Third Sonata, Rosenberg sets a course of impassioned determination reminiscent of Ernest Bloch which he maintains the length of three movements. The work is rich in chordal material, double stops and other technical hurdles for the player, yet Rosenberg keeps his eye fixed on the broad lines of his essentially melodic inspiration. A high point in modern Swedish chamber music, Rosenberg's Third Sonata has been called a seventy-year-old's youthful, intensive affirmation to life.

SONATA FOR SOLO FLUTE (1959)

Rosenberg has produced all sorts of music for all sorts of reasons, so why not join his colleagues in new music for one of Scandinavia's most eminent soloists, the late Norwegian flute virtuoso Alf Andersen? In two extended movements, Rosenberg's contribution is expertly realized, but non-flutists may find the piece too strenuous a study in serious flute gymnastics.

WIND QUINTET (1959, rev. 1966)

The wind quintet has become such an established tradition in Nordic music that nothing in this department from a composer as prolific as Rosenberg would almost be unthinkable. Yet his response in this form took long in coming. The opening moments are quite striking, a long, poetic horn solo acting as a sort of prelude to the varied instrumental dialogues to follow. All told, the piece consists of seven uninterrupted movements built on twelve-tone melodic material and polyphonic interplay. Rosenberg ruminates in a pastoral mood at several points but closes on a note of good cheer. Racy wit and French frippery make no appearance here, rather Rosenberg's Quintet impresses more for its Swedish earnestness and solid craftsmanship.

Keyboard Music

ELVA SMÅ FÖREDRAGSSTUDIER (Eleven Small Performance Studies) (1925)

Personal mastery of both organ and piano guarantees as much authority in Rosenberg's keyboard compositions as in his more renowned orchestral and vocal works. The present set of moderately difficult pianoforte sketches have instruction as their principal purpose, yet they reveal a welcome amount of tuneful vitality.

IMPROVISATIONS (1939)

Taking departure from an austere but promising motive, Rosenberg develops a musically solid and pianistically interesting piece by means of a chain of étude-like free variations. As with some of Carl Nielsen's piano works, *Improvisations* stands a long distance from the school of Scandinavian picture postcard writing.

FANTASY AND FUGUE FOR ORGAN (1941)

The first of Rosenberg's sporadic contributions to organ literature, *Fantasy and Fugue* represents idiomatic, quality work if offering nothing particularly new to this traditional, well-worn coupling.

Vocal Music

DEN HELIGA NATTEN (The Holy Night) (1936)

A Yuletide cantata for popular consumption, *The Holy Night* has long been a staple item for Swedish radio's Christmas broadcasts. Simplicity and directness, therefore, guide this narrated musical account of the birth of Christ based on texts drawn from Luke, Matthew and John. Following a brief orchestral Prologue, alto solo and chorus present a Northerner's knowing picture of winter night's chill air and panoply of twinkling stars. Essentials of the Christmas story then are taken up as narration over orchestral accompaniment allowing time for ample reverent musical interludes bringing in Mary, the Wise Men, shepherds, Joseph and Herod. Use of punctuating fanfares becomes tedious as the cantata progresses, but clichés run second to effective moments especially the moving concluding number, "Song to the Star."

MARIONETTER (Marionettes) (1939)

The bright overture to Rosenberg's second opera quickly took its place as one of the composer's best-known concert pieces, but following the 1939 premiere *Marionettes* as an opera languished. But the 1967–68 Stockholm opera season witnessed a revival; nobody was more surprised than the composer himself to see his resurrected work win the enthusiastic acclaim of a new generation of opera-goers.

Based on the Jacinto Benavente play, *Los interesas creados,* Rosenberg's three-act *opera buffa* harks back to the commedia dell'arte with added twists of social satire. Two adventurers "flying from justice" (Crispin and Leandro) enter a small town where they soon find ample opportunity to unleash their store of tricks and deceptions on the hapless locals. A romancing couple becomes involved and plot complications finally lead to love triumphant over pettiness.

In *Marionettes,* the usually stern-faced symphonist and erudite producer of string quartets presents a completely different face. Rosenberg revels in the horseplay enlivening Act I where Crispin and his sidekick dupe a gullible innkeeper. He rises to heights of ravishing lyricism in the gorgeous love music of Act II described as a "night for poetry," and he draws all threads together with full mastery in Act III where a well-fashioned ballet episode embellishes his score. The Third Act arias for the two female leads Columbina and Silvia also deserve highest praise.

Marionettes may well be a worthy successor to Nielsen's *Maskerade*; certainly, an opera of this quality should become known far and wide.

MOTETS (1949)

After World War II, Swedish art circles received encouragement for contemporary design and adornments for church use; new liturgical music was also welcomed. Actually, Rosenberg stood ready with a dozen or so a cappella motets such as *Om I vänden* (In Returning and Rest) and *Se, såsom en handsbredd* (Behold, Thou Hast Made My Days as Handbreadths) from Psalm 39. In these examples, the composer achieves a high degree of serene intimacy.

For Further Exploration

Symphony No. 5 ("The Gardener); Symphony No. 7; Symphonic metamorphoses (3); *Riflessioni* for strings (3); Concertos for strings (4); "Bianca-nera" Overture; Piano Concerto; Viola Concerto; Cello concerto; Sinfonia Concertante; Violin/Piano Sonatas (2); Piano Sonatas (4); Sonatina for piano; *Joseph and His Brothers; Lycksalighetens ö* (The Isle of Bliss); *The Portrait*; songs.

HARALD SAEVERUD (b. 1897)

Like his American counterparts Roy Harris and Aaron Copland, the Norwegian composer Harald Saeverud has successfully applied the secrets of defeating old age, but added years of vigor have been accompanied by declining interest in the music of each. When Saeverud reached his seventieth birthday congratulatory messages poured in from all quarters. But all the back-pats, press interviews, special performances and *Festschriften* generated by this occasion could not blow away the unhappy fact that the world, Scandinavia included, has yet to grant Saeverud his due.

Saeverud is more than a regional composer; he is a strikingly original composer who prefers living and working in his native land. Individuality, not compositional method, defines his position above all else; Sir John Barbirolli put his finger on this fact when he said: "Whether you like the music of Saeverud or not there is no mistaking who wrote it, and this can be said of we composers of the present day." Saeverud's early, almost eccentric approach to writing music changed profoundly during the German occupation to become simpler, more direct and decidedly humanistic. But a streak of wild Norwegian stubbornness has always run through Saeverud's basically homespun idiom which can crackle with the cantankerousness of an angry troll. Born in Bergen and largely self-taught, Saeverud grew up fully aware of Norway's rich folkloric tradition of which he says, "I could never disavow that in words, nor in my music." But Saeverud would quickly add that he has "never tried to be Norwegian in any but my own way."

Orchestral Music

SYMPHONY NO. 2 IN C MINOR (1923, rev. 1934)   (20′)

Harald Saeverud's first orchestral music began reaching the public when he was only in his teens, and this precocious youngster seriously disturbed the Old Guard. However, Nina Grieg looked upon the young radical as the spirit of a new Norway while Carl Nielsen spread further calm when he assured the anxious by saying: "Just as Norwegian as Grieg's music, but in a different way." A key work in Saeverud's development, his Second Symphony contains sprouting seeds of his strongly individual style. Generally speaking, this music is harsh, discordant and uncompromising in contrapuntal vigor. Powerful rhythmic impulses sputter from the piece with telegraphic terseness and contrast with passages of cool lyricism at times flavored with curiously oriental sensuality. None of the symphony's three movements (Entrata dramatica, Andante mesto, Sonata grande) contain specific Norwegian references.

202

SINFONIA DOLOROSA (1942) (14')

Numerically sixth in a canon of nine, *Sinfonia dolorosa* is the composer's direct reaction upon hearing the fate of his friend Audun Lavik who was tortured, then murdered by the Nazis. This "Symphony of Sorrows" mirrors personal grief as well as smouldering resentment and defiance of the oppressors. Like the preceding Fifth or "Resistance" Symphony, the urgency of Saeverud's wartime messages demanded concise, stripped-down, single-movement construction with non-essentials cast aside. In this instance Saeverud employed a freely treated rondo based on two significant themes; these grow from heartfelt elegy to epic climax.

SALME (Psalm Symphony) (1945) (20')

Corresponding to Saeverud's Seventh Symphony, *Salme* forms a deeply sincere tribute to those fathers and mothers of Norway who endured five years of wartime privation and suffering. Although played as one continuous movement, the composer has designated five well-defined episodes: Hymns, Yuletide variations, Stave church chimes, Fugue and Glorification. Once again Saeverud builds by means of characteristic repetition-variation technique; this, coupled with his melodic forthrightness, imparts an almost crude strength to his symphonic thinking.

GALDRESLÅTTEN (The Sorcerer's Dance) (1943) (9')

English rendering of this title varies; designation as *Sorcerer's Dance* can be no worse than other suggestions like "The Enchanter's Ballad" or "The Witchcrafter." Said to have taken inspiration from the magic and sorcery of ancient Norse mythology, this typical Saeverud opus comes out a sardonic scherzo in three interconnected sections: symphonic dance, passacaglia and concluding dance. Specific programmatic allusions, as in the Sibelius tone poems, do not seem present. Saeverud's themes dovetail with ingenious unity, and he gives the piece a feeling of rapid motion by telling use of gallop rhythm.

KJEMPEVISESLÅTTEN (Ballad of Revolt) (1943) (5½')

This vehement piece offers a good example of Saeverud the forceful melodist. One day during the Occupation he came upon a German army barracks cluttering up the beautiful countryside near Bergen which blew his short Norwegian fuse. He began cursing under his breath; this took a pattern; suddenly the composer stopped short realizing he had a new musical idea. Originally for piano (Op. 22, No. 5), a postwar version for orchestra has traveled far even to popularity among Israeli patriots. *Ballad of Revolt* consists almost entirely of a relentless, repeated theme which gathers strength and builds toward defiant climax, a rising tide of protest structurally borrowing from a pattern found in Norwegian folk dance. According to the composer, the work's gradual crescendo must be "firm as steel in its drive."

PEER GYNT SUITE NO. 1 (1950) (18')

Grieg was neither the first nor Saeverud the latest composer motivated to bring music to the aid of Ibsen's famous satirical play *Peer Gynt*. Saeverud's purpose when fitting out appropriate incidental music for a radically different production of the play (Oslo, 1948) was not, as he put it, to "compete in a horse race" with the venerable Grieg score. Any comparison between the two composers on the subject of *Peer Gynt* must recognize that Grieg concentrated on the play's tragic aspects and colorful exoticism, while Saeverud went along with the producer's concept of a "de-romanticized" *Peer Gynt* with raw nerves fully exposed.

In his prickly *Peer Gynt Suite No. 1,* which generally conforms to the action through the first half of the play, Saeverud meets the challenge of unmitigated realism head on, although in a sometimes heavy-handed way as in the opening numbers, The Devil's Five-Hop and Dovretroll Jog. But the composer's sharp wit takes over when he comes to Mixed Company, a collage of national airs and anthems fleshing out Ibsen's original wish for an entre'acte musically compressing Gynt's global wanderings. Solveig Sings emerges as a stark, simple melody reminiscent of some ancient ballad. As for the sultry Bedouin charmer Anitra, Saeverud sounds as contrived as Grieg, although one critic commented that Saeverud had painted a more life-like picture of the girl, "dirty feet" and all.

PEER GYNT SUITE NO. 2 (1957)   (19')

Saeverud's Second Suite emits less boisterousness than the troll-laden First Suite, but does include the opening number for the whole play coyly designated Peer-ludium. Otherwise various scenes from the last part of *Peer Gynt* are deftly sketched with considerable cleverness shown by the composer in the handling of his small, pit-size orchestra.

Keyboard Music

LETTE STYKKER FOR KLAVER (Easy Pieces for Piano) (1939)

Saeverud's unique, economical keyboard style by and large carries forward the Kjerulf-Grieg legacy of brief character pieces suitable for amateur and professional alike. Most of his piano pieces show a diatonic melodic line interwoven with two-part polyphony and quaint, freely modal harmony. The first set of *Lette Stykker* offers seven numbers including memorable gems like *Syljetone* (Peasant Heirloom Brooch), *Li-Tone* (Hillside Melody) and the charmingly impressionistic *Vindharpe-slåtten* (Aeolian Harp Tunes). Main attraction, however, is the wistful *Rondo Amoroso,* probably the most popular single piece of twentieth-century Scandinavian piano music. This listener first heard *Rondo Amoroso* from the composer's hands; as he played he remarked with baffled wonderment, "If they gave me 100,000 Crowns I could never do this again."

A second "set" of *Lette Stykker* (1942) contains only a single piece: *Småfugl-vals* (Little Bird's Waltz), a further characteristic example of Saeverud's good-humored piano style.

SLATTER OG STEV FRA "SILJUSTØL" (Dances and Tunes from "Siljustøl") (1943)

Saeverud's stone and timber hilltop home "Siljustøl" lies about a half hour's drive from Bergen. Here in the early forties, during the dark days of the Occupation, he worked on five volumes of short piano pieces influenced by his country's folk music. Of these angular, generally animated compositions only *Ballad of Revolt* (later orchestrated) makes specific reference to those trying wartime years. In fact, most of the pieces seem an escape into homespun sentiment, humor and daydreaming. Particularly delightful examples include *Revebjølle* (Digitalis purpurea), *Brudemarsj* (Bridal March), *Hamar-Tor slåtten* (Thor the Hammerer) and *Bjonn' Støkk-Lokk* (Beware Bear). In *Den siste bå'nlåt* (Her Last Cradlesong), Saeverud indicates a closer affinity to Grieg than generally seems realized.

SIX SONATINAS FOR PIANO (1948–50)

Budding pianists rather than ordinary listeners are most likely to benefit from these piquant bitonal mini-sonatas, collectively a sort of Norwegian counterpart to Bartók's celebrated *Mikrokosmos*. Despite Saeverud's dry, laconic manner of piano writing, melodic impulses are by no means suppressed, notably Sonatina No. V designated "Quasi una fantasia."

Vocal Music

SJA SOLI PA ANARIPIGG (Shepherd's Farewell) (1952)

Generally speaking, Saeverud has sidestepped the northland's great song and choral tradition, but *Shepherd's Farewell*, a brief a cappella choral work, has enjoyed considerable popularity along the Scandinavian concert circuit. The composer's craftsmanship with mixed choir lies beyond complaint, his mood one of mild nostalgia.

For Further Exploration

Symphonies Nos. 1, 3, 5 ("Quasi una fantasia"), 8 ("Minnesota Symphony"), 9; *Gjetlevisevariasjoner* (Variations on a Shepherd's Tune); Sinfonia Concertante "Allegria"; Piano Concerto; Violin Concerto; Bassoon Concerto; *Entrata regale; The Rape of Lucretia* (incidental music); *Bluebeard's Nightmare* (ballet); 20 small duos for violins (or winds).

CHRISTIAN SINDING (1856–1941)

Although raised by a widowed mother in the old Norwegian mining town of Kongsberg, all three of the Sinding boys heeded the call of art — Christian in music while his brothers made names for themselves in painting and sculpture. For a while Christian Sinding received training at home from Ludvig Mathias Lindeman, but his musical personality became more decisively shaped in the great German music centers: Leipzig, Berlin, Dresden, Munich. Sinding knew them all. His artistic temperament became strong, assertive; to admirers he held forth the image of the fighter, man of action and composer-as-hero. While Sinding's music usually shows unmistakable Nordic tendencies, his style only occasionally incorporated deep Norwegian feeling, setting him a good distance from Grieg. The viking blood determination, chivalric spirit and face-to-the-gale determination of his symphonic and chamber music once found great favor in foreign concert halls particularly in Germany and the United States. Conductors like Felix Weingartner and Arthur Nikisch helped spread his fame on the Continent while Americans got to know him firsthand when he became a professor at the Eastman School of Music in Rochester, New York (1921–1922).

But tastes change. Sinding's name became scarce on concert programs by the late twenties as audiences wearied of musical sauerbraten. Finally, mutual admiration between Sinding and Germany turned into a bitter pill when the befuddled octagenerian let himself be used as a propaganda tool by the Nazis; understandably, this act dampened enthusiasm for the old master's music in Norwegian quarters. With talk about a "romantic revival," however, the music of Christian Sinding shows some signs of a comeback. This can only be viewed as heartening because some of his works, particularly what he wrote between 1880 and 1890, contain inherent worth and repay looking into.

Orchestral Music

SUITE IN A MINOR (1888)

Grieg held keen admiration for the music of his younger countryman; he not only appreciated Sinding's harmonic boldness and command of larger forms, but also took delight in the way he could decant old baroque legacies into new bottles much the way Grieg did himself in the *Holberg Suite*. Sinding's Suite in A minor amounts to a restyled Bach-like violin concerto written with dazzling skill if not excessive reverence. The opening Presto demands a true virtuoso at the helm if only to maintain the merciless indicated tempo. This swift movement also displays ample contrapuntal ingenuity. The broad handling of lyricism in the Adagio well demonstrates the stylistic differences between Sinding and Grieg. In the

206

finale (Tempo giusto), Sinding works violinistic brilliance into a dance pattern built up toward a resolute conclusion.

Keyboard Music

VARIATIONS FOR TWO PIANOS IN E-FLAT MAJOR (1886)

Both the virtues and faults of Sinding's style become manifest in his duo-piano variations (Op. 2), a work lying very close to the German tradition via Brahms. On the credit side, the composer starts with a short motive first heard in the bass which proves ideal for variation expansion. What follows is music of manly strength and striking harmonic imagination. But, like Max Reger, Sinding suffered from the habit of sometimes not leaving a good thing well enough alone. In these piano variations texture grows increasingly dense, points once made are relentlessly hammered home, the two keyboards thunder under a barrage of counterpoint. Yet if a certain amount of late-romantic excess can be overlooked (after all, Sinding was a child of his time) the work provides interesting discourse demonstrated by firm assurance and thoughtful musicianship.

SOLO PIANO MUSIC

Sinding's work for solo piano makes up a sizable pile of scores running through approximately a dozen opus numbers. Most of these pieces show fairly simple construction with designations split between generic and suggestive titles. Most famous of all is, of course, *Rustle of Spring* (Op. 32, No. 3) composed in 1887 and known throughout the world both in original form and numerous arrangements. Of the smattering of Sinding's other piano pieces heard so far, this listener finds the Prelude in A-flat (Op. 34, No. 1) typical of the composer's Nordic hero stance, a virile outpouring of rolling chromatic arpeggios in the left hand topped by full, rich chords in the right. Melodie in G (Op. 32, No. 2) and Nocturne in F-sharp (Op. 118, No. 4) seem confined to romantic conventions. Nocturne in B-flat (Op. 53, No. 2), on the other hand, stands out for particularly memorable melody. The little mood picture Crepuscule in F minor (Dawn, Op. 34, No. 4) almost modulates itself out of existence. Sinding moves closer to Grieg and Mendessohn in Caprice in F minor (Op. 44, No. 13), a captivating type of scherzo calling for fleet-fingered dexterity.

Chamber Music

QUINTET IN E MINOR FOR PIANO AND STRINGS (1885)

A sensation in its day, the Sinding Opus 5 Piano Quintet bristles with what once seemed like outrageous harmonic audacity. Tchaikovsky, according to anecdote, proved himself a musical prude upon ruffling through the score; in shocked tones he pronounced the work full of wrong notes. Well before the nineteenth century had ended, however, the piece had made the rounds of most of the world's music centers to firmly establish Sinding as one of the more important younger composers of Europe.

Whatever the reasons for the Quintet's long absence from the standard chamber music repertoire, the fault does not lie with the composer; he produced a masterpiece in the quintet class. The opening Allegro ma non troppo, almost symphonic in concept, can trace lineage to the Brahms-

Schumann school but with new, highly imaginative transformation. Material already presented receives further treatment in the songful Andante. Movement three (Intermezzo, Vivace) brings further delight, a youthfully energetic scherzo skipping happily along like a child released in a garden. First movement strength resumes in the Finale, a rapidly delivered yet elaborate peroration of rugged Norse disposition. On all counts the Sinding Piano Quintet makes a worthy addition to what Brahms, Franck and Dvorák contributed to the genre.

Vocal Music

SONGS

Sinding stands as one of Scandinavia's major song composers. Yet both during the 78 rpm days and in the LP-tape era to date recorded representation of his some 250 works for solo voice with accompaniment can only be described as wretchedly inadequate. Pending a change in this state of affairs, the bulk of his songs must remain unknown to the phono-graphic explorer. Today, Sinding the song writer holds attention mainly through his heartfelt *Sylvelin* (words by the minor Norwegian author Vetle Vislie, not Sinding himself as some accounts have it). This song shines with soft radiance, a mood of adoration sustained by the composer's dis-creet use of glissando in his accompaniment. Sinding's songs have been spoken of as Grieg-like, but this hardly seems the case when comparing versions of Vilhelm Krag's poem *Der skreg en fugl* (Scream of a Bird). With Grieg, the whole message is conveyed elementally, like a rapidly com-pleted charcoal sketch; Sinding paints the full picture, a song filled with romantic melancholy.

Of the lesser-known Sinding songs, *Leit etter livet og liv det* (Take Hold of Life and Live It) treads the broad, hearty path so typical of the composer. Norwegian folk spirit, not common in Sinding's music, comes out full-blown in *Den Jomfru gik i valmuvang* (A Maiden Strolls in the Poppy Fields), a gay and thoroughly charming song. Sinding the out-spoken patriot may be heard in *Vi Vil Os Et Land* (We Will Have Our Land).

Although Sinding tried his hand in a couple of operas, his major vocal production was largely devoted to song; unlike most Norwegian composers of his generation, he left little of importance in the realm of choral music.

For Further Exploration

Symphonies (3); Piano Concerto in D-flat major; Violin Concertos (2); *Suite: In Olden Style; Episodes chevaleresques; Rondo infinito;* String Quartet; Piano Trios (3); Piano Sonata; Variations "Cantus doloris"; *Der heilige Berg* (The Holy Mountain); *Titandros;* piano music; songs; folk-song arrangements.

WILHELM EUGEN STENHAMMAR (1871-1927)

An aroma of aristocracy surrounded Stenhammar. The man upheld and his music reflected a patrician attitude accompanied by a deep sense of artistic responsibility and instinctive feeling for superior craftsmanship. (Stenhammar's bearing had a basis in fact: his mother's side of the family descended from the Vasa kings). His earlier works paid due homage to the German monarchs — Wagner, Brahms, Bruckner — but maturity brought him closer to the frail thread of a true Swedish musical tradition which Stenhammar traced back to Berwald; he carried this line forward, a Swedish presence linking the disparate worlds of his good friends Sibelius and Carl Nielsen.

More and more Stenhammar looms as one of Scandinavia's major musical figures. Although by no means as powerful a symphonist as Sibelius or Nielsen, his orchestral music is estimable, the songs superlative, the chamber music without peer in the North. Stenhammar could turn out patriotic pieces and the lilt of folk song sometimes flitted across his pages, but the essential Swedish nature of his music was born of the refined sensibilities of the man himself. Folklore as such held only limited fascination for Stenhammar, and while not despised, his artistic aims went beyond mere ethnic glorification. He became wary of committing his entire creative philosophy to narrow restrictions; he doubted the "liberating effect" of folk music at a time when these sources were fast drying up. Stenhammar clearly saw that the best urbanized society could do for folk music would be to keep it alive by artificial respiration. Loftier ideals were needed to renew music in Sweden, and time has since proven the validity of Stenhammar's foresight.

Orchestral Music

SYMPHONY NO. 2 IN G MINOR (1915)   (45')

Stenhammar completed two symphonies. The First (F major) rarely reaches performance, but the Second Symphony composed some twelve years later impresses this listener as the outstanding Swedish work in this form to appear between Berwald and Rosenberg. The opening movement (Allegro energico) beautifully exemplifies the Nordic sound, a strong, saga-like statement surging with drama and impassioned earnestness. Similar outgoing vigor characterizes the third movement, a scherzo (Allegro ma non troppo presto) which recalls Bruckner in its energy and solidity. In a late-romantic symphony of this type, the center of gravity might be expected to rest in the slow movement, but Stenhammar prefers a comparatively restrained Andante; he shifts main emotional strength to the finale, an architecturally complex movement where seven intertwined episodes build on fugue, variations and thematic evolution. Sometimes sheer weightiness impedes the flow and the movement strains heavily forward. Yet the grandeur and nobility of Stenhammar's ideas eventually win through.

SERENADE FOR LARGE ORCHESTRA (1913, rev. 1919)   (33')

Stenhammar's concept of a "serenade" drifts considerably from classical Viennese models; no "a little night music" here. Like Reger and Dvorák, his serenade becomes expanded almost to symphonic proportions, although heroics retire in favor of more subdued moods and melodies. Not unreasonably, this piece might be considered Stenhammar's pastoral symphony. Movements entitled Overtura and Finale anchor stem and stern with center of the *Serenade* held by a block of three movements played without pause (Canzonetta, Scherzo, Notturno). The rhythmic kick of the Scherzo with its delightful horn passages proves immediately attractive. Equally inspired pages appear in the Notturno and buoyant Finale. Although eclectic and long-winded in spots, Stanhammar's *Serenade* remains a choice example of late-romantic Swedish music.

CONCERTO NO. 2 FOR PIANO AND ORCHESTRA (1907)   (30′)

Revived interest in the blood-and-thunder romantic piano concerto might swing the spotlight of international attention back to sadly neglected pieces like this worthy Stenhammar opus. Resounding chords, bravura chromatic passages, opulent melody once again command the interest of serious listeners all over the world. These elements find their way into Stenhammar's Second Concerto, music of vintage similar to MacDowell or Rachmaninoff, but Stenhammar distinguishes himself by not falling victim to prolixity or overdrawn sentiment. He moves through a gamut of poetic feelings supported by intimate knowledge of the pianoforte, casting his concerto in four movements yet welding them together as a whole played without pause. Inspiration never falters as this concerto continues on course with confident determination.

The A minor Piano Concerto by Grieg by no means exhausts the romantic concerto in Scandinavia. Sinding, Palmgren and others also contributed highly interesting entries in this field. Stenhammar must be added to this company, for his strong Second Piano Concerto ranks among the best from Nordic sources.

MELLANSPEL UR "SÅNGEN" (Intermezzo from "The Song") (1921) (6′)

Performances of the complete cantana *Sången* (composed for the 150th anniversary of the Swedish Royal Academy of Music) are rare, but recent years have seen the mid-point Intermezzo attain status as one of Stenhammar's best-known orchestral works. The ecstatic mood, stately pace and pauses for brass chorales found here bear uncanny likeness to the style of Anton Bruckner. As short Scandinavian concert pieces go, this one rates a gold star.

SUITE FROM "CHITRA" (1921)   (14′)

This pleasant, but pallid music for Rabindranath Tagore's forgotten play about the legendary Princess Chitra adds little to Stenhammar's stature.

TWO SENTIMENTAL ROMANCES FOR VIOLIN AND ORCHESTRA (1910) (12′)

Sharing the same year of composition and opus number, this pair of contrasting long-songs for soloist with orchestra was evidently conceived as a single piece. Both offer the more generally familiar Svendsen Romance substantial competition. No. 1 (in F minor) sings eloquently; No. 2 (in A major) delves deeper into impassioned argument with more than a hint of ruffled waters.

Chamber Music

STRING QUARTET NO. 2 IN C MINOR (1896)

Without disrespect for the earnest poetry of Grieg or the acuity of Carl Nielsen (not to mention such later dedicated practitioners of Nordic chamber music as Vagn Holmboe and Hilding Rosenberg), a personal impression singles out Wilhelm Stenhammar as the one Scandinavian composer who has written most naturally and *con amore* for string quartet. In this area Stenhammar developed his ideas within the great European classical tradition, and his Second String Quartet clearly proceeds from archtypes of Beethoven's "Rasoumovsky" period. The twenty-five-year-old Stenhammar more than showered credit on his model. His Second Quartet seems driven by restless, questioning energy impeccably portioned out to the four voices. Outer movement rises in emotional temperature find balanced contrast in the seraphic slow movement and the peaceable conclusion. This is rich, eloquent and sometimes passionate music; a distinguished quartet by any standard.

STRING QUARTET NO. 3 IN F MAJOR (1900)

In his Third Quartet Stenhammar turns from classical poise to a more robust romantic attitude. In the work's four movements he advances on his goals with unstilted directness: an opening Quasi andante of warm, singing character, then a flying scherzo (Presto molto agitato), next relaxation in a deeply felt Lento sostenuto. The final word emerges from a context of dramatic agitation (Presto molto agitato/moderato). Evidence at hand points to the Stenhammar Third Quartet inching its way into the international chamber music repertoire where this magnificent music most assuredly belongs.

STRING QUARTET NO. 5 IN C MAJOR: SERENADE (1910)

Discovery of Stenhammar's six string quartets can lead to many hours of enrichment. His fifth member of the series makes an ideal starting point, a vivacious and comparatively lighthearted work which enthralls at once, like the sudden burst of a northern Spring. Organization is concise and masterful. In place of the customary four-movement plan, Stenhammar dispensed with the slow movement to substitute a striking set of variations on the folk song *The Knight Finn Komfusenfej,* one of the few occasions when he made open use of such material. No two of Stenhammar's quartets are alike, a sure sign of his broad command of this difficult art form.

SONATA IN A MINOR FOR VIOLIN AND PIANO (1900)

Considering Stenhammar's powerful capabilities as a pianist and his close familiarity with the performance of chamber music (through his long association with the Aulin Quartet), a duo sonata from his hand naturally would arouse great expectations. Unfortunately, this is not the case. His sole violin/piano sonata seems a merely pleasant, unhurried gesture avoiding the sharp contrasts and emotions found in the string quartets. Delicate

211

charm and intimate reflections emerge, but the total effect is disappointingly flat, like a passionless love letter. Much of this music may remind listeners of the aloof, restrained romanticism of Fauré.

Keyboard Music

THREE FANTASIES (1895)

Although fully capable of exploiting the resources of the piano, Stenhammar never produced works for his chosen instrument comparable to the best of Chopin, but it seems reasonable to consider him a sort of Nordic Rachmaninoff. The *Three Fantasies* provide good examples of Stenhammar's fully aroused late-romantic feelings, music which glances inwardly at some points but much of it seems born of almost urgent emotional pressure. In the first, strikingly emotive number (Molto appassionato) a commanding melody sweeps across the keyboard, one glowing with full, rich chords and assertive progressions. An almost sober playfulness occurs in the second fantasy (Dolce scherzando). The unmistakable cadences of Swedish folk song look up from the pages of the concluding number (Molto espressivo e con intimissimo sentimento).

SENSOMMARNÄTTER (Late Summer Nights) (1914)

Supposedly written as Stenhammar's answer to the popular piano characterizations by Peterson-Berger, these five short pieces have a somewhat dry and studied quality (most apparent in the first three); they only prove that vignettes for popular consumption were not Stenhammar's forte. The fifth number, however, designated Poco allegretto, does veer close to the "lyric piece" idiom and even manages to sound a bit Griegish. What really makes this collection memorable is piece number four (Presto agitato), a veritable tiny diamond among rhinestones; here Stenhammar brings some of his most fragrant poetry to bear.

Vocal Music

SONGS

In Wilhelm Stenhammar the listener encounters one of Scandinavia's most engaging, and important, contributors to art song. Stenhammar not only revealed himself as a child prodigy at the piano, but by the age of sixteen he was an established songwriter. The developmental years brought him into personal contact with the major poets energizing Sweden's literary renaissance of the 1890s, notably Oscar Levertin and Verner von Heidenstam. Musical inspiration also came from the poetry of Runeberg, Fröding and Karfeldt, but special affinity arose for his closer contemporary Bo Bergman, the prime source of Stenhammar's song texts.

No other Swedish song composer — not even Ture Rangström — outstripped Stenhammar in his clear, musical perception of poetic values. The mood and meter of the verse itself closely directed the melody, harmony and rhythm of Stenhammar's songs. Most of them can be called "through composed" while accompaniments tend toward simplicity and discreet use of color. In almost no instance can Stenhammar be accused of fitting words to preconceived melodies, a dangerous practice sometimes charged against Peterson-Berger.

Stenhammar's aristocratic outlook and elevated artistic purpose might seem to set barriers against any popularization in his art, but this was not always the case. His pen produced one of the most beloved of all Swedish songs, the devoutly patriotic *Sverige* (Sweden, 1905), originally part of the cantata *Ett folk*. This has virtually become a second national anthem.

Comprehensive treatment of Stenhammar's many songs in recorded form remains a project for the future, but enough of them have reached discs to gauge the composer's mastery of this genre. His first published song retains a reasonable degree of currency: *I skogen* (In the Forest), a Schumannesque charmer from Stenhammar's teen-age years. *Flickan kom från sin älsklings möte* (The Maiden Came from the Tryst) also comes from the composer's youthful period, but a song showing mature understanding of Runeberg's poem even when compared to the far more widely known setting by Sibelius. Runeberg displayed interest in folk materials in his group of poems known as "Idyls and Epigrams," reflected in the Stenhammar song *Flickan knyter i Johannenatten* (Girl Knitting on St. John's Eve). In *Fylgia* (poem by Fröding) Stenhammar produced a stunning vocal masterpiece, one of the truly great Swedish art songs where tragic undercurrents underlie a gorgeous melodic outpouring.

Like Stenhammar, the poet Bo Bergman clung to a patrician view of the world. His earlier writings dealt with fatalistic pessimism joined to escapist imagery, a way of looking at things which exerted much influence on Stenhammar. In *Adagio* poet and composer speak as one voice projecting a melancholic mood which yearns to join a flight of wild swans in the sky. *Stjärnöga* (Starry Eyes), one of Stenhammar's more popular songs, seems a lesser offering. Of later Stenhammar/Bergman songs from the years 1906–1909, special attention must go to *Jungfru Blond och jungfru Brunett* (Blonde and Brunette Maidens), a song of balladic character and to the delightfully light-hearted *Det far ett skepp* (There Sails a Ship). Bo Bergman's outspoken love affair with his native Stockholm found sympathetic response from Stenhammar when he set some of the *Stockholm Poems* during 1918. One of these, *En positivvisa* (Hurdy-Gurdy Song), has become one of Stenhammar's most often-performed songs.

THREE A CAPPELLA CHORAL SONGS (1890)

Two of these Danish poetry settings (after J.P. Jacobsen) sound frugal and merely meditative, namely, *September* and *I Seraillets Have* (In the Seraglio Garden). The final number, however, conveys more spark of life. *Havde jeg, a havde jeg en dattersøn* (Oh, If I Had a Grandson) demonstrates smooth part writing augmented by a whiff of folk tone.

For Further Exploration

Symphony No. 1; *Excelsior*; String Quartets Nos. 1, 4, 6; *Sången*; *Gildet på Solhaug* (The Feast at Solhaug); *Midvinter*; *Ett folk*; Piano Sonata in A-flat major; songs.

213

JOHAN SEVERIN SVENDSEN (1840–1911)

Nineteenth-century Norway cradled several interesting composers, but at least two merit front rank positions: Edvard Grieg and Johan Svendsen. Their backgrounds and talents, however, differed in many ways. Svendsen was an East Norwegian, born in Christiania. He grew up a poor boy earning money from an early age playing the fiddle at dances and weddings and following his father's footsteps for a while as a military bandsman. These boyhood experiences were similar to those of Carl Nielsen, a common bond cementing friendship in later years when Svendsen the prominent conductor generously encouraged Nielsen the fledgling symphonist.

A seasoned musician by twenty-one Svendsen laid plans for a concert violinist's career, but a crippling condition in one hand forced his path toward conducting and composition. Constant moves occupied much of his early career. Stopovers included the Leipzig Conservatory where his genius bloomed, the violin section of Musard's Odéon Orchestra at Paris, Bayreuth and New York to get married. Along the way Svendsen made friends with Liszt, Wagner, Sarasate and other members of Europe's musical elite.

The years 1872–1877 (his most productive as a composer) found Svendsen back in Christiania helping conduct the Music Society concerts and doing much to improve a still provincial musical climate. Grieg relished his presence, but much as Svendsen loved his native land, restless ambition required more than Norway could provide. When offered the coveted post of conductor at Copenhagen's Royal Theater Svendsen found the opportunity impossible to refuse. Unfortunately his move to Denmark in 1883 for all intents and purposes shut the book on his creative life; he lost all further desire to compose and quit on the threshold of great fame. But what Svendsen did complete securely fixes his name to the laureate list of Nordic musicians.

Orchestral Music

SYMPHONY NO. 1 IN D MAJOR (1866)   (35')

Svendsen's First Symphony clearly shows what Grieg lacked, Svendsen possessed — the ability to organize large musical structures and move comfortably within them. Written when still a student at the Leipzig Conservatory, anecdote indicates that Svendsen dashed off the symphony as an act of "one-upmanship" against some snide remarks from his composition teacher (Carl Reinicke). True or not, this robust, outgoing music contains a wealth of appropriate ideas developed in a climate of spontaneity and formal balance. Both outer movements move with a strong, virile stride while the rich slow movement and light-footed third movement

214

(Allegretto scherzando) glow with inspiration not entirely remote from Norwegian associations.

SYMPHONY NO. 2 IN B-FLAT MAJOR (1876)   (25')
In his second statement in symphonic form, Svendsen displays greater subtlety and emotional involvement than in his First Symphony, but at the expense of youthful drive. Overt national romanticism held limited influence over Svendsen's work, but his Second Symphony supposedly sums up an artist's life and inward reflections in a reawakened Norway. This conclusion finds most convincing realization in the heartfelt Andante which swells to a great lyrical outburst.

CARNIVAL IN PARIS (1872)   (12')
If not necessarily his best, *Carnival in Paris* has proven Svendsen's most durable opus, one of the few nineteenth-century scores from Norway not by Grieg to remain on active duty with the world's orchestras. Indebted to Berlioz, the piece essentially consists of a vibrant scherzo split by an extended lyrical section, music reflecting the composer's love for the life and nostalgic memories of the great city where he worked and studied in his younger years. The superb orchestration of this reliable showpiece still commands admiration.

NORWEGIAN ARTISTS' CARNIVAL (1874)   (6½')
This rousing, but not particularly memorable Svendsen enterprise acts as a sort of sequel to *Carnival in Paris* with locale shifted to a peasant wedding in the Norwegian mountains. But despite some healty whiffs of the *Halling* and *Springdans,* events seem forced and contrived.

FESTIVAL POLONAISE (1873)   (8')
Still a widely-known "pops" concert favorite, Svendsen's *Festival Polonaise* honored a state visit to Christiania by the newly crowned Swedish-Norwegian monarch Oscar II. A fine example of Svendsen's command of the orchestra, the opulent *Festival Polonaise* creates the distinct impression of gilt-edged ballet music. This obvious fact required time to sink in, but choreographic possibilities were finally realized when Harald Lander used this music for his ballet *Fest-Polonaise* (Copenhagen, 1942).

ZORAHAYDA (1873)   (14')
Atypical Svendsen, one of the subtlest and possibly the most beautiful orchestral piece from Norwegian sources, *Zorahayda* takes inspiration from Irving's *The Legend of the Rose of the Alhambra.* Openly programmatic, this tone poem depicts a supernatural encounter beside one of the Alhambra's splashing fountains. A Christian maiden meets the cursed ghost of a long-dead Moorish princess (Zorahayda). The ghost begs for baptism; the maiden feels pity and sprinkles water from the fountain over the head of the phantom. "Then Zorahayda, her countenance transfigured, laid her silver lute down gently by the fountain, folded her white arms over her bosom and, smiling on the young girl with a tenderness ineffable, disappeared . . . ." But her silver lute remained behind. Svendsen allows

215

ample time for requisite ethereal mood to unfold and moves toward an impassioned climax with steady control. His orchestra paints the full picture aided by complex subdivisions among the strings.

NORWEGIAN RHAPSODIES (4) (1872–1877)

For a composer in Norway during the 1870s to have ignored the national romantic outpouring would have been superhuman. In this climate Svendsen's four *Norwegian Rhapsodies* became inevitable. These pieces followed the Second Symphony, but somehow the composer does not seem entirely committed to ethnic material, pleasant as he makes these rhapsodies thanks to colorful and lucid orchestration. The national romantic side of Johann Svendsen is perhaps more convincingly represented by his arrangements of Ole Bull and the Scandinavian airs arranged for strings (Op. 20).

ROMANCE FOR VIOLIN AND ORCHESTRA (1881)   (7½')

Time has muffled Svendsen's two early concertos (one for violin, one for cello), but his *Romance* carries on in the favor of violinists the world over. A determined publisher, so the story goes, brought impatience to an end by locking the procrastinating Svendsen in a room until he finished this score. A touch of genteel sadness clings to this music, maybe a sign that Svendsen knew this to be his swan song as a composer. At any rate, the *Romance* is beautifully poised and entirely uncomplicated, a long-spun cantilena over discreet orchestral support, lovely music as fresh as the day it was written.

Chamber Music

STRING QUARTET IN A MINOR (1865)

In decided contrast to Grieg, who more than once claimed he hated the place, Svendsen declared his student days at the Leipzig Conservatory "the happiest of my life." Certainly this optimism shines from the important works (First Symphony and chamber music) which Svendsen completed during these years of formal study. The A minor String Quartet (Op. 1), Svendsen's sole essay in this form, became eclipsed by a more popular string octet written about the same time. This seems an undeserved fate because, in some ways, the more tightly-knit quartet comes off as the superior work. While hardly electrifying, the quartet offers smooth part writing, positive outlook and a dash of Norwegian heartiness.

OCTET FOR STRINGS (1866)

At one time a frequently performed piece in Germany as well as Scandinavia, the Octet finds youthful zest matched by skill in instrumental writing. Yet four full movements and a paucity of truly toothsome melodic material create more the feeling of an overenthusiastic ramble. On the other hand, Svendsen did not set out to compose a divertimento, but rather a serious piece for eight strings on the model of Mendelssohn and perhaps as a proving ground for the gestating First Symphony. In these goals he succeeded with distinction.

Vocal Music

Song writing belonged to Svendsen's lesser efforts, and the few he produced lie tucked away in odd corners of his works list. *Lang Sel* (Waiting) and *Venetian Serenade* still receive occasional performance. In *Violen* (The Violet) the composer set a poem by Mrs. Svendsen.

For Further Exploration

Sigurd Slembe (overture); *Romeo and Juliet* (fantasy overture); Cello Concerto; Violin Concerto: String Quintet.

FARTEIN VALEN (1887–1952)

Fartein Valen, Norway's most rarified composer, first reached general attention during the 1947 ISCM convocation at Copenhagen. He was then in his sixties, a fact which alone raised curiosity in vanguard circles about his place in the musical firmament. Since then, ample biographical and works information has become available, but sometimes fuzzed by idolatry. Was Valen truly a significant twentieth-century pathfinder or merely a peculiar type of introvert who made a nice try? To the cultic faithful, Valen stands on a pedestal, a musician of consummate importance. According to Bjarne Korsten, a particularly ardent disciple: "Fartein Valen must undoubtedly be reckoned as the leading Norwegian composer since Grieg and Svendsen." But, even in Norway, not everyone is yet ready to accept such opinions hands down.

In some ways Valen can be likened to Charles Ives. Each developed an intensely personal, unorthodox style ahead of its time. Their works were produced in comparative isolation and suffered near-total misunderstanding from the public whenever presented. But where Ives could leap from his seat to berate a hostile audience with salty ripostes like the famous "Shut up, you damn sissies, and listen!" unfriendly reactions from press or public would deeply wound Valen, almost a personification of Caspar Milquetoast. Faced with rejection of his music, Valen was known to run, hide and console himself in the pages of the Bible. Yet back of this timid, retiring exterior lay a true intellectual, an erudite man with deep religious faith and consistent artistic convictions.

Except for Denmark's Jørgen Bentzon, who wavered in the face of full atonal commitment, Valen pushed forward on his own to stake out rightful claim as Scandinavia's first and most dedicated non-tonal composer prior to the 1950s. Much of his mature music was penned under isolated — one is tempted to say secretive — conditions in Valevaag, a lonely family farm about a hundred miles down the coast from Bergen. Before his retirement from a music librarian's post at Oslo University, Valen built up a local reputation as a composition teacher. But Klaus Egge, Sparre Olsen and others who came to him at various times showed scant inclination to carry on their teacher's free-wheeling atonal idiom. Valen, like Rosenberg in Sweden, had picked up the revolutionary significance of Schoenberg in Berlin during the 1920s, but his admiration never ran too deep. Keeping Schoenberg's system at arm's length, Valen proceeded to elaborate his own brand of atonality based on free canonic treatment of terse motives having only approximate functions of the Schoenbergian note row. His music became linear, moving through a web of dissonant counterpoint with an ascetic's horror of orchestral coloration.

He became masterful in his ability to condense his thoughts (almost to the point of dessication) and balance tension and release. The results sometimes recall late Mahler or Alban Berg.

Two decades after his death, Valen's art remains abstruse, the composer still a "special case." While the average listener may never warm up to the singular music of Fartein Valen, concentrated listening can yield the satisfaction of getting to know a bold pioneer with a very pure soul.

Orchestral Music

PASTORALE FOR ORCHESTRA (1930) (5')

The first of Valen's nine essays or tone poems for orchestra, *Pastorale* won unexpected praise when first performed in Oslo soon after composition — a rare event for Valen. David Monrad Johansen added to the favorable reception by saying, "Valen's *Pastorale* is like a shot fired into the future." While the tonal ambiguity of Valen's piece may well have sounded radically different to his countrymen, his own conception was merely to shape his feelings aroused by the coming of Spring to his beloved rose garden.

SONETTO DI MICHELANGELO (1932) (5')

Much of Valen's music takes inspiration from poetry, nature, and religious-philosophical meditation. Musically, his ideas pour out in long strands of interwoven polyphony, cross rhythms and austere soloistic orchestration. Concentration of expression forms another hallmark of his style. All these elements are at work in *Sonetto di Michelangelo,* disturbed, vaguely tormented music moodily commenting on a lover's lament by the famous Renaissance poet-sculptor who, like Valen, also loved solitude to feed upon his own soul. Although terse motives achieve points of climax, most of this piece keeps to the quiet side with Valen's subtle reflections, released only with reluctance.

CANTICO DI RINGRAZIAMENTO (Song of Thanksgiving) (1933) (7')

Valen's orchestral pieces often seem to have come from the same cookiecutter, but in *Song of Thanksgiving* deep religious sensibilities attain distinctive eloquence. In contrast to some of the other symphonic poems, Valen inserts more sharply etched motivic material and builds it up to a substantial climax by means of a five-part fugue. Form of the piece shows characteristics of a motet and pays homage to Valen's favorite composer (J.S. Bach).

NENIA (1932) (4')

"Nenia" means a lament, in this instance a type of funeral procession song chanted by the ancient Romans. Idea for this piece jelled one night in Valen's mind when he saw his sleeping nephew's face bathed in moonlight, a reminder of "The Dying Gaul," a statue once seen in Rome. Appropriately as cool as marble, the sorrowful nature of *Nenia* evolves from dialogues between strings and woodwinds with brass entering before Valen's typical abrupt break-off.

AN DIE HOFFNUNG (1932) (6')

A companion work to *Nenia,* this essay took inspiration from John

Keats' poem "To Hope." But fearing mistranslation into Norwegian at the time of the premiere, Valen decided to shift the title into its German equivalent. Add his uncompromising atonal idiom and it is no wonder audiences were baffled. Musically, *An die Hoffnung* offers Valen's usual dense message, neither the best nor the worst of his symphonic poem series. One minor detail: the last six bars mark one of the very few spots where Valen used the harp in his restricted orchestral palette.

LA CIMETIÈRE MARIN (Graveyard by the Sea) (1934)   (9')

Vivid, concrete imagery has helped place *La Cimetière Marin* in first place as Valen's most widely accepted single score. His own notes for the Oslo first performance in 1935 remain useful as an aid to better understanding: "The inspiration for *The Graveyard by the Sea* came to· me when I was staying in Mallorca and read a translation of Paul Valery's famous poem ("La Cimetière Marin") in the Spanish paper *El Sol* for May 8th, 1933 . . . . This made me think of another graveyard back in Norway where cholera victims had been buried, by the sea in West Norway, just near where I live [Valestrand]. The music does not follow the poem programmatically, but seeks to voice the reflections which arise wherever Man stands face to face with death."

Little comment is needed. Valen's moody, restless polyphonic surges have never been put to better use than in this exceptional work sketching the forlorn and dilapidated cemetery starkly contrasted against the ceaseless undulation of the nearby sea.

LA ISLA DE LAS CALMAS (The Silent Island) (1934)   (5')

Multilingual titles for his pieces serve as a reminder of Valen the philologist and master of many foreign tongues. The idea behind *La Isla de las Calmas* occurred to Valen when aboard ship off Mallorca. With the island about to drop behind the horizon, a flock of white doves were released; they fluttered, soared over the ship and then swung back towards a fog-shrouded cloister on the island. Valen saw this dramatic flight of homebound birds as a symbol of the soul returning to a merciful God. A Mahler-like struggle emerges from this music, a feeling of hope pitted against intense yearning, but Valen manages to have his say within a far more condensed framework.

ODE TO SOLITUDE (1939)   (8')

Valen became a symphonist fairly late in his career, which helps explain the feeling for sonata form in *Ode to Solitude,* his last tone poem, completed the same year as the First Symphony. Otherwise little else distinguishes this piece from its companions, the usual Valen opus awash with pensive spirituality and intense longing.

VIOLIN CONCERTO (1947)   (12')

Circumstances surrounding Valen's concise, single-movement Violin Concerto correspond almost exactly to the more renowned atonal concerto by Alban Berg. Both works convey the profound grief caused by the death of a beloved child with resolution coming as a quoted old chorale. This beautiful concerto deserves a more prominent place in the world repertoire.

PIANO CONCERTO (1953)   (12′)

Valen's last major work, for piano and chamber orchestra, holds a special position among his disciples because the dedication reads to Aleksandr Helman, pianist and founder of the Fartein Valen Society. Listeners not members of the "in" group might feel the title presumptuous in view of the sparse musical substance offered. Really a highly concentrated concertino, three wispy movements run together over dry, reserved orchestral accompaniment so self-effacing as to be hardly noticeable. This emaciated little opus is not recommended as a general introduction to the music of Fartein Valen.

Chamber Music
SERENADE FOR FIVE WIND INSTRUMENTS (1951)

Valen composed for all forms except opera, with his chamber music largely bunched in his early years although central to the evolution of his singular style. His Piano Trio (Op. 5, 1924) marked his takeoff into atonal flight. The *Serenade,* however, is late Valen, essentially the first movement of a projected but uncompleted wind quintet planned for some Danish players. What remains is set up in the usual Valen manner: a mix of motive-bound twelve-tone material more or less following a sonata plan. Toothsome counterpoint develops, but the overall mood is unrelentingly somber. As wind quintets go, Valen gets badly outclassed by the far pithier discourse of Carl Nielsen and Arnold Schoenberg, two good reasons why Valen may have failed to complete his project.

Keyboard Music
FOUR PIANO PIECES (1935)

Although trained as an organist, like so many other Scandinavian composers, Valen's main effort as a keyboard composer favored the pianoforte. If listeners feel Valen orchestral music is dry, wait until they sample his piano pieces! More dessicated music would be difficult to imagine. This holds true, as here, even when he makes use of evocative titles; Night Piece, Valse Noble, Song Without Words and Gigue.

VARIATIONS FOR PIANO (1936)

Advanced stuff from the land of Grieg, but a tough nut to crack. Economy and tight discipline follow these dozen variations on an original twelve-tone theme all the way. But here Valen's harmony has been enriched by more generous use of chord complexes.

PRELUDE AND FUGUE (1937)

Supposedly a boat trip down the Norwegian coast touched off the inspiration for this piece, but a reading of Spitta's biography of Bach would seem more probable. Valen's choice of a baroque model helps to make the rigors of his parched counterpoint more palatable.

PASTORALE FOR ORGAN (1939)

Valen the organist personally disliked organ music; only two short pieces for the King of Instruments appear on his works list. Unlike the Sahara desert atmosphere of the piano music, *Pastorale* for organ manages a more personal, even touching, integration of atonal materials. A specific image, El Greco's "Adoration of the Shepherds," apparently accounts for the favorable effect of Valen's meditation. Sometimes *Pastorale* for organ (Op. 35) gets confused with *Pastorale* for orchestra (Op. 11); each is an entirely separate composition.

Vocal Music

AVE MARIA (1921)

Valen's output for solo voice and orchestra carries greater weight than generally realized; without access to the songs, the picture of this unique composer is incomplete. In some ways the songs introduce Valen's art more effectively than his work in other forms, the literary element forming a smooth coating over his intensely personal orchestral speech. Valen paid close attention to the setting of carefully selected texts and polished his songcraft with exceptional diligence. Curiously, only the soprano voice is specified.

Ava Maria, one of the loveliest of Valen's creations, appeared just before his plunge into atonal waters.

ZWEI CHINESISCHE GEDICHTE (Two Chinese Poems) (1926)

Here is one instance where the Nordic sound might have come straight from *Mitteleuropä*; both songs (*Expectation of Friends* and *Farewell to Friends*) derive from the same source as Mahler's *Das Lied von der Erde,* namely Hans Bethge's collection, *The Chinese Flute.* But similarities do not end there. A Mahlerian sense of exalted sadness directs the vocal line with forebodings of doom seldom absent from the orchestral infrastructure. Interesting moods, but greater tempo contrasts between these two songs would have been welcome.

DAREST NOW O SOUL (1928)

In addition to his other accomplishments, the scholarly Fartein Valen was master of several languages and their literatures. In this instance he dipped into American literature for a poem by Walt Whitman. The song is entirely characteristic of the composer's style and outlook on life and the hereafter.

DIE DUNKLE NACHT DER SEELE (1939)

The Dark Night of the Soul is the next-to-last item in Valen's soprano/orchestra song series. Literary source in this instance comes from the sixteenth-century Spanish mystic St. John of the Cross, whose lyrical spirituality held great appeal for a man like Valen. For some reason, the composer felt some of St. John's verses too strong so he eliminated them and translated the remainder from the original Spanish into German. In some ways the most engrossing single song from Valen, the premiere was nevertheless delayed until 1971.

For Further Exploration

Symphonies, Nos. 1 through 4; *Epithalamion*; Sonata for Violin and Piano; Piano Trio; String Quartets Nos. 1 and 2; Second Piano Sonata; Goethe amd Mörike songs; choral motets.

LARS JOHAN WERLE (b. 1926)

One of the more intense members of the Swedish younger generation, Lars Johan Werle has advanced to maturity on the strength of a slim list of works, but each succeeding piece has added something to his stature. Pending future developments, Werle's most representative music exhibits close control and refinement of classic serial methodology, often exploited for specific dramatic purpose. Drama, in one form or another, seems the stuff on which Werle feeds.

Werle's training has included musicology at Uppsala and counterpoint under Sven-Erik Bäck, but for the most part Werle can be considered self-taught, thanks to a keen ear for Continental developments of the 1950s and 1960s era. In some ways he appears to follow Blomdahl, but with the attitudes and technique of another generation. Some of Werle's activities have included affiliation with radio and film music for Ingmar Bergman.

Orchestral Music

SINFONIA DA CAMERA (1961)   (15′)

Werle's debut orchestral composition shows full-fledged expertise in music of crystalline texture and fluent technique. Moments of sensuous atonal lyricism, particularly some fine passages for solo woodwind, temper the fragmentation and atomization so typical of orchestral scores written in the shadow of Webern. Elements of optional pitch and reverberational effects also add a dash of contemporary cachet. But an attentive listener can get the feeling from this piece of a composer sure of his way, not a mere follower of others.

SUMMER MUSIC FOR ELEVEN STRINGS AND PIANO (1965)   (7½′)

Summer Music illustrates another of those "quickies" which today's composers find necessary to slip their names onto concert and festival programs in place of longer pieces unsuited for crowded performance schedules; but this is a good one, what might be considered as an extension of the Scandinavian "pastoral suite" tradition. Werle's must have been a stormy summer, judging from the jolting block chords, fluttering after-tones and "shattering glass" sonorities crossing this landscape. Although Darmstadt-type syntax freely raises its head, Werle jells his piece with considerable skill and decided éclat.

Keyboard Music

ATTITUDES FOR PIANO (1965)

A serialist étude of modest presumption, the gentle introspection of *Attitudes* dissolves in a midpoint climax of carefully spaced jabs of dissonance.

223

Vocal Music
CANZONE 126 DI FRANCESCO PETRARCA

Werle produced several choral pieces during the 1960s, presumably *Canzone 126* among them. Written for unaccompanied mixed choir, the work's opening stanzas prove completely disarming — chaste, limpid Renaissance polyphony! With the sonnet's second verse, however, Werle reminds the listener of his true point in time. The music fragments into variable meters with the chorus exchanging spoken as well as sung material. Reassembly approximates the archaic beginning, but the spoken word provides the final touch.

DRÖMMEN OM THÉRÈSE (Vision of Thérèse) (1964)

Werle's two-act opera-in-the-round has become the most discussed work of its type in Scandinavia since Blomdahl's *Aniara*. Audience involvement is total, with seats arranged around a circular stage and the whole auditorium ringed by live orchestra players and loudspeakers — a spatial arrangement apparently pioneered by John Cage.

The plot (taken from Émile Zola's novelette *Pour une nuit d'amour*) boils down to a series of deadly games played out to a murderous finish by the arrogant, voluptuous Thérèse and the drab, flute-playing clerk Julien. His fatal obsession leads to his ruin. Told in cinematic flashbacks with constant coming and going of the actor-singers and supporting players, the opera creates a fluid milieu all its own and one charged with neurosis. Werle's closely integrated score covers a full gamut of emotions from beguiling tenderness (the second-act "Ballad") through a jocose grenadier's scene (recalling *Wozzeck*) to moments of raw-nerved passion as Julien's erotic fantasies turn into nightmares.

However one may wish to gauge *Vision of Thérèse* — opera, lyric drama, musical theater or whatever — all gears mesh. Werle's sharp sense of theatrical projection, firm command of contemporary musical tools and courage to experiment achieve the desired effect, the unforgettable portrait of a dangerous woman.

For Further Exploration
Pentagram; *Die Reise* (The Journey); *Tintomara*; *Zodiac*; *Nautical Preludes*.

CHRISTOPH ERNST FRIEDERICH WEYSE (1774–1842)

Weyse hailed from Altona, a town in the German-Danish borderland. Because of a fit of ill humor from old C.P.E. Bach, he backtracked to pursue his musical studies in Copenhagen instead of Germany, a turn of events highly important in the subsequent development of Danish music. While practically nothing from Weyse has drawn sustained attention abroad, his songs, above all, enshrine his name in the Danish Pantheon and have reached all levels of national consciousness. Weyse became the leading figure in early Danish romanticism, the direct heir of J.A.P. Schulz; an industrious court composer and organist with a large list of works to his credit — popular operas, singspiels, bravura piano pieces, a half dozen symphonies and religious music.

Through close collaboration with Hans Christian Andersen and other figures of Denmark's literary "Golden Age," Weyse moved with his times, yet he imbibed the heady wine of the romantic movement in smaller, more cautious sips than his German counterparts. Not that he was insensitive to the human passions (a thwarted love affair almost destroyed him), but his musical perception seldom extended beyond the established conventions of the late eighteenth century. He venerated Mozart but held Beethoven suspect; younger, up-and-coming Danes, like Gade, he found incomprehensible. Yet Weyse's feeling for the gentler side of romantic poetry proved so keen that as a songwriter he is sometimes mentioned in the same breath as Schubert, a comparison not entirely presumptuous.

Orchestral Music

SOVEDRIKKEN OVERTURE (The Sleeping Potion) (1809)

Titles and theater overtures need not match. Certainly, no hint of drowsiness accompanies this forceful, bright-eyed curtain-raiser to a two-act singspiel of Adam Oehlenschläger which Danes still number among their classics. Musically, this overture is worthy of Haydn. For theater use, Weyse sometimes pirated his earlier symphonies which may explain the substantial quality of the piece.

Keyboard Music

ETUDES FOR PIANO (1831)

Posterity has treated Weyse the songwriter better than Weyse the keyboard composer, which gives an unbalanced perspective of his abilities. Not only did Weyse serve as organist to the cathedral of Copenhagen, but his skill as an improvisor at the pianoforte also gained recognition from such authorities as Liszt and Schumann. After perusing some of the Danish composer's Etudes, the great Moscheles ventured the opinion that Weyse ranked among the best pianoforte writers of his time. On the basis of two Études (No. 1 in E and No. 2 in E minor) from the Opus 60

225

Book (1831) this listener would not go so far; the first is an exercise in velocity while the second displays true romantic pathos. But the obscurity of Weyse's piano music no longer seems warranted.

Vocal Music

SONGS

Weyse's songs have become an integral part of Denmark's cultural heritage. Drawn from various ballad operas, cantatas and assorted collections, they generally extend the homely simplicity and folk tone cultivated by his mentor J.A.P. Schulz. Classical restraint, sparing accompaniments, strophic form and genuine feeling for tender romantic poetry typify Weyse's songs which did so much to set the character of the Danish *romanse*. Music more inherently Danish is hard to come by.

Although Weyse's tendency toward measured, hymnic dignity can sometimes prove tedious, some true gems may be culled from his songs written for the theater. This listener has in mind *Tommeliden* (Tom Thumb) and the idyllic *Der er en ø i livet* (There Is an Island in Life), both from the opera *Ludlams Hule* (Ludlam's Cave). The subdued *En elskeoverklaering* (Declaration of Love) and the barcarolle *Natten er så stille* (The Night Is So Silent) are survivors from the operetta *Et Eventyr i Rosenborg Have* (A Fairytale in the Rosenborg Gardens) which whets curiosity about the work as a whole. One of Weyse's most renowned songs comes from *Sovedrikken* (The Sleeping Potion), namely *Skøn Jomfru, luk dit Vendue op* (Fair Lady, Open Your Window).

The collaborative efforts of Weyse and Hans Christian Andersen were not always free of stress, but one of their most successful projects was a singspiel based on Sir Walter Scott's *The Feast at Kenilworth* produced in 1836. The little pastorale romance from the second act, *Hyrden graesser sine far* (The Shepherd Takes His Flocks to Graze), may be praised as one of Weyse's brightest diamonds.

Of separate songs, practically every Danish schoolchild has sung *Kommer hid, I piger små!* (Gather Round, Little Girls) which honors the memory of the rash, but brave, Lieutenant Willemoes who died in battle against the invading British fleet.

But for the ultimate distillate of Weyse's songcraft, attention turns to the fifteen *Morgen- og Aftensang* (Morning and Evening Songs) composed in the later years of his life. Evidently intended for the moral uplifting of children, these mini-hymns to the words of the romantic poet Bernhard Severin Ingemann project a love of nature and devotion to God all out of proportion to their deceptive simplicity and naivete. They might be seen as a kind of Danish counterpart to *The Little Flowers* of St. Francis.

Taken together, the songs of Weyse add a unique, distinctive dimension to the many facets of the Nordic sound.

For Further Exploration

Symphonies; *Faruk*; *Floribella*; *Ludlams Hule* and other stage works; pianoforte sonatas and études; organ music; cantatas.

DAG WIRÉN (b. 1905)

Like the animals on Noah's Ark, the pairing of composers often seems the result of divine command with musical literature full of conjunctives like Bach-Handel, Bruckner-Mahler and Debussy-Ravel. The linkage of Dag Wirén and Lars-Erik Larsson affords a Scandinavian variant of this bad habit. "Why do they always put us together when, really, we are so different?" was the mild complaint heard from Wirén himself.

There are similarities, of course: Wirén and Larsson rank with Sweden's most representative composers, both belong to the same generation, and they maintain homes fairly close by in the Stockholm suburbs. During the 1930s, without collusion, both sidestepped the more heated issues in modern music to offer audiences easily digested music sometimes described as their "divertimento" style. Afterwards, however, the paths followed by Wirén and Larsson diverged. Basic temperamental differences became clearer. Larsson moved from the fringes of post-romanticism into a type of respectable serialism in line with an increasing academic outlook. Wirén, on the other hand, sought renewal in the traditions of Nielsen and Sibelius leading to the metamorphic and cyclical features of his later work, a philosophy which brought him close to the thinking of Denmark's Vagn Holmboe. Yet the precise calibration of neo-classicism remained paramount.

Wirén's identification with neo-classic precepts stems from his student years in Paris when he made direct contact with the work of Stravinsky, Honegger and Prokofiev, who were, like himself, drawn to the magnetic vitality of Parisian musical life during the 1920s.ʻ Wit, elegance and meticulous craftsmanship — essential parts of the neo-classicist's creed — came to lie at the heart of Wirén's elegant style. Among composers, Dag Wirén cannot be called a giant, but his work, the product of ruthless revision and pruning, includes some of the most civilized music of the twentieth century.

Orchestral Music

SINFONIETTA IN C (1934)   (18′)

Wirén's compact *Sinfonietta* indulges in some parodic nose-thumbing after the manner of Prokofiev's *Classical Symphony,* but more than frolicsome levity emerges from this highly polished, beautifully proportioned score. The slow movement turns to Nordic seriousness (Andante espressivo) while the peppery finale (Molto allegro) makes telling use of strong rhythms reinforced by snare-drum flourishes. Although an early piece, *Sinfonietta* belongs with the composer's front rank scores.

SERENADE FOR STRINGS (1937)   (15′)

Music of intuitive Swedish feeling without benefit of folk song, this

227

suave and often ironic piece won the composer international recognition. The Nordic mood reaches highest pitch in the pulsating ground bass and lyric flight of the slow movement, while the irony becomes least veiled when Wirén struts Tempo di marcia in his finale. Precision string writing, sharp-edged melody and wry humor which never becomes forced or stale make Wirén's *Serenade* an outstanding composition, a highly recommended portal of entry into more recent Scandinavian music.

SYMPHONY NO. 4 (1952)   (18')

Hilding Rosenberg may be the strongest, but by no means the only successful symphonist of his generation in Swedish music. Dag Wirén's Third (1944) and Fourth Symphonies also have received a fair share of attention both at home and abroad. To some extent the Fourth is a symphony affirming tonal principles. The work is monothematic with all material evolving out of an austere opening motive coming, like the prow of a ship, out of a fog bank. Transformation of the germinal idea requires three fairly concentrated movements hewing close to metamorphosis technique yet classical enough for a slow-fast-slow pattern. Events build climactically, then subside again with the original motive dissolving back into its murky origins.

Chamber Music

STRING QUARTET NO. 2 (1935)

Dag Wirén has devoted close attention to the cultivation of chamber music with particular emphasis on the string quartet. The Second Quartet is non-problematic, music reflecting the composer's "divertimento" style of the 1930s. The work opens with a captivating, singing melody of gentle simplicity followed by a set of warm and winning variations. The second movement comes as a perky scherzo with a wistful midsection interlude. The finale (Prestissimo) proves deft while reserving moments for poetic reflection.

STRING QUARTET NO. 4 (1953)

A good example of Scandinavian "middle way" modernism, Wirén's highly organized Fourth Quartet serves as a casing for a dry little chromatic sequence brought up immediately by the viola. In one guise or another, this germ material integrates all five concise, strongly contrasted movements including two "intermezzi" inserted for essential bridging. Although neither formidable nor vexing, the interplay of the Fourth Quartet finds the composer more cerebral than soulful.

STRING QUARTET NO. 5 (1970)

A set of spare and understated comments from an elder statesman, the Fifth Quartet soberly sticks to the point without a trace of garrulousness. Material showing both warmth and flickers of ironic humor grow out of one movement into the next with all connections showing the refinement and skill so characteristic of this composer's work. No new ground is broken, no new challenges confronted; the Fifth Quartet rests its case on the evidence of distilled wisdom.

LITTLE SERENADE FOR SOLO GUITAR (1964)

The phenomenal revived interest in the guitar and its varied literature has not gone unnoticed by some of the twentieth century's more prominent composers, but in this instance Wirén only gets a "C" for effort. Considering the pithy humor and melodic facility so evident in other compositions, the Guitar Serenade merely strums lethargically.

Keyboard Music

IRONISKA SMÅSTYCKEN (Ironical Miniatures) (1942)

That touch of witty impudence often stealing into Wirén's music steps into broad daylight in these five easy-to-take capsules. All of them show animated rhythm and racy harmony. The final number may strike some ears as a miniature paraphrase on a familiar Gershwin opus.

Vocal Music

TITANIA

Comparatively few songs or choral pieces have issued from Wirén, but *Titania,* an a cappella gem, makes this listener wish for more. Setting a poem by Fröding, the piece shows the Fairy Queen magically dancing by the silvery light of a midsummer moon; then, all of a sudden, Titania simply evaporates.

For Further Exploration

Symphonies Nos. 3 and 5; *Triptyk* for small orchestra; Violin Concerto; Piano Concerto; Cello Concerto; *Oscarian Ball* (ballet); String Quartet No. 3; Sonatina for piano; *Three Poems of the Sea* for chorus; Karfeldt songs.

PART III

SELECTIVE INTERNATIONAL DISCOGRAPHY

GENERAL INFORMATION

The erratic, capricious nature of the commercial recording industry renders any discography obsolete almost as soon as it is written. Making no pretense at completeness, the following discography serves only to mirror the substance of *The Nordic Sound,* a sort of microgroove bibliography designed to stimulate and assist the listener in his own explorations. Unless otherwise indicated, all recordings given are 33 1/3 rpm without distinction made between monaural or stereo; but where a more modern, stereo pressing of a given work exists, preference has been given to it. While every effort has been made to include recordings generally available, many have been deleted and may be almost impossible to obtain. Still others may sink below the surface only to later reappear on some different label and even at budget price.

Despite attrition, a substantial selection of Scandinavian music exists in modern recorded form. The outflow of pressings covering this field has shown a striking upward curve in recent years. So, if every disc listed cannot be obtained on a moment's notice through the usual commercial channels, the listener should cultivate the collector's perseverance, scan catalogues and haunt record shops. Scarce records have a strange way of popping up. When local resources fail, the listener must turn to Scandinavia. The inventory and overseas service of the following firms can be recommended:

Copenhagen
    FONA
    Vimmelskaftet 46
    Copenhagen K, Denmark
Oslo
    Norsk Musikforlag A/S
    Karl Johans Gate 39
    N-Oslo, Norway
Stockholm
    AB Nordiska Musikförlaget
    Drottningg. 37
    101 30 Stockholm 1, Sweden.

For general information about all aspects of music within each of the three Nordic countries, the listener is referred to:

Wilhelm Hansen Musikforlaget
Gothersgade 9-11
DK-1123 Copenhagen K, Denmark

Society for Danish Music
c/o Dan Fog Musikforlag
Graabrødretorv. 7
DK-1154 Copenhagen K, Denmark

Norwegian Composers Society
Klingenbertggt. 5
Oslo, Norway

Swedish Music Information Center
STIM
Tegnérlunden 3
111 85 Stockholm, Sweden

Catalogues

Although vast archives of recorded music may be found in each of the Nordic countries, particularly at the state radio services, no general catalogues of these resources as yet exists. More Scandinavian music than may be realized, however, circulates in the international record market. Most of these pressings find entry into the three major world catalogues: Schwann (U.S.A.), Gramophone (Great Britain) and Bielfelder (Germany).

The picture magnifies markedly, at least for Swedish music, when reference is made to the beautifully organized catalogue *Svensk Ton På Skiva* (Swedish Sound on Records) issued by the Swedish Music Information Center. While the Norwegian Composers Society offers nothing comparable, their book *Contemporary Norwegian Orchestral and Chamber Music* gives appropriate recordings. They also can furnish a useful flyer on their admirable recording project with Phillips. In regard to Danish music, information must be gathered in bits and pieces with a request to FONA for their catalogue *Seriøse Danske Plader* (Classical Danish Records) as a starting point. The little bulletin *Musical Denmark,* issued at sluggish intervals, frequently contains a great amount of useful information about Danish musical artists and recordings of Danish music. To get on the *Musical Denmark* mailing list write to: Det Danske Selskab (The Danish Society), Kultorvet 2, 1175 Copenhagen K, Denmark.

Abbreviations

For record label:

Ang. = Angel
ASA = ASA Records (Denmark)
BLR = BLR Record Co. (Norway)
Cap. = Capitol

Col. = Columbia
Cr. = Crossroads
Dec. = Decca (England)
DGG = Deutsche Grammophon Gesellschaft
EMS = EMS Recordings
Folk. = Folkways
GMM = Great Masters of Music
HMV = His Masters Voice (Electrical Music Industries)
Lon. = London
Lou. = Louisville
Lyr. = Lyrichord
Main. = Mainstream
Mer. = Mercury
MGM = Metro-Goldwyn-Mayer
MHS = Musical Heritage Society
None. = Nonesuch
NM = National Museum (Denmark)
Phi. = Phillips
RIKS = Rikskonserter (Expo Norr, Sweden)
RCA = Radio Corporation of America, Victor
RCA VICS = Radio Corporation of America, Victrola
SR = Sveriges (Swedish) Radio
SWS = Swedish Society Discophil
Turn. = Turnabout
Van. = Vanguard
ZAC = ZAC Recordings (Denmark)
Other labels given in full
For performing organizations:
Orch. or orch. = Orchestra
Phil. = Philharmonic or Philharmonia
Qt. = Quartet
Quint. = Quintet
Sym. = Symphony
Other:
alt. = alternate listing

HISTORICAL PERSPECTIVES

Ancient Wellsprings
Lappish Joik Songs from Northern Norway. Folk. FE 4007
Joik (Lapp Folk Music). SR RELP 1029 1/14 (seven discs)
Music Blown from Lurs from the Danish Bronze Age. NM 67-001
(10")
Anonymous: *St. Magnus Hymn*
Prague Madrigal Singers: "Old English Vocal Music." Cr. 22 16 0144
Middle Ages Ballads. SR RELP 5003/06
Medieval Ballads of Norway. BLR NO. FO. 1
Norwegian Folk Ballads. RCA (Norway) FLP 101/2 (7" 45 rpm)
(two discs)
Courtly Patronage
Buxtehude, Dietrich
Aperite mihi portas justitiae
Collegium Sagitarii + concert. Oryx EXP 26
Düben, Gustav
Veni Sancte Spiritus
Ericson, Radio choir + Albrici. SR RAEP 5 (7" 45 rpm)
Odae Sveticae (selections)
Dorow, S.B. Taube: "Pastime with Good Company." Odeon SCLP
1038
Wedar, Arnér, B. Ericson. SR RAEP 6 (7" 45 rpm)
Music at Drottningholm: Naumann, Roman, Uttini
Björlin, Drottningholm Theater Orch. None. 71213
Kraus, Joseph Martin
Funeral Cantata for Gustav III of Sweden
Soloists, chorus, Jenkins, Clarion Concerts Orch. Van. C-10065
Romanticism and National Assertion
Songs and choral music. See Collections
Kuhlau, Friederich
Elverhøj (Elf Hill), excerpts
Hye-Knudsen, Danish Royal Orch. + Lange-Muller. Turn. 34230
Danish Theater Music: du Puy, Weyse, Kuhlau, J.P.E. Hartmann, Heise,
Hornemann
Hye-Knudsen, Danish Royal Orch. Turn. 34308
Hartmann, Johan Peter Emelius
Gulhornene (The Golden Horns)
Reumert, Ase, Radio Orch. Tono LPX 35008
Lumbye, Hans Christian
Tivoli Music
Felumb, Tivoli Orch. Vox 512840 (alt. Fona VIBE PW 1003)
Hammelboe, Danish Orch. Mer. 90461 (alt. Phi. PY 841901)
Friisholm, Copenhagen Sym. HMV (Denmark) SXLP 30057

Backer-Grøndahl, Agathe
Piano Music
   Pines + Chaminade. Genesis GS 1024
Almqvist, Carl Jonas Love
Songs and Fantasies
   Sjöstrand, S.B. Taube. HMV (Sweden) SCLP 1074
Söderman, August
Six Songs in Folkstyle
   Ericson, Radio Choir. HMV (Sweden) EBS 28 (7" 45 rpm)
A Country Wedding
   Ericson, Orphei Drängar. Barben BEP 58 (7" 45 rpm)
Skillingtryck (Broadside ballads)
   S.B. Taube. HMV (Sweden) SCLP 1015
Sjögren, Emil
Sonata No. 1 for Violin and Piano
   Berlin, Erikson + Schumann, Sibelius. SWS SLT 33201
Folk Trails
Folk Music of Norway. Folk. FM 408
Norwegian Folk Songs. Folk. FW 8725
Songs and Dances from Denmark. Fiesta FLPS 1522
Folk Fiddling from Sweden. None. H-72033
Ancient Swedish Pastoral Music. SR RELP 5017
Music from the Far.North. Argo ZRG 533
   NOTE: The more than casually interested folklorist is urged to investigate the large number of authentic folk music Extended Play (45 rpm) recordings issued by RCA (Norway and Denmark) and the Swedish Radio.
Late Romanticism
Langgaard, Rued
Music of the Spheres
   Soloists, chorus, Comissiona, Stockholm Phil. "Nordic Music Days 1968," Vol. 2. HMV (Sweden) CSDS 1087
Halvorsen, Johan
Fossegrimen Suite
   Fjeldstad, Oslo Phil. + Suite Ancienne. Mer. 90001
Eggen, Arne
Olav Liljekrans (excerpts)
   Buntz, Gruner-Hegge, Oslo Phil. + Braein, Jensen, Johansen, Olsen. Mer. 90002
Jensen, Ludvig Irgens
Symphony in D minor
   Fjeldstad, Oslo Phil. + Japanese Spring. Phi. 6507 005
Hall, Pauline
Circus Pictures
   Bergh, Norwegian Broadcasting Orch. + light music. Phi. 839.239 AY

237

Tveitt, Geir
Hundred Folk Tunes from Hardanger Suite No. 1
  Grüner-Hegge, Oslo Phil. HMV (Norway) NCLP 4
Olsson, Otto
Te Deum
  Levén, church choir, Stockholm Phil. + choral music.
  SWS SLT 33169
Koch, Erland von
Saxophone Concerto
  Rascher, Westerberg, Munich Phil. + Scandinavian Dances.
  HMV (Sweden) 4E061-34016
Frumerie, Gunnar de
När du sluter mina ögon (When I close my eyes)
  Meyer, Bonneau + Brahms, Sibelius, Rangström. HMV (Sweden)
  FALP 568
Toward the New Musics
Karkoff, Maurice
Landscape of Screams
  Lindholm, Rosenbluth, Bäck with instrumental ensemble + Morthenson, Deak, Bark. SUEC PS 2
Pettersson, Allan
Symphony No. 7
  Dorati, Stockholm Phil. Lon. 6740
Barefoot Songs
  Sjunnesson, Larsson. RIKS EP 3 (7" 45 rpm)
Lundsten, Ralph
Winter Music (electronic music) + Ludsten-Nilson. HMV (Sweden)
  CSDS 1085
Naumann, Siegfried
Riposte II
  Naumann, instrumental ensemble + Hermanson, Nilsson, Welin.
  SUEC PM 1
Bark, Jan and Rabe, Folke
Bolos for Four Trombones
  Bark, Rabe + Bäck, Hambraeus, Morthenson, Nilsson. Artist
  (Sweden) ALP 102
Tarp, Svend Erik
Symphony in E Flat
  Caridis, Radio Orch. + Te Deum. Odeon PASK 2009
Lewkovitch, Bernard
Il cantico delle creature
  Chamber Choir — Nordic Music Days 1968, Vol. 4 + Rydman,
  Pergament. HMV (Sweden) CSDS 1089
Brustad, Bjarne
Symphony No. 2
  Fjeldstad, Oslo Phil. + Kielland. CRI 160

Olsen, Sparre
Seven Krokann Songs
  Skram, Levin + Choir Songs, Wind Quintet. Phi. 6507 011
Arnestad, Finn
Cavatina cambiata
  Andersen, Bergen Orch. + Kvandal, Bull, Berge. Phi. 6507 031
Johnsen, Halvard
Symphony No. 3
  Andersen, Bergen Orch. + Baden. Phi. 6507-019
Bibalo, Antonio
Sinfonia Notturno
  Andersen, Bergen Orch. + *Autunale.* Phi. 6507 015
Kolberg, Kåre
Plym-Plym
  Mixed choir, soloists quartet, speaker + G. Sønstevold, Andersen,
  M. Sønstevold, Berge. Phi. 6507 018
Fongaard, Björn
Homo sapiens for tape + P. R. Olsen, Mellnäs, Sigurbjörnsson —
  Nordic Music Days 1968, Vol. 3. HMV (Sweden) CSDS 1088
Nilsson, Torsten
Seven Improvisations for Organ; Deuteroskopi
  T. Nilsson, Arnér, Welin. Proprius PROP 7714/15 (two discs)
Hermanson, Åke
In Nuce
  Westerberg, Radio Orch. + Rosenberg. SWS SLT 33215

COMPOSERS GALLERY

Alfvén, Hugo
Symphony No. 2 in D
Segerstam, Stockholm Phil. SWS SLT 33211
Symphony No. 3 in E
Grevillius, Stockholm Phil. SWS SLT 33161
Symphony No. 4
Malmborg, Wilkström, Grevillius, Stockholm Phil. SWS SLT 33186
Symphony No. 5 (First Movement only)
Westerberg, Radio orch. + *Tale of the Skerries.* SWS SLT 33174
Swedish Rhapsody "Midsommarvaka"
Ormandy, Philadelphia Orch. + Sibelius, Grieg. Col. MS-7674
Uppsala Rhapsody
Rybant, Berlin Orch. + Atterberg, Eriksson, Lindberg, Udden, Weis-
lander. Cupol CLPN 344
Dalecarlia Rhapsody
Westerberg, Stockholm Phil. + *Festpel, Midsommarvaka.* SWS SLT
33145
The Prodigal Son
Alfvén, Swedish Royal Orch. + *The Mountain King.* SWS SLT
33182
Gustav II Adolph Suite
Westerberg, Radio Orch. SWS SLT 33173
Sonata for Violin and Piano
Saulesco, Solyom + Songs. HMV (Sweden) 4 E 061-34024
Choral Pieces
Academy Choir — Swedish Choral Songs. Phi. PY 842 557
Atterberg, Kurt
Symphony No. 2 in F
Westerberg, Stockholm Phil. SWS SLT 33179
The Wise and Foolish Virgins Suite
Grevillius, Stockholm Phil. + Lindberg. SWS SLT 33192
Suite for Violin, Viola and Strings
Westerberg, Radio Orch. + de Frumerie, Wirén. SWS SLT 33167
Suite Barocco
Atterberg, Radio Orch. + *Suite Pastorale.* SWS SLT 33175

240

Bäck, Sven-Erik
Sinfonia per archi
Bäck, chamber orch. + Hinemith, Martinu. SR RELP 1062
Sinfonia da camera
Blomstedt, Stockholm Phil. + Blomdahl, Wirén. SWS 33123
A Game around a Game
Ehrling, Stockholm Phil. + Nystroem, Larsson. Phi. DSY 839277
Favola
Janson, percussion ensemble + Carlstedt, Werle. RIKS LP 18
String Quartet No. 3
Frydén Qt. + Bark-Rabe, Hambraeus, Morthenson, Nilsson. Artist ALP 102
Kattresan
Eriksson, Gothenburg chamber choir and ensemble + Johanson. HMV (Sweden) SCLP 1079
The Crane Feathers
Bäck, soloists, chamber choir and Norrköping Orch. SWS SLT 33183
The Bird
Bäck, soloists, Norrköping Orch. SWS SLT 33195
Motets
Ericson, Radio choir + Lidholm, Hambraeus. SR RLMP 1096
Ericson, Radio choir + Swedish church music. CAN 640 224
Bellman, Carl Michael
Fredman's Songs and Epistles
S.B. Taube, Björlin, chamber ensemble, Vol. 1. HMV (Sweden) SCLP 1003
S.B. Taube, Björlin, chamber ensemble, Vol. 2. HMV (Sweden) SCLP 1018
Clauson. Polydor LPHM 46246
"Bellmania" (arr. orch.) — Westerberg, chamber orch. SWS SLT 33155
Bentzon, Jørgen
Symphonic trio
Friisholm, Collegium Musicum + Høffding, Riisager. Odeon MOAK 10
Mikrofoni No. 1
Cold, chamber ensemble + Berg, Høffding, T. Nielsen. Odeon PASK 2005
Racconto No. 1
Rousseau, chamber ensemble + Ibert. Coronet 1709
Racconto No. 5
Danish Wind Quint. + Nielsen, Høffding. Phi. 6578 001
Bentzon, Niels Viggo
Symphonic Variations
Semkow, Royal Danish Orch. + Chamber Concerto for 11 Instruments. Turn. 34374

Pezzi Sinfonici
  Whitney, Louisville Orch. + Piston, Van Vactor. Lou. 58-6
Mosaïque Musicale
  Chamber ensemble + Holmboe. Triola TDLP 207,
String Quartet No. 6
  Danish Qt. + Olsen, Westergaard, Holm. Fona TF 126
Sonata No. 3
  Bentzon + Toccata, Woodcuts, Paganini Variations. Wilhelm Hansen Ed. LPWH 3015
Sonata No. 4
  Bentzon + Sonata No. 5. Fona TF 117
The Tempered Piano
  Bentzon. Fona LPK 540/541 (Two discs)
Sagn
  Eckart-Hansen, chorus, Tivoli Orch. + J.P.E. Hartmann, Gabold, Holmboe. Fona TF 131
Berwald, Franz
Symphony in G Minor ("Sérieuse")
  Schmidt-Isserstedt, Stockholm Phil. + "Singulière." None. 71087
Symphony in D ("Capricieuse")
  Dorati, Stockholm Phil. + Rosenberg, Blomdahl. RCA VICS-1319
Symphony in C ("Singulière")
  Ehrling, London Sym. + Symphony in E-flat. Lon. 6602
Piano Concerto
  Erikson, Westerberg, Swedish Orch. + Piano pieces. Genesis 1011
Estrella di Soria: Overture
  Ehrling, Radio Orch. + Queen of Golconda Overture, Polonaise, tone poems. None. 71218
String Quartet in G Minor
  Fryden Qt. + Quartet in A minor. SWS SLT 33180
String Quartet in A minor
  Copenhagen Qt. + Sibelius. Turn. 34091
String Quartet in E-flat
  Saulesco Qt. + Mozart. SWS SLT 33178
Grand Septet
  Vienna Octet Members + Kreutzer. Lon. 6672
Piano Trio No. 1
  Berwald Trio + Trio No. 3. TR TRS 11038
Piano Quintet in C Minor
  Riefling, Benthien Qt. + Quintet in A. None. 71113
Borup-Jørgensen, Axel
Music for Percussion + Viola
  Frisholm, Collegium Musicum + P.R. Olsen, Koppel. Odeon MOAK 12
Nordic Summer Pastorale
  Friisholm, Radio Orch., + Holm, Jørgensen, P.R. Olsen. Odeon PASK 2004

String Quartet "Torso"
    Danish Qt. + Nørholm, Stravinsky, Penderecki. ASA LS 102
Blomdahl, Karl-Birger
Symphony No. 3 "Facets"
    Ehrling, Stockholm Phil. + Rosenberg. Turn. 34318
Chamber Concerto
    Ehrling, London Sym. + Lidholm, Rosenberg. Dec. SXL 6180
Forma ferritonans
    Commissiona, Radio Orch. + Sisyphos. RIKS LP 16
Dance Suite No. 2
    Instrumental ensemble + Bäck, Wirén. SWS LT 33123
Game for Eight
    Björlin, Stockholm Phil. + Prelude and Allegro; Five Italian Songs.
    Ang. S-36576
Suite for Cello and Piano
    Helmerson, Negro + A. Berg, de Frumerie, Liszt. RIKS LP 19
Trio for Clarinet, Cello and Piano
    Janson, Blöndahl-Bengston, Baekkelund + de Frumerie. SWS LT
    33147
In the Hall of Mirrors
    Ehrling, soloists, chorus, Stockholm Phil. RIKS LP 6
Aniara
    Janssen, soloists, chorus, Vienna Volksoper Orch. Phi. AL 1522/
    1523 (two discs)
Aniara: "Electronic Suite"
    Janssen, Vienna Volksoper Orch. with electronic and concrete effects
    by Swedish Radio (in album "2001 A Space Odyssey"). Col. MS
    7176
Altisonans
    Electronic music + Johnson. SR LPD 2
Carlstedt, Jan
Symphony No. 2
    Westerberg, Stockholm Phil. HMV (Sweden) YE 055 34424
Eight Duets for Two Violins
    Crafoord, Nordin + Five chorales; Six songs. Tel. LT 43075
Sonata for Solo Violin
    Dekov + Eklund, Karkoff, Linde. SWS SLT 33199
String Quartet No. 2
    Slovak Qt. + Bäck, Werle. RIKS LP 18
Egge, Klaus
Symphony No. 1
    Grüner Hegge, Oslo Phil. HMV (Norway) NCLP 3
Symphony No. 2 ("Sinfonia giocosa")
    Fjeldstad, Oslo. Phil. + Groven, Monrad-Johansen, Svendsen. Phi.
    838.052 AY

Symphony No. 3
Whitney, Louisville Orch. + Harris. Lou. 602
Symphony No. 4
Ehrling, Oslo Phil. + Mortensen, Hovland. Phi. 6507 010
Piano Concerto No. 2
Riefling, Fjeldstad, Oslo Phil. + Sonata. Phi. 6507 014
Violin Concerto
Wicks, Fjeldstad, Oslo Phil. + Sonata No. 2; Fantasies. Phi. 839.238 AY
"Draumkvede" ("Dream Vision") Sonata
Knardahl + Piano Concerto No. 2. Phi. 6507 014
Piano Sonata No. 2 ("Sonata patetica")
Baekkelund + Halling and Springar Fantasies; Violin Concerto. Phi. 839.238 AY
Sonata for Violin and Piano
Tellefsen, Glaser + Grüner-Hegge. Phi. 6507 009
String Quartet No. 1
Hindar Qt. + Nystedt. Phi. 839.253 AY
Wind Quintet
Norwegian Wind Quint. + Baden, Janson, Brustad. Phi. 839.249 AY
Gade, Niels
Ossian Overture
Hye-Knudsen, Royal Danish Orch. + Nielsen, Riisager. Turn. 34085
Symphony No. 1 in C Minor ("Zealand's Fair Plains")
Hye-Knudsen, Royal Danish Orch. Turn. 34052
Blue Grotto Scene from "Napoli"
Grondahl, Radio orch. + Henriques. HMV (Denmark) 45-X 8392 (7" 45 rpm)
Bridal Waltz from "A Folk Tale"
Ase, Radio orch. + Mendelssohn. HMV (Denmark) 45-X 8378 (7" 45 rpm)
Sonata No. 2 for Violin and Piano
Sachsenskjold, Rasmussen + Hartmann. Fona TF 106
String Quartet in F Minor
Copenhagen Qt. + Grieg. Turn. 34270
String Quartet in D
Copenhagen Qt. + Nielsen. Turn. 34187
Three Novelettes from Op. 29
Göbel Trio + Godard, Sitt. MHS 1159
Fantasy Pieces for Clarinet and Piano
Sigurdsson, Blyme + Kuhlau, Nielsen, Høffding, Holmboe. Fona TF 118
Sonata in E Major
Johnsson + Aquarelles, Foraarstoner, Arabesque. DCM SM 93121
Aquarelles (Books 1/2, Op. 19); Arabesque (Op. 27)
Ruiz + Sinding. Genesis 1003

Organ Works
   Hansen + Church arias. Fona TF 101
   Prip + Matthison-Hansen. Principal PLP 1005
Elverskud (The Erl King's Daughter)
   Soloists, chorus, Hye-Knudsen, Danish Royal Orch. Turn. 34381
Grieg, Edvard
In Autumn Overture: Old Norwegian Melody with Variations (arr. orch.)
   Beecham, Royal Phil. + Schubert. Ang. 35339
Piano Concerto in A Minor
   Rubinstein, Wallenstein, RCA Sym. + Rachmaninoff. RCA LSC-3338
   Baekkelund, Grüner-Hegge, Oslo Phil. + Peer Gynt. RCA VICS-1067
Sigurd Jorsalfar Suite
   Karajan, Berlin Phil. + Peer Gynt Suites 1 & 2. DGG 2530243
Peer Gynt: Incidental Music
   Armstrong, Ambrosian Singers, Barbirolli, Hallé Orch. Ang. S-36531
Peer Gynt Suites Nos. 1 and 2
   Barbirolli, Hallé Orch. + Norwegian Dances. Ang. S-36803
Holberg Suite
   Munchinger, Stuttgart Chamber Orch. + Mozart. Lon. STS-15044
Two Melodies (Op. 53)
   Neel, Boyd Neel Orch. — "Light Music." Unicorn LP 1038
Music of Grieg: Wedding Day at Troldhaugen; Cowkeeper's Tune and Country Dance; Two Elegiac Melodies
   Mackerras, London Proms Orch., + Sibelius. Lon. STS-15159
Symphonic Dances
   Gould, New Phil. + Norwegian Dances. RCA LSC-3158
Lyric Suite
   Weldon, Royal Phil. + Norwegian Dances; Piano Concerto. Sera. S-60032
Sonatas for Violin and Piano, Nos. 1, 2, 3
   Loveday, Cassini. Saga XID 5296
Sonata for Cello and Piano in A Minor
   Mantel, Frieser + Piano Sonata; Wedding Day. MHS 1179
String Quartet in G Minor
   Guarnari Qt. + Mendelssohn. RCA LSC-2948
String Quartet in F: "Unfinished"
   Hindar Qt. + Quartet in G minor. Phi. 839-241 AY
Piano Music "Complete"
   Mourao. Vox SVBX 5457/5458 (Six discs)
Funeral March for Rikard Nordraak (arr. brass and percussion)
   Philip Jones Brass Ensemble — "Classics for Brass " Argo ZRG 731
Piano Music (Performed by Edvard Grieg)
   "Famous Composers Play Their Own Works." Tel. HT 18

"Composers at the Keyboard Play Their Own Compositions." Allegro LEG-9021

Songs
Flagstad. Lon. 5263
Flagstad. Sera. 60046
Flagstad. Decca (England) ECS 622
Roessel-Majdan. West. 18089
Myrvik. EMS 501
Nilsson. Lon. 25942
Skram. Phi. 6507 001
Prytz. RCA (Norway) LPNE 54

Haugtussa, Song Cycle
Thallaug, Baekkelund + Kjerulf, Hurum, Jensen, Sinding. Phi. 854.006 AY

Four Psalms
Norwegian Soloist Choir + Egge, Lammers, Sommerfeldt, Saeverud. Phi. 854.001 AY

Groven, Eivind
The Bridegroom
Soloists, chorus, Fjelstadt, Oslo Phil. + Margjit Hjuske. Phi. 839.055/56 (two discs)

Hjalarljod Overture
Fjeldstad, Oslo Phil. + Monrad-Johansen, Egge, Svendsen. Phi. 838.052 AY

Mot Ballade
Chorus, Kram, Oslo Phil. + Egge. Mer. 90003

Hambraeus, Bengt
Transfiguration
Gielen, Radio orch. + Fresque sonore. SWS SLT 33181

Rota II; Tetragon. RIKS LP 7S

Transit II
Instrumental ensemble + Back, Bark-Rabe, Morthenson, Nilsson. Artist ALP 102

Interferences for Organ
Hambraeus + Constellations. Phi. DSY 839278

Responses
Solen, Hambraeus, Welin, Ericson with choir and organ + Reger. SR RMLP 1093

Motetum Archangeli Michaelis
Radio choir + Back, Lidholm. SR RMLP 1096

Rencontres
Westerberg, Stockholm Phil. + Larsson. RIKS LP 32

Holmboe, Vagn
Symphony No. 8 ("Sinfonia boreale")
Semkow, Danish Orch. + Nørgård. Turn. 34168

Concerto No. 11
Surinach, Chamber orch. + Glanville-Hicks. MGM 3357
String Quartet No. 1
Copenhagen Qt. + Quartet No. 4. Fona TF 109
String Quartet No. 3
Copenhagen Qt. + Quartet No. 6. Fona TF 111
String Quartet No. 7
Copenhagen Qt. + Quartet No. 8. Fona TF 108
String Quartet No. 8
Copenhagen Qt. + Nielsen. Turn. 34217
Primavera
Danish instrumentalists + N.V. Bentzon. Triola TDLP 207 (10")
Quartetto Medico
Danish instrumentalists + Gade, Kuhlau, Høffding. Fona TF 118
Quintet for Brass Instruments
Danish Brass Quint. + A.J. Jørgensen, Roikjer, Schmidt. Fona TF
125
"Suono da Bardo"
Blyme + Sonata for solo flute. Fona TF 123
"Inuit" — Three Igloo Songs
Cold, Student Choral Society, percussion + Hartmann, Gabold, N.V.
Bentzon. Fona TF 131

Høffding, Finn
Evolution
Frandsen, Radio orch. + J. Bentzon, Riisager. Odeon MOAK 10
Dialogues
Wolsing, Erichsen + Riisager. HMV (Denmark) 7R K21 (7" 45
rpm)
Chamber Music
Danish instrumentalists + J. Bentzon, Berg, T. Nielsen. Odeon PASK
2005
Wind Quintet
Danish Wind Quint. + Nielsen, J. Bentzon. Phi. 6578 001

Hovland, Egil
Music for Ten Instruments
Bruland, Oslo Phil. members + Nordheim. Forum FORLP 6100
Lamenti per orchestra
Fjeldstad, Oslo Phil. + Egge, Mortensen. Phi. 6507 010
Suite for Flute and Piano
Øien, Knardahl + Bergh, Jordan, Berge, Kvandal, Olsen, Mortensen.
Phi. 6507 020
Wind Quintet
Norwegian Wind Quint. + Fongaard, Mortensen, Nystedt, Valen.
Phi. 839.248
Varianti per due pianoforte
Haase, Zerah + Mortensen. Ny Musikk NM-1

247

Johansen (Monrad-Johansen), David
Symphonic Fantasy
Fjeldstad, Oslo Phil. + Groven, Egge, Svendsen. Phi. 838.052 AY
Pan
Andersen, Bergen Sym. + Saeverud, Nystedt. Phi. 6507 007
Flute Quintet
Øien, Hindar Qt. + Janson, Hall, Sommerfeldt. Phi. 839.256 AY
From the Gudbrandsdal Valley, Suite No. 2
Baekkelund + Sommerfeldt, Kvandal. Phi. 6507 012
Voluspaa
Soloists, Norwegian Soloists Choir, Fjeldstad, Oslo Phil. Phi. 854.002 AY
Nordlands Trompet
Ebrelius, Johansen + Five Biblical Texts. Phi. 631.092 AL
Kjerulf, Halfdan
Songs
Prytz + Grieg. RCA (Norway) LPNE 54
Piano Music. Genesis(in preparation)
Lange-Müller, Peter
Sulamite and Solomon, Song Cycle
Halding, Gürtler + J. Nørgaard. Odeon MOAK 11
Once Upon a Time
Soloists, chorus, Hye-Knudsen, Royal Danish Orch. + Kuhlau. Turn. 34230
Songs
Westi. Phi. AY 836752
Larsson, Lars-Erik
Little Serenade; Concertino for Double Bass and Strings
Ossoniak, Stockholm chamber orch. +Roman. SWS SLT 33187
Pastoral Suite; Little March
Westerberg, Stockholm Phil. + Wirén. SWS SLT 33176 (alt. Lon. 6430)
Epilogue from "A Winter's Tale"
Westerberg, Radio orch. + Björkander, Sköld, Björklund. SR RAEP 19 (7" 45 rpm)
Melody from "Dangerous Roads"
Jelvings, orch. — "Svensk Folkton." HMV (Sweden) SCLP 1010
Music for Orchestra
Westerberg, Stockholm Phil. + Hallnäs, Werle. Phono Suecia PS 4
Violin Concerto
Gertler, Frykberg, Radio orch. + Fernström, Blomdahl. Telestar 11014 (alt. Lon. International 91091)
Orchestral Variations
Ehrling, Radio orch. + Karkoff. SWS SLT 33164
Lyric Fantasy; Pastoral Suite
Björlin, Stockholm Phil. + Roman, Uttini. HMV (Sweden) CSDS 1084

Concertino for Horn and Strings
Lanzsky, Otto, Chamber ensemble + Hermanson, Hindemith. RIKS LP 17
Concertino for Clarinet and Strings; Little Serenade
Janson, Ehrling, chamber orch. + Roman. SWS SLT 33187
Concertino for Trombone
Smith, Kuehefuhs + Bordogni, Hartley, Haydn, Hasse, Ravel. Coronet 1711
Due Auguri
Westerberg, Radio orch. + Hambraeus. RIKS LP 32
Quattro tempi
Stockholm Philharmonic Wind Quintet + Lundquist, Welin, Nilsson. Orfeus 2-73-3-A/B
Sonatina No. 1
Scheja + Rangström, Stenhammar, Wirén. RCA LSC-3119
Sonatina No. 2
Baekkelund + Blomdahl, Bäck, Carlid, Lidholm. Sonet SLP 2032
Croquiser ("Espressivo" only)
Larsson — "Composers at the Piano." SWS SLT 33184
The Disguised God
Soloists, chorus, Westerberg, Radio Orch. SWS SLT 33146
Missa Brevis
Ericson, Chamber choir + Olsson. SWS LT 33130

Lidholm, Ingvar
Toccata e canto; Songs for Soprano and Orchestra (1940-1945)
Rodin, Blomstedt, Stockholm Phil. + Stenhammar. HMV (Sweden) SCLP 1072
Concerto for String Orchestra
Bäck, Chamber orch. + Bach, Geminiani, Hassler, Rameau, Roman. SR RELP 1061
Music for Strings
Kyndel Qt. + Stenhammar. SR RELP 1038
Ritornell
Schmidt-Isserstedt, Stockholm Phil. + Blomdahl, Rosenberg. SWS LT 33135
Riter
Ehrling, London Sym. + Blomdahl, Rosenberg. Dec. SXL 6180
Poesis
Blomstedt, Stockholm Phil. + Rosenberg. SWS SLT 33160
Four Pieces for Cello and Piano
Gerhard, Kirsten + Holewa, Rosenberg. HMV (Sweden) E 055-34629
Piano Piece (1949)
Baekkelund + Blomdahl, Bäck, Carlid, Larsson. Sonet SLP 2032
Stamp Music (organ and vocal versions)
Dorow/Welin. Interdisc IPS 1193

Laudi
Ericson, Radio choir + Bäck, Hambraeus. SR RMLP 1096
Four Choruses
Ericson, Radio choir. SR RAEP 4 (7" 45 rpm)
"Canto LXXXI"
Andersson, Bel Canto Choir + Bäck, Rabe, Werle. Artist ALP 103
From the a cappella book
Ericson, Radio choir — "Swedish Choral Songs." HMV (Sweden) SCLP 1032
Nausikaa ensam
Söderström, Westerberg, Radio orch. + Rosenberg, Stenhammar. RIKS LP 22

Mortensen, Finn
Fantasy for Piano and Orchestra
Haase, Ehrling, Oslo Phil. + Egge, Hovland. Phi. 6507 010
Sonata for Solo Flute
Andersen + Rosenberg, Jolivet, Varèse. Phi. 631 053 NL
Five Studies for Solo Flute (three only)
Oien + Hovland, Bergh, Jordan, Kvandal, Berge, Olsen. Phi. 6507 020
Fantasy and Fugue for Piano
Baekkelund + Hovland, Fongaard, Knystedt, Valen. Phi. 839.248 AY
Sonata for Two Pianos
Haase, Zérah + Hovland. Ny Musikk NM-1

Nielsen, Carl
Little Suite for Strings
Garaguly, Tivoli orch., + Quartet No. 2. Turn. 34149
Symphony No. 1 in G Minor
Previn, London Sym. + Saul & David Prelude. RCA LSC-2961
Symphony No. 2 ("The Four Temperaments")
Garaguly, Tivoli Orch. Turn. 34049
Symphony No. 3 ("Sinfonia espansiva")
Bernstein, Royal Danish Orch. Col. MS-6769
Symphony No. 4 ("Inextinguishable")
Martinon, Chicago Sym. + Helios. RCA LSC-2958
Symphony No. 5
Horenstein, New Philharmonia + Saga Dream. None. 71236
Symphony No. 6 ("Sinfonia semplice")
Ormandy, Philadelphia Orch. + Maskarade Overture. Col. MS-6882
Violin Concerto
Varga, Semkow, Royal Danish Orch. Turn. 34043
Clarinet Concerto
Drucker, Bernstein, New York Phil. + Flute Concerto. Col. MS-7028

Helios Overture; Pan and Syrinx; Rhapsody Overture "An Imaginary Journey to the Faeroes"
Ormandy, Philadelphia Orch. + Symphony No. 1. Col. MS-7004
At the Bier of a Young Artist (Andante lamentoso); Modern Prelude; Serenata in vano
Hye-Knudsen/Jensen, Danish Orch. + Symphony No. 2. Odeon MOAK 30006
Aladdin Suite
Felumb, Tivoli orch. + Lumbye. Col. (Denmark) 33 KSX 1
String Quartet No. 1
Copenhagen Qt. + Gade. Turn. 34149
String Quartet No. 3
Copenhagen Qt. + Serenata in vano. Turn. 34109
String Quartet No. 4
Copenhagen Qt. + Holmboe. Turn. 34217
Quintet for Strings in G
Telmanyi Quint. Odeon PASK 2003
Wind Quintet; Serenata in vano; Fantasy Op. 2; Canto serioso; Moderen (excerpts)
Lark Woodwind Quint. Lyr. 7155
Sonata No. 1 for Violin and Piano in A
Telmanyi, Schiøler + Sonata No. 2. Odeon MOAK 30003
Sonata No. 2 for Violin and Piano
Laursen, Møller + Prelude & Theme with Variations; Preludio e Presto. Washington WLP 462
Piano Music
Rasmussen. Vox SVBX-5449 (three discs)
Commotio
Hansen + Organ Preludes. Turn. 34193
Maskarade
Lembek, Frey, Bastian, Hartmann, Jorgensen, Danish orch.
(NOTE: At time of writing a generally available stereo recording of Nielsen's opera has yet to appear. The two-disc, private edition set listed here (N-401 A/D), however, boasts a strong performing cast with good recording made in 1964).
Maskarade Suite
Jensen, Radio Orch. Decca BR 3111
Songs
Schiøtz. Sera. 60112
Schiøtz. Odeon MOAK 4
Westi, Winther et al., Wöldike cond. Phi. AY 836750
Fynsk Forår
Soloists, chorus, Wöldike, Radio Orch. + Songs. Mer. 90450 (alt. Phi. AY 836750).
Three Motets
Wöldike, Madrigal Choir + Commotio. Lon. LL 1030

Nilsson, Bo
Frequenzen; Szene III
Travis/Maderna, Darmstadt and Hamburg Chamber ensembles +
Xenakis, A. Clementi, Schoenberg, Kotonski, Takahashi. Main.
MS/5008
Szene II
Travis, Stockholm Phil. + Hermanson, Naumann, Welin. Phono
Suecia PM 1
Revue
Björlin, Nörrköping Orch. + Bartók, Stravinsky. HMV (Sweden)
061-34007
Déjà-vu
Stockholm Phil. Wind Quint. + Larsson, Lundquist, Welin. Orfeus
2-73-3-A/B
Quantiäten; Rendezvous
Klein + Nørgaard, Nordheim, Janson, Bibalo. Phi. 6507 022
Stenogramm
Welin + Bark-Rabe, Back, Hambraeus. Artist ALP 102
Stunde eines Blocks
Dorow, Staern, instrumental ensemble + Langgaard, Jordal — "Nordic Music Days 1968," Vol. 2. HMV (Sweden) CDS 1087
Letter to Gösta Oswald
Dorow, Sebon, Travis, Berlin Radio Orch. Phono Suecia PS 3
Nordheim, Arne
Canzona per orchestra; Epitaffio
Blomstedt, Oslo Phil. + Response I. Phi. 839.250 AY
Colorazione
Kolberg, Thorsen, Nordheim, Rudnik + Solitaire; Signals. Phi. 854.
005 AY
Listen
Klein — "Modern Scandinavian Music." Phi. 6507 022
Aftonland
Skaug, Bruland, Oslo Phil. ensemble + Hovland. Forum-FORLP
6100
Eco
Valjakka, Ericson. Blomstedt, chorus, children's choir, Radio Orch.
+ Kokkonen — "Nordic Music Days 1968," Vol. 1. HMV (Sweden)
CSDS 1086
Nørgård, Per
Constellations
Semkow, Danish Orch. + Holmboe. Turn. 34168
Le Jeune Homme à Marier
Vetö, Prisme Ensemble. Wilhelm Hansen LPWH 3012
Quartetto Brioso
Koppel Qt. + Holmboe. Wilhelm Hansen LPWH 3011

Waves; Rondo
Lylloff, percussion group + Lylloff, Varèse. Cambridge 2824
Le Bal Sonambule; Introduction and Toccata for Accordion
Bjarne, Pilsl, Arntzen. ZAC ZEPK 5007 (7" 45 rpm)
Sonata in One Movement; Grooving
Klein + Sketches, Studies, Fragments. Wilhelm Hansen LPWH 3013
Piano Sonata No. 2
Klein + Nilsson, Nordheim, Janson, Bibalo — "Modern Scandinavian Music." Phi. 6507 022
Nystedt, Knut
The Seven Seals
Fjelstadt, Oslo Phil. + Kvandal, Arnestad. Phi. 839.254 AY
String Quartet No. 3
Norwegian Qt. + Kjellsby. Triola TNLP 4
String Quartet No. 4
Hindar Qt. + Egge. Phi. 839.253 AY
De Profundis
Nystedt, Norwegian Soloists Choir +Kvandal, Hovland, Sløgedal, Beck, Olsen, Groven, Monrad-Johansen. Phi. 839.235 NY
The Moment
Skaug, chamber ensemble + Hovland, Fongaard, Mortensen. Phi. 839.248 AY
The Burnt Sacrifice
Chorus, Andersen, Bergen Sym. + Saeverud, Monrad-Johansen. Phi. 6507 007
Nystroem, Gösta
Sinfonia del mare
Söderström, Westerberg, Radio Orch. SWS SLT 33207
Theater Suite No. 4 "Merchant of Venice"
Ehrling, Radio Orch. + Berwald. SR RHLP 1105
Sinfonia concertante
Blöndahl-Bengtsson, Westerberg, Radio orch. + Koch. SWS SLT 33136
Concerto ricercante
Lareti, Ehrling, Stockholm Phil. + Back, Larsson. Phi. DSY 839277
Songs by the Sea
Rautavaara, Mann, Radio orch. + Theater suite. SWS LT 33103
Songs from "Soul and Soil"
Meyer, Eyron + de Frumerie, Rangström, Stenhammar. SWS SLT 33171
Peterson-Berger, Wilhelm
Symphony No. 3 "Same Ätnam"
Frykberg, Radio Orch. SR REXLP 5001
Violin Concerto
Pierrou, Westerberg, Radio orch. + Romance. HMV (Sweden) CSDS 1083

Arnljot (excerpts)
  Hagegard, Thallaug, Asker, Jerhlander, Kamu, Stockholm Phil. —
  HMV (Sweden) E 06134925
Frösöblomster
  Ribbing. HMV (Sweden) SCLP 1002
Songs
  Björling. RCA LSC-9884
  Gedda. Electrola (Germany) C 063-28023
  Gedda. RCA LSC-10034
  R. Björling. Odeon PMES 552
  Söderström/Saedén. Telestar 11067
Karfeldt Songs
  R. Leanderson, H. Leanderson. Rival RILP 03
  Hagegard, Eyron. HMV (Sweden) 161-34197/98 (two discs)
Rangström, Ture
Symphony No. 1 "August Strindberg in Memoriam"
  Mann, Stockholm Concert Assn. Orch. Lon. LLP 514
Divertimento elegiaco
  Westerberg, Royal Swedish Orch., + King Erik's Songs. SWS LT
  33149
Lake Mälar Legends
  Scheja + Larsson, Wirén. RCA LSC-3119
Songs
  Nilsson. Lon. 25942
  Meyer. SWS SLT 33171
  R. Leanderson. RCA VICS-1603 (Sweden)
Riisager, Knudage
Primavera
  Jensen, Radio orch. + J. Bentzon, Høffding. Odeon MOAK 10
On the Occasion of —
  Friisholm, Randers City Orch. + Høffding. HMV (Denmark) 7R
  K21 (7" 45 rpm)
Concertino for Trumpet and Strings
  Johnson, Ormandy, Philadelphia Orch. — "First Chair Encores." Col.
  MS-6791
Qarrtsiluni; Étude
  Semkow, Royal Danish Orch. + Gade, Nielsen. Turn. 34085
Serenade for Flute, Violin, Cello
  Rafn, Svendsen, Honnens + Nielsen, Debussy. Triola TDL 204
  (10")
Roman, Johan
Sinfonia in D; Sinfonia in E Minor
  Westerberg, Chamber orch. + Drottningsholm Music. SWS SLT
  33140
Sinfonia in B: Violin Concerto in D minor
  Stockholm Phil. ensemble + Larsson. SWS SLT 33187

Sinfonia No. 1 in G
  Lillefors, Stockholm ensemble + Bach, Zellbell. Aurora ARS 7101
Drottningholm Music
  Björlin, chamber orchestra + Naumann, Uttini. None. 71213
Oboe Concerto in B Major
  Gillblad, Björlin, Stockholm Baroque Ensemble + Larsson, Uttini.
  HMV (Sweden) CSDS 1084
Oboe d'amore Concerto
  Nilsson, Verde, chamber orch. + Larsson, de Frumerie. Fermat
  FLPS 10
Assaggio No. 6; Sonata No. 8 in A
  Ofverström, Hallhagen, Ericson + Berwald. SR RELP 5008
Chamber Sonata No. 6
  Edlen, Pro Arte Antiqua + Nichelmann. GMM 077 (Supraphon
  SUF 20131)
Jubilate
  Weman, Uppsala Cathedral Choir with orch. — "Nova Cantica."
  HMV (Sweden) SCLP 1026
God Is Our Refuge
  Ericson, choir — "Swedish Church Music." Cantata 640 224
Rosenberg, Hilding
Symphony No. 2 ("Sinfonia grave")
  Blomstedt, Stockholm Phil. + Wirén. Turn. 34436
Symphony No. 3
  Blomstedt, Stockholm Phil. HMV (Sweden) SCLP 1071
Symphony No. 4 "Revelations of St. John"
  Saeden, chorus, Blomstedt, Radio orch. HMV (Sweden) SCLP 1059/
  60 (two discs)
Symphony No. 6 ("Sinfonia semplice")
  Westerberg, Stockholm Sym. + Blomdahl. Turn. 34318
Concerto for Orchestra No. 3 "Louisville Concerto"
  Whitney, Louisville Orch. + Wen-Chung, Guarnieri. Lou. 56-1
Journey to America Suite
  Dorati, Stockholm Phil. + Berwald, Blomdahl. RCA VICS-1319
Orfeus in Town Suite
  Westerberg, Stockholm Phil. + Lidholm, Stenhammar. RIKS LP 22
String Quartet No. 5
  Kyndel Qt. + Quartet No. 6. SWS LT 33122
String Quartet No. 7
  Kyndel Qt. + Quartet No. 8. RCA LM 9913
Sonatas for Solo Violin (Nos. 1, 2, 3)
  Barter, Berlin, Spierer. RIKS LP 10
Sonata for Solo Flute
  Andersen + Jolivet, Mortensen, Varèse. Phi. 631 053 NL
Wind Quintet
  Stockholm Phil. Wind Quint. + Lidholm, Alldahl, Holewa. HMV
  (Sweden) E 055-34629

Eleven Small Piano Studies
Ribbing — "Swedish Piano Compositions." HMV (Sweden) SCLP
1052
Improvisations
Carlson + Mozart, Karkoff. Fermat FLPS 1
Fantasy and Fugue for Organ
Lundkvist — "Vox Humana." Proprius 25 04-02-0007
The Holy Night
Ericson, soloists, choir, Radio Orch. SR RELP 5007
Marionettes: Overture
Schmidt-Isserstedt, Stockholm Phil. + Blomdahl, Lidholm. Dec. SXL
6180
Motets
Ericson, Radio choir. — "Swedish Church Music." Cantata 640-224
Saeverud, Harald
Sinfonia dolorosa
Andersen. Bergen Sym. + Monrad-Johansen, Knystedt. Phi. 6507
007
Salme
Grüner-Hegge, Oslo Phil. + Jensen. Triola TNLP 2
Galdreslåtten; Rondo Amoroso
Fjeldstad, Oslo Phil. + Valen. Mer. MG 10149
Ballad of Revolt
Grüner-Hegge, Oslo Phil. + Svendsen, Jensen, Tveitt. Phi. 838.050
AY
Peer Gynt Suite No. 1
Caridis, Oslo Phil. + Peer Gynt Suite No. 2. Phi. 6507 006
Dances and Tunes from Siljustøl; Easy Pieces (including *Rondo
Amoroso, Ballad of Revolt*)
Andersen. Triola TNLP 3
Rondo Amoroso
Ribbing — "Nordisk Pianolyrik." HMV (Sweden) SCLP 1007
Six Sonatinas for Piano
Kayser + Jordan, Hurum. Phi. 6507 004
Sinding, Christian
Suite in A Minor
Heifetz, Wallenstein, Los Angeles Phil. + Brahms, Ravel. RCA LM-
2836
Variations for Two Pianos
Levin, Baekklelund + Grieg. DGG 2538 090
Solo Piano Music
Ruiz + Gade — Genesis 1003
Rustle of Spring
Ribbing — "Nordisk Pianolyrik." HMV (Sweden) SCLP 1007
Dragon, Hollywood Bowl Sym. — "Viking!" Cap. SP 8562

Piano Quintet
Knardahl, Hindar Qt. Phi. 854.003 AY
Songs
Flagstad. Dec. Eclipse (England) ECS623
Thallaug (Sylvelin only) + Grieg. Phi. 854.006
Stenhammar, Wilhelm
Symphony No. 2
Mann, Stockholm Phil. RCA (Sweden) LSC 9854
Serenade for Large Orchestra
Kubelik, Stockholm Phil. Heliodor S-25086 (alt. DGG SLPM 108579)
Piano Concerto No. 2
Solyom, Westerberg, Munich Phil. +Liszt. HMV (Sweden) E 063-34284
Interlude from "Sången"; "Chitra" Suite
Blomstedt, Stockholm Phil. + Lidholm. HMV (Sweden) SCLP 1072
Sentimental Romances for Violin and Orchestra
Tellefsen, Westerberg, Radio orch. + Rosenberg, Lidholm. RIKS LP 22
String Quartet No. 2
Kyndel Qt. + Lidholm. SR RELP 1038
String Quartet No. 3
Borodin Qt. Telestar 11023
String Quartet No. 5
Kyndel Qt. + Three Choral Songs, Sensommarnätter. SR RELP 5010
Sonata for Violin and Piano
Saulesco, Solyom + Three fantasies. HMV (Sweden) SCLP 1058
Three Fantasies
Scheja + Rangström, Larsson, Wirén. RCA LSC-3119
Sensommarnätter
Roos + Eklund, Hindemith, Liszt, Mozart. RIKS LP 20
Songs
Söderström. SWS SLT 33171
Leandersen. RCA (Sweden) VICS 1603
Rödin. HMV (Sweden) 061-34015
Sverige
Björling, Grevillius, Royal Opera Orch. + recital. RCA LM 9884
Gedda, Grevillius, Stockholm Phil. + recital. RCA LSC 10034
Svendsen, Johan Severin
Symphony No. 1; Zorahayda
Grüner-Hegge, Oslo Phil. 838.051 AY
Symphony No. 2
Kramm, Oslo Phil. + Norwegian Rhapsodies Nos. 2 & 3. Mei. 90001
Carnival in Paris
Fjeldstad, Oslo Phil. + Halvorsen, Valen, Braein. Phi. 838.053 AY

Norwegian Artists' Carnival
Fjeldstad, Oslo Phil. — "Norwegian 'POP' Concert." Mer. MG10150
Festival Polonaise
Fjeldstad, Oslo Phil. + Egge, Monrad-Johansen, Groven. Phi. 838. 052 AY
Romance for Violin and Orchestra
Grumiaux, de Waart, New Phil. + Beethoven, Berlioz, Tchaikovsky, Wieniawski. Phi. 6580047
String Quartet in A Minor
Copenhagen Qt. + Grieg. Fona TF 105
Octet for Strings
Members of Hindar Qt. with associates. Phi. 854.004

Valen, Fartein
Pastorale for Orchestra; Sonetto di Michelangelo; Cantico di ringraziamento; Nenia; An die Hoffnung; Le cimetière marin; La isla de las calmas; Ode to Solitude; Ave Maria; Two Chinese Poems; Darest Thou Now O Soul; Die dunkle Nacht der Seele
Dorow, Cardis, Oslo Phil. Phi. 6754 001 (two discs)
Piano Concerto
Riefling, Fjeldstad, Oslo Phil. + Svendsen, Braein, Halvorsen. Phi. 838.053 AY
Violin Concerto
Wicks, Fjeldstad, Oslo Phil. HMV (Norway) DBN 11909
Serenade for Five Wind Instruments
Norwegian Wind Quint. + Hovland, Fongaard, Mortensen, Nystedt. Phi. 839.248 AY
String Quartet No. 2
Julliard Qt. + Piano music. Argo RG 81
Piano Music
Weydahl. Epic BC 1368
Pastorale for Organ
Boysen + contemporary Norwegian organ music. Phi. 854.000 AY

Werle, Lars Johan
Sinfonia da camera
Björlin, Norrköping Sym. + Björlin, Ravel. HMV (Sweden) E 061-34211
Summer Music
Miedel, Stockholm Phil. + Larsson, Hallnäs. Phono Suecia PS 4
Attitudes
Ribbing — "Svensk Pianolyrik," Vol. 1. HMV (Sweden) SCLP 1052
Canzone 126 di Francesco Petrarca
Andersson, Bel Canto Choir + Bäck, Lidholm, O'Månson-Rabe. Artist ALP 103
Vision of Thérèse (excerpts)
Hallin, Malmborg, Jehrlander, Saeden, Gielen, Royal Swedish Orch. SWS SLT 33177

Weyse, Christoph Friederich Ernst
Sovedrikken Overture
Hye-Knudsen, Royal Danish Orch. — "Danish Theater Music."
Turn. 34038
Two Etudes (Op. 60 Nos. 1 & 2)
Westergaard + Kuhlau. Phi. 6578 002
Songs
Schiøtz. Odeon MOAK 4
Various artists. Polyphon LUP 802 (10")
Nuppenau. RCA CAS 10135
Wirén, Dag
Sinfonietta in C
Westerberg, Radio orch. + Atterberg, de Frumerie. SWS SLT 33167
Serenade for Strings
Somary, English Chamber Orch. + Grieg. Van. C-10067
Westerberg, Stockholm Phil. + Larsson. Lon. 6430 (alt. SWS SLT 33176)
Symphony No. 4
Ehrling, Radio orch. + Rosenberg. Turn. 34436
String Quartet No. 2
Saulesco Qt. + Wikmanson. HMV (Sweden) SCLP 1069
String Quartet No. 4
Kyndel Qt. + Nilsson, Bäck, Lidholm. SR RELP 5002
String Quartet No. 5
Saulesco Qt. + Shostakovich, Welin. RIKS LP 24
Little Serenade for Guitar
Bengtsson + recital. SWS LT 33165
Ironical Miniatures
Scheja + Larsson, Rangström, Stenhammar. RCA LSC-3119
Titania
Ericson, Chamber choir + Swedish choral music. HMV (Sweden) SCLP 1043
Collections
The Art of Aksel Schiøtz. Odeon MOAK 3, 4, 5, 19, 20 (five discs)
Studentersangerne. Phi. NE 423800
Den Danske Romance. Phi. AY 836751
Det Norske Solist Kor. Phi. 839.235 NY
Det Norske Solist Kor. Phi. 854.001 AY
Contemporary Music from Norway (organ). Phi. 854.00
Swedish Church Music. Cantata 640 224
Sveriges Vackraste Körlyrik. Telestar TRS 11105
Orphei Drängar. RCA VICS 1602
Stockholm University Chorus. Phi. PY 842 557
Jenny Lind Songs (Söderström). Lon. 25949
Songs from Norway (Flagstad). Lon. 25103
Svensk Pianolyrik (Ribbing) HMV (Sweden) SCLP 1052/53 (two discs)
Air Norvégien (Tellefsen/Levin). Phi. 839.236 NY

INDEX

263

264